Dis/Closures

New York University Ottendorfer Series
Neue Folge Band 24

unter Mitarbeit von
Helmut Brackert (Frankfurt/M.),
Peter Demetz (Yale), Reinhold Grimm (Wisconsin)
Walter Hinderer (Princeton)

herausgegeben von
Volkmar Sander

PETER LANG
New York · Berne · Frankfurt am Main

Katherine Goodman

Dis/Closures

Women's Autobiography in Germany
Between 1790 and 1914

PETER LANG
New York · Berne · Frankfurt am Main

Library of Congress Cataloging in Publication Data

Goodman, Katherine:
Dis/Closures: Women's Autobiography in Germany
Between 1790 and 1914.

(New York University Ottendorfer Series; n. F.,
Bd. 24)
«Translation»: p.
Bibliography: p.
1. German literature – Women authors __ History and
criticism. 2. Autobiography – Women authors.
3. Women – Germany – Biography. I. Title. II. Series.
PT167.G66   1986   830'.9'9287   86-10687
ISBN 0-8204-0398-9
ISSN 0172-3529

CIP-Kurztitelaufnahme der Deutschen Bibliothek

Goodman, Katherine:
Dis/Closures: Women's Autobiography in Germany
Between 1790 and 1914 / Katherine Goodman. –
New York; Berne; Frankfurt am Main: Lang,
1986.
(New York University Ottendorfer Series;
N. F., Bd. 24)
ISBN 0-8204-0398-9

NE: New York University: New York University . . .

Printed by Lang Druck., Inc., Liebefeld/Berne (Switzerland)

jec
5-27-87

For J.C.B.

ACKNOWLEDGEMENTS

For their support of the research for this book I am indebted to the Alexander von Humboldt-Stiftung of the Federal Republic of Germany and to the National Endowment for the Humanities in the United States.

For her technical assistance and moral support I would like to express my gratitude to Judith Brown.

CONTENTS

Introduction
WOMEN AND AUTOBIOGRAPHY:
METHODOLOGICAL CONSIDERATIONS . . . . *i*

Chapter 1
THE CASES OF BALDINGER, ENGEL, AND WALLENRODT . . 1

Chapter 2
THE CASES OF RECKE AND STÄGEMANN 31

Chapter 3
THE CASES OF VARNHAGEN AND ARNIM 73

Chapter 4
THE CASES OF ASTON AND MEYSENBUG 121

Chapter 5
THE CASES OF LEWALD AND EBNER-ESCHENBACH 147

Chapter 6
THE CASES OF POPP, WEGRAINER, AND VIERSBECK 187

Conclusion 209

Translations 215

Notes 233

Introduction

WOMEN AND AUTOBIOGRAPHY: METHODOLOGICAL CONSIDERATIONS

Nineteenth-century England boasts strong capable women in many fields: from brilliant novelists like George Eliot to dedicated political economists like Harriet Martineau. Nineteenth-century France vaunts nearly as many: from influential novelists like George Sand to outstanding scientists like Marie Curie. It is difficult to find women of equal strength and force in nineteenth-century Germany. The present study will not answer the question of *why* this should be so, but it will seek some answers regarding *what* happened to women and their voices in that time and place, which at least as far as women's history is concerned, remains somewhat more dimly lit than for England or France, and also the United States. For the most part the women whose lives will be discussed were educated, middle-class women, whom one might have expected to play a more "significant" historical role. But the lives of some working-class women will also be examined.

The source for answers of what happened to women will be the life histories they wrote of themselves. But it is a problematic source, especially for women. And just because the genre theory for autobiography has proven itself so problematic a vehicle for the understanding and expression of women's experience, this study will necessarily undertake a dual task. It will draw attention to the experience of particular women in nineteenth-century Germany, but it will also need to critically re-examine the standards by which any work is labeled "autobiography". For reading these works requires redefining the categories of the genre. In the end, in this case, these tasks are in fact one. The attempt to grasp something of the experience of these women *is* the effort to perceive them explaining their lives in the context of an autobiographical tradition which had not evolved forms adequate for them. It is to observe them in the act of defining their lives in and for the culture in which they lived.

The desire to understand women of past centuries seems naturally to draw readers to autobiographical sources in hope of discovering what *did* happen to them, as though their personal remarks would yield the clearest, most authentic answers. We expect them to disclose their authors' secrets. We want them to reveal their authors' "real" inner selves. We want to know how they perceived their lives. But the moment we sit down to read such a work we encounter endless difficulties diciphering the subject we have in front of us. Without doubt any autobiographer assumes a pose and creates a "second self" — at least to a certain extent. However since women have traditionally been obliged to conform to particularly limiting cultural conventions, as autobiographers they have also been subject to special pressures to mold their lives into certain patterns. The problem becomes the difficult if not impossible one of knowing where that fictional persona ends and real experience begins. Clearly, we need to read autobiographies as critically as anything else. But for this we need certain analytical tools, and therefore these introductory remarks will be addressed to the question of autobiography as a source of knowledge about women's lives.

There are particular difficulties surrounding the reading of any autobiography. Like history, this genre (after all, the narration of *personal* history) pretends to portray "reality", and not some fictional tale. Modern readers tend to be sceptical and generally accept the fact of subjective perspective in historical narration. Whether an historical account is contemporary or belongs to an earlier era, the viewpoint of the author — and the times — makes itself felt in the selection and treatment of material. And while the inclination to accept the existence of perspective in historical writing may be greater than for scientific writing, even in this most "objective" of fields modern historians — at least since Thomas S. Kuhn — have begun to recognize the influence of factors external to experimentation on scientific theories.

However, the situation is quite different and far more methodologically complex for autobiographical writings. An autobiographer *knows* her/his subject matter in a very different manner than a scientist or historian. As both subject and object of an investigation, the autobiographer speaks with an authority which is difficult to question. For example, it is possible to argue with historians or scientists on the basis of mutually observable phenomena; but, while it is possible to dispute an autobiographer's interpretation of her own life in those few cases where facts may contradict her assertions, it is virtually impossible in most incidences. And yet the very same kinds of forces which influence historical and scientific writing work to shape any autobiographer's understanding of her/his own life.

At first the challenge would seem to lie in finding what Patricia Meyer Spacks has called "selves in hiding". But the theoretical situation is no longer so relatively straight-forward, for precisely the "self" is no longer an unproblematic concept. Under the strains of the recent invasion of French Critical Theory, the authenticity of any "self" or "I" has been radically questioned – even if it is not for the first time in history. And when the very notion of "subject" has been undermined, women must needs take note. For those who want to become *subjects* of history in the Hegelian and/or Marxist sense, and no longer its *objects*; for autobiographers who want to become the subjects of their own life histories; for women who struggle with the "difficulty of saying I" such a theory is necessarily threatening. The very moment women set out to take matters in their own hands, they are told the relationship to history which they seek is and always has been an illusion. Why then should they struggle? In its most radical forms this theoretical invasion is, in fact, inimicable to the more political interests of women; and it would be tempting, indeed, simply to try to repel the assault were it not for the fact that some aspects of this theory may actually aid in the re-evaluation of women's lives and autobiographies.

This attack on the integrity of any "self" is, of course, central to the issue at hand. Undermining the authenticity of the "self" has necessarily and in turn placed the entire genre and genre theory of autobiography in question. The concept of an autobiographical "self" or experience is not something that historians of the genre have doubted. Indeed traditional theory of autobiography – from the grandfather of all such research, Georg Misch, to more recent scholars, like Roy Pascal, Wayne Schumaker, and Georges May – is predicated on the assumption of just such an authenticity. However, lest one be inclined to think that the traditional predication of the concept of "self" is advantageous to the appreciation of women's lives and a just evaluation of their autobiographies, let it be stated from the first that, although such an appreciation will require *something* from traditional theory of the genre, it is categorically not the case that that traditional theory has proven itself capable of evaluating women's contributions. This will require some elaboration.

The study of autobiography as a literary genre actually began with the recognition of the partiality of the narrator and an appreciation of subjectivity and individual self-consciousness per se. While all but a few historians around 1900 dismissed the genre as factually unreliable, in an atmosphere of anti-positivism it was precisely the "psychologische Poesie" of the genre that attracted other scholars.[2] In Germany in 1893 Friedrich von Bezold emphasized and praised the subjectivity of the genre: "Die Selbstbiographie im engeren Sinne hat es vor allem mit der inneren Entwicklung ihres Helden zu tun; sie ist nicht nur Rückschau auf das Durchlebte, sondern zugleich und vorwiegend Innenschau."[3] In 1903 Hans Glagau maintained that without their more lively, personal traits Rousseau's *Confessions* and Goethe's *Dichtung und Wahrheit* would be bare skeletons and very dull indeed. Overlooking the pietist tradition, he maintained that since Rousseau the essence of modern autobiography had become the inner history of a person: "die Bildung seiner Seele und die Entwicklung seines Charakters".[4] Written in the same vein, the first — and still most comprehensive and influential — history of the genre appeared in 1904, after winning the competition for the best history of autobiography designed in 1900 by the Prussian Academy of Sciences. It was Georg Misch's *Geschichte der Autobiographie.*

The traditional definition of autobiography assumes not only the existence, but also the evolution of a "soul" or a "self"; and the essential subjectivity of the genre characterized its treatment from the first. For instance, ever since Bezold and Glagau — and continuing into the present — scholars of the genre have tended to distinguish between Memoirs and Autobiography.[5] *By definition* Memoirs relate external events in which the narrator was involved or which were witnessed by the narrator: court intrigues, military campaigns, political or professional struggles. Autobiographies recount internal events: the evolution of a religious, philosophical, intellectual position. To be sure, the classic example of the genre in German, Goethe's *Dichtung und Wahrheit*, is presented as a grand and universal synthesis of historical, professional, intellectual, and personal struggles. However, critics would not consider it autobiography without its internal dimension. Just this is the aspect of the genre that most commonly interests readers searching for the emergence of a consciously female "self", for women who asserted their individuality and could say "I".

No scholarly work illustrates this theoretical tendency better than Georg Misch's classic study of the history of autobiography in Western civilization. It was nothing less than the attempt to outline the emergence of a self-conscious "self", of the awareness of individuality: "die schier unbegrenzte Mannigfaltigkeit des autobiographischen Schrifttums in dem universalgeschichtlichen Zusammenhang der Entwicklung des menschlichen Geistes in der europäischen Kultur".[6] Autobiography, he maintained, arose out of the individual's need for expression and self-assertion. He aimed to recount the history of this need, for: "Die Geschichte der Autobiographie ist in einem gewissen Sinne eine Geschichte des menschlichen Bewußtseins."(I,11) He sought to reveal the history of that sense of personality which a human being possesses when s/he perceives both her/his uniqueness and her/his contribution/debt to the whole.

In actuality Misch's study necessarily severely limited the significance he accorded women's experience and their autobiographies. He appointed himself the task "das Geschichtliche als vernünftig zu begreifen, das Zufällige als organisch zu verstehen".(IV/2, 926) If history was rational it not only had an idea, it also had a goal. That implicit goal was the creation of fully self-conscious individuals. The issue of gender did not complicate his understanding of that evolution. In his idealist and teleological view, the representative human consciousness of any age resided in the works of its "significant personalities". The self-awareness of an age was expressed by its dominant culture and its dominant figures. He aimed to study "den Menschen in der Kunst der grossen Individuen".(I,15) It goes without saying that while this did not de jure ban consideration of women's autobiographies, it did so de facto.

Indeed, it is virtually predictable that Goethe's autobiography comes to represent the epitome of this development, as if all of modern history had converged on this telos. It is not only women's autobiographies which are relegated to the status of mere predecessors or successors to Goethe's, it is also the personal histories of less inclusive bourgeois autobiographies and proletarian autobiographies. To his credit, Misch admitted his difficulty—but then proceeded anyway: "An Goethes Autobiographie heranzutreten als ein geschichtlich bestimmtes Werk und Glied einer sich fortentwickelnden Gattung, hält schwer. . . [wir] spüren. . .den Künstlergeist, den organisierenden Willen, das Welt- und Menschenverständnis, das in dieser Erzählung waltet, und die Geschichte. . .stellt sich als das große in sich ruhende Kunstwerk dar, in dem zum ersten Mal die ganze Wirklichkeit eines Individualdaseins als Selbstzweck wahrhaft geschichtlich aufgefaßt ist."(IV/2, 917) History is sublated, the telos of world evolution is achieved. What can happen next? Only decline.

Probably no woman in history could have begun even to approach the all-inclusive self-identity which Misch perceives in *Dichtung und Wahrheit*. If this is the model for the genre, to all purposes it is impossible, by generic definition, for a woman to write any but a highly flawed example of autobiography.

But Misch's study of autobiography makes the inclusion of women's works difficult for another reason as well. For Misch—and more recent German scholars, too[7]—autobiography after Goethe resumed its uninteresting nature, void of that individualism and full interiority Goethe had so successfully conveyed. That included the last two-thirds of the nineteenth century and the twentieth century—precisely the period in which increasing numbers of women began to write and publish their autobiographies. Indeed, as will become evident in the course of this study, any teleological view of history virtually assures the subordination of women's experience to dominant culture and dominant trends. Women's lives and the experience they represent are generally not accorded significance in such interpretations. Nor does there appear to be any telos to the direction taken by the history of women's experience. The theoretical and historical hurdle represented by *Dichtung und Wahrheit* has posed problems for all scholars who have attempted to study German autobiography in the nineteenth century, but it challenges particularly anyone interested in women's autobiography. Both the particular conceptualization of "self" and the teleological view of history have mediated against the consideration of issues of gender in autobiography.

In actuality, however, part of Misch's analysis—the very concept of experience—is necessary to evaluate and appreciate women's autobiography. Ultimately this concept derives from his mentor and father-in-law, Wilhelm Dilthey (1833-1911), the originator of the German school of "Geistesgeschichte"—frequently translated as history of ideas. In reaction to prevailing interest in positivism in the latter part of the nineteenth century, Dilthey sought to understand and formulate originary experience as "Erlebnis". His philosophy represents an effort not only to recapture something of the richness of German idealism, by emphasizing areas of human life ignored by positivists, but also to ground idealism's discussion of morals in something concrete, rather than abstractly rational—namely personal experience, that which—according to him—we best know. Considering the second or third class status accorded women and women's experience within "Geistesgeschichte" it is somewhat ironical that it is precisely the emphasis on personal experience that will prove valuable for a consideration of women's autobiography.

In his effort to mediate idealist subjectivism and positivist objectivism Dilthey drew heavily on the German romantic tradition with its pietist roots, in particular on the writings of Friedrich Schleiermacher (1768-1834). (Indeed it was Dilthey's biography of this Romantic theologian that launched the new method of historical inquiry known as "Geistesgeschichte".) Pietists had traditionally examined the soul minutely in search of authentic experience of God. Secular manifestations of the tradition sought to uncover the hidden workings of the soul, the psyche, or the "self". With an extensive history of interior investigation this movement was a logical source for Dilthey's positing of interiority and subjectivity. It was a realm of human life untapped by positivists, whose concern for experience was restricted to the reactions of the senses and that which could be measured by external observers and was therefore "scientific". For Dilthey, experience included the realm in which feelings were located: imagination, emotion, and intuition. Characteristically it is this most readers seek in autobiography. For Schleiermacher feelings had been precisely the source of interior knowledge, the mediator between real and ideal, conditioned and absolute. As a means to knowledge, of course, this method of inquiry was unacceptable to positivists because the subject and the object of investigation were identical. They deemed it "unscientific" and as invalid as any modern French critic could claim. However, it is precisely this understanding of experience which became the core of Dilthey's and Misch's definition of autobiography. And precisely this concept, the authenticity of experience, remains vital to the re-evalution of women's autobiography. Like Misch, however, Dilthey also failed to allow room for revelations of qualitatively different experience. And it is here that the present critique of Misch's and Dilthey's assumptions will begin.

If Dilthey's study of the soul was not absolutely subjectivist at all points in his intellectual evolution, his most influential writings were. The emphasis on intuitive and impressionistic means of cognition relegated rationally explainable phenomena to the periphery.[8] True knowledge was ephemeral, indefinable, and issued only from the intensity of experience. For this reason Dilthey especially valued letters and autobiographical forms as direct personal expression of "self". However, as far as he was concerned, only poets possessed the ability to express pre-rational, hence true, experience. The critic's task consisted in intuiting and re-experiencing that "truth". Dilthey was less concerned with matters of artistic form than with the eternally pulsing stream of life of immediately articulated expression.[9] By the end of his life, as he witnessed the irrational extremities of subjectivist approaches, Dilthey re-emphasized objective knowledge. He complained: "There has arisen recently a subjective, limitless vortex of emotions. Every day more books appear which promise salvation through a subjective view of the world based upon some kind of introspection or self-immersion of the subject in itself. Everywhere the conviction is growing that objective, methodical knowledge is impossible."[10] He seems, ultimately, to have favored some mediating ground. As a critic he wanted both to reflect and to create reality, to be "ein schaffender Spiegel".[11]

Heavily influenced by Dilthey, Misch's study proceeds chronologically but remains devoid of specific historical associations. Moreover, the evolution of the immediate expression of the soul occurs not only in an historical vacuum, it occurs in a formal one as well: "Die Selbstbiographie ist keine Literaturgattung wie die anderen. . . keine Form ist ihr fremd."(I, 6) His study therefore ignores any concrete evolution of literary form; it includes indiscriminantly prayers, rhetorical declamations, reports, poetry, confessions, letters, family chronicles, courtly memoirs, novels, biographies, epics, dramas, and more: "in all diesen Formen hat die Autobiographie sich bewegt, und wenn sie so recht sie selbst ist und ein originaler Mensch sich in ihr darstellt, schafft sie die gegebenen Gattungen um oder bringt von sich aus eine unvergleichliche Form hervor". (I, 6) Despite the emphasis on experience, Misch's investigation is idealist in the Hegelian tradition. It follows neither the evolution of concretely defined experience (as in class or gender) nor that of concretely defined literary genres, but rather that of the elusive, but eternally pulsing stream of life. "Life", some will undoubtedly argue, is a more concrete understanding of history than the "Idea". But, for this author, the degree of abstractness with which it is viewed binds it more closely to idealism than materialism.

Naturally this quasi-Hegelian view of history, of human consciousness (and of autobiography) could not and has not gone unchallenged. However the difference with which this and similar views have been countered in West Germany and in France is of particularly current interest. In the 1920s and particularly the 1970s German (mainly post-war West German) scholars of autobiography sought to correct some of the historical failings of Misch's impressive study by concretizing the history of the genre. In studies by Mahrholz, Neumann, and Müller its evolution was identified with the emergence of the bourgeois affirmation of or struggle for "self" in the 16th and 18th centuries.[2] Thus it was associated with a particular historical and class event. These studies, all issuing from a more concrete sociological understanding of the autobiographer, were supplemented by a more formalist approach when Günter Niggl examined concretely the evolution of 18th century autobiographical forms. Although all of these efforts made the evolution of the expression of individuality and subjectivity more concrete and less abstract, they remain refinements of Misch's view. Despite the fact that some have attempted to dismantle the hurdle represented by *Dichtung und Wahrheit*, that work appears repeatedly as the summation of autobiographical evolution, the historical and formal goal after which the form (and presumably bourgeois consciousness) disintegrates. That hurdle is held together by the supposition of an uncomplicated view of subjective expression as well as a teleological view of history. Even the studies of proletarian autobiography only modify the formula slightly. Continuing the interest

in the ascension to historical subjectivity, these emphasized the further evolution of the expression of individuality among workers.[13] Underlying all
remains the assumption of a meaningful course of history (if not always
a teleological one) and an uncomplicated view of subjective expression. In
none of them are the difficult questions raised by the issue of gender even
asked. However, as we shall see in the study of nineteenth-century women's
autobiography, such assumptions simply will not permit the inclusion of
works by women. They force women's autobiographies to be categorized
as historical aberrations.

Precisely the concept of a historical subject as well as the assumption of
meaning in history have been the targets of recent French theories. It is a
matter of historical irony that those German thinkers they frequently cite
(Schleiermacher, Dilthey, Nietzsche, Heidegger) also firmly believed in a
"self". But that is a different issue, and this study accepts Barthes and Foucault as two of the most recent critics of "self" and teleology. Indeed, their
emphatic re-formulation of these issues re-opens possibilities for the interpretation of women's autobiography. In their own reaction to other
philosophies, however, these critics may have gone too far. Not only are
historical subjects and teleological histories in dispute, the very existence
of interiority, or subjectivity—as posited by Schleiermacher, Dilthey, and
Misch and assumed by the German scholars of the 1920s and 1970s—has
been called into question. When Roland Barthes asks of a Balzac text, "Who
is speaking thus?" he determines—as Nietzsche had for God—that the Author is dead. He postulates that authorial interiority is "pure superstition".[14]
"Writing is that neutral, composite, oblique space where our subject slips
away, the negative where all identity is lost, starting with the very identity
of the body writing."(142) The "prestige of the individual", the "human person" had been discovered, as Misch would have agreed, only since the Middle
Ages (143). Except that for Barthes it is a pure fiction. In that "humanist"
tradition, exemplified so well by Dilthey's study of Schleiermacher or Misch's
of *Dichtung und Wahrheit*, "[t]he *explanation* of a work is always sought
in the man or woman who produced it, as if it were always in the end, through
the more or less transparent allegory of the fiction, the voice of a unified
individual, the *author* confiding in us." (143) As this quote suggests, however, for Barthes this discovery is an illusion. Indeed he ventures to assert:
"Linguistically, the author is never more than the instance writing, just as
I is nothing other than the instance saying *I*: language knows a subject, not
a person, and this subject, empty outside of the very enunciation which defines it, suffices to make language hold together, suffices, that is to say, to

exhaust it." (145)

It is difficult to imagine a concept of writing more in antithesis to the traditional definitions of autobiography, or to recent feminist concerns with women's experience. The very authenticity of the subject women seek in writing — and readers usually seek in their autobiographies — is disputed: "Did [an author] wish to *express* himself, he ought at least to know that the inner thing' he thinks to translate' is itself only a ready-formed dictionary, its words only explainable through other words, and so on indefinitely [. . .]." (146) Indeed in *Sade, Fourier, Loyola* (1971) Barthes specifically ridicules the very idea of biography as untrue to life because it posits a conterfeit integration of its subject.

There are some things, however, for which such a theory can give no account, or only poorly. If a human person neither exists nor possesses a history outside the presence of the text, how does one explain historical change or individual innovation and difference — or even choice of words. For Barthes the answer actually appears somewhat mystical. For him it is the "instance" which defines the subject, but what is the "instance"? As Barthes uses it, without explaining it, the term would seem to imply a particular — can we assume historical? — congruence of linguistic agreement. Although this "instance" fully expresses the subject, he never proposes in what it might consist. In order to understand women's autobiography, however, the concepts of choice, innovation, and difference will be crucial. And as an explanation for them only a concept of individual experience suffices.

Barthes is by no means alone among the modern French critics in supposing the discontinuity of the "self". And if he pronounced the Author dead, Foucault sought to bury "him". This critic noted that, despite Barthes' pronouncement, the mystique surrounding the concepts of a "work" or of "writing" (*écriture*) continually resuscitated the notion of Author. For Foucault writing was an "interplay of signs, regulated less by the content it signifies than by the very nature of the signifer".[5] But Foucault also questioned the nature of a "Work". Why not include Nietzsche's notation about a laundry bill among his collected works? In questioning both the existence of "authors" and the definition of "works", he sought to radically dismantle the relationship of the Author's name to a text.

Naturally traditonal interest in autobiography lies precisely in the association of the text to a real person. But for any text Foucault wanted to distinguish author from writer from first person narrator. For autobiography that would eliminate the connection between the autobiographer and the life described. The historical specificity of the author would not matter at all. A writer – and on this point Foucault included not only texts of recognized literary value, but also functional texts, such as reports of scientific experiments – creates "a second self". "It would be as false to seek the author in relation to the actual writer as to the fictional narrator [. . .]." (129) The *idea* of the "subject" becomes the center of a disembodied discourse. Applying this logic, an autobiographer would be a disexperienced linguistic construction. In the end Foucault answers the question of who is speaking with a question originally posed by Beckett: "What matter who's speaking?" (138)

To be sure Barthes, Foucault, and others have alerted critics to the pitfalls of assuming a cohesive author or subject. Such a warning is clearly valuable in the study of women's autobiography, because it relieves the reader of the obligation of trying to reconcile all aspects of the author's personality under one cohesive and harmonious interpretation, one dominant culture. It permits the surfacing of contradictory elements of personality. In the context of such a theory, an autobiographer would also be considered to write within a situation of defining plots, texts, or conventions. It is unquestionably useful in reading women's autobiography to be aware of which plots, texts, or conventions were current when the autobiography was written. For, like other autobiographers, women adopt those poses and plots for their life histories which are current and socially acceptable – or indeed intellectually thinkable. And, importantly, these theoretical tendencies have also led some thinkers to extend the notion of "scripts" or "texts" to actual lives: in daily life people live out particular and available plots or life patterns. A limited number of life patterns are thinkable at any particular time. It is not just that women – and men, as well – perceive their lives and experience in the intellectual currency of the times, they actually use that currency as guidelines for living their lives. These concepts of determining literary and/or real plots are ones which express the situation in which many women have felt themselves to be living for centuries.

We can grant the usefulness of all this and still not be satisfied, especially with the extremity of the position. There is, as objected before, no adequate explanation for innovation or difference. In addition, however, feminists – and others, too – have known for some time that it makes a great deal of difference who is speaking. The discourses of authority, of patriarchy, of morality can be spoken very differently from various vantage points. Women have known things about themselves men have never known when they participated in the discourse on the family or women. Women would formulate – and have formulated, as we shall see – their perspectives with difference. But to propose this is to suggest a concreteness to women's (and men's) existence and an ability to articulate it which exceeds the concepts of discourse and the dissolution of the author offered by Barthes and Foucault. It suggests some degree of authenticity to the concepts of subjectivity and experience, some degree of correspondence between self and text. Women have spoken and do speak from a different place, indeed from different places, and they are not ones that are merely negative or absent.

All of this is to say that the desire to *absolutely* dismantle the concept of the subject is ultimately not in women's interest. It abysmally ignores the interjections that women have made. This, in turn, does not mean Dilthey's concept of subject or individual, as manifested in his adulation of Goethe, is still theoretically viable. Clearly it can no longer claim, in its all-consuming, unifying perspective, to represent the full truth about an age. The present study of women's autobiography in nineteenth-century Germany will illustrate just why it is necessary to postulate a "self", though it be a fragmented one. It asserts the authenticity of experience, though not of all expression of experience. In no other way can these works be adequately explained or incorporated into our understanding of the world.

Foucault offers yet more assistance to this project. For him the denial of the subject occured in the context of a critique of history. Drawing heavily on Nietzsche and juxtaposing genealogy to history, he called for an overthrow of history and the foundation of genealogy.[16] That is, he pronounced linear, meaningful, teleological interpretations of history to be shams. Taking to the barricades three years after May, 1968 he assaulted the concept of a timeless and essential secret or idea behind history as well as the very concept of progress proposed by "radicals" of the day. The "adolescent quest" (143) (including Sartre's!) represented by such ideas contrasted a history of erroneous understanding with the revelation of contemporary truth. According to him, it was a position of arrogance — and ignorance as well, since these histories were "free from the restraints of positive knowledge".(143) Writing, so it seems, in reaction to any metaphysical, neo-Hegelian, or neo-Marxist interpretations of history, he perceived that intellectuals were now emerging from the history of truth and gradually realizing there was none to be articulated. He proposed the relativism of all times and ideas.(144) The genealogical approach to history would answer these needs by studying "descent" in history and without applying pre-conceived notions of "meaning":

"Where the soul pretends unification or the self fabricates a co-

herent identity, the genealogist sets out to study the beginning
[. . .]. The analysis of descent permits the dissociation of the self,
its recognition and displacement as an empty synthesis, in liberating a profusion of lost events.[. . .] An examination of descent
permits discovery, under the unique aspect of a trait or a concept, of the myriad events through which — thanks to which,
against which — they were formed. Genealogy does not pretend
to go back in time to restore an unbroken continuity that oper-
ates beyond the dispersion of forgotten things [. . .] Genealogy
does not resemble the evolution of the species and does not map
the destiny of a people. On the contrary, to follow the complex
course of descent is to maintain passing events in their proper
dispersion[. . .]." (145-6)

There is room in an "historical" approach to take stock of what is normally
relegated to the peripheries of dominant history. There is room to ask why
women's experience and women's autobiographies have been ignored. There
is room to give them their own value and not permit them to be relegated
to the peripheries. Such an approach also obliges us not to reconstruct another "history", giving dominance to another position, even if it is a "feminist" one. It obliges us to perceive the dispersion of all "history". Analysing
descent need not deny the connection between events, nor the presence of
domination, nor even the infusion of values. It can mean opening the "un-
stable assemblages of faults, fissures, and heterogeneous layers"(146).

Strangely and despite other philosophical differences, Barthes and Foucault share with positivism a distrust of introspective observation and the
concept of subjectivity. Indeed at least in the late 1960s and early 1970s some
French leftists referred to Foucault's philosophy as a "new positivism". And,
to be sure, he shared other traits with the old nineteenth-century variety as
well. It, too, pretended pure devotion to the object (Foucault, 147); promoted
absolute relativity; opposed the imposition of metaphysical meaning or tran-
scendental values. In contrast to the older positivism, however, the new one
denied historical progress and denied that anyone ever has privilege to the
"truth", in essence denied the possibility of establishing any laws of historical or human behavior. Indeed one critic perceptively referred to Foucault's
work as *un positivisme désespéré*.[17] However neither the new nor the old
positivism believed the individual could contribute with intention to the
course of history. Individuals remain the instruments of some instance of
history.

It was precisely against such dry, valueless, positivistic investigations that

Dilthey had reacted. He criticized the fact that for positivists and empiricists "The self-active 'I' is. . .an illusion of the intuitive standpoint".[8] We may not like the particularities of Dilthey's formulation of the concept of "self", but positing one need not return us to Dilthey's universals. Foucault held that the very interpretation of history (and we might draw parallels with personal history, autobiography) was a form of domination, "the violent or surreptitious appropriation of a system of rules, which in itself has no essential meaning, in order to impose a direction" (151-2). In autobiography this would refer to the author's imposition of interpretation on events of her own life. The search for genealogical descent (consider again the implications for personal narration) does not build imposing structures or pronounce "apocalyptic objectivity". On the contrary it disturbs what was previously considered immobile, it fragments what was thought unified; it shows the heterogeneity of what was imagined consistent within itself.(147) History (read autobiography) must not "compose the finally reduced diversity of time into a totality fully closed upon itself".(152) Genealogy refuses the certainty of absolutes. It possesses a "glance that distinguishes, separates, and disperses, that is capable of liberating divergence and marginal elements — the kind of dissociating view that is capable of decomposing itself, capable of shattering the unity of man's being through which it was thought that he could extend his sovereignty to the events of his past."(153) Genealogy excludes the rediscovery of ourselves as self-identical individuals.(153) For the purposes of this study of women's autobiography: It must dis/close the "self". The imagination, dreams, and creativity of the "self" experienced and expressed (or unclearly expressed) may not represent the "whole" self, but they deserve to be considered as part of it. They are usually present in autobiography.

Surely Dilthey's concept of "Geistesgeschichte" is included in Foucault's condemnation: "An entire historical tradition (theological or rationalistic) aims at dissolving the singular event into an ideal continuity — as a teleological movement or a natural process."(154) While feminists need to posit a subject, women have no stake in resurrecting or maintaining such a monolithic history. There is no room for their history within it.

Foucault's genealogy claims to recognize no constants.(153) He claimed everything that is considered immortal or immutable — even sentiment, instinct, the body — has, as Nature had for Feuerbach, a descent. And yet, perhaps because he drew a little too heavily on Nietzsche, there is one constant, one law, for Foucault: "the endlessly repeated play of dominations".(150) Those forces dissatisfied with the status quo phrase their demands in the language of their oppressors with the aim of subverting them, but they only end by restructuring domination. Certainly, feminists do recognize the constancy of male domination to date and for this reason find it difficult to accept totally Foucault's assertion of the "singular randomness of events".(154) For them domination has been all too specific and not at all abstract. There has been too much consistency in the single principle of male domination to consider that random. However, it remains to be seen whether women's strategies for subversion have remained within the "endlessly repeated play of dominations", or whether some have not managed to create something new.

Ultimately this study of women and autobiography in nineteenth-century Germany will take from the categories of both history and genealogy. Insofar as it assumes some connection between writer and autobiographer and focuses on individuals and their conception of self — even though they are not the "purest individuals"(155) — it falls into Foucault's category of "history". In other respects, however, it hopes to have benefitted from the critique of the concepts of "self" and "history". It does not posit, even as a goal, the principle of a unified, harmonious individual. Rather it recognizes the inevitable fragmentation of the self as well as the existence of imposed structures. It also seeks to avoid a teleological, unidirectional account of the "history" of women's autobiography. Although the autobiographies have been selected from the full range of time between 1790 and 1914, this is not intended to represent a linear development of women's autobiographical forms. It is rather a recognition of the fact that certain life patterns and literary forms cannot emerge until other events make them thinkable or even possible.

In the end Foucault may after all have reaffirmed a concept of the "self", for he affirms knowledge as perspectival, not universal truth. Genealogy would recognize the bias of the viewer. History discreetly effaces the subject before the objects to be observed. Genealogy, writes Foucault, does not seek laws because it gives equal weight to its own sight and objects. "A characteristic of history is to be without choice." (157) Historians obscure preferences, their own taste; they lack individuality in the face of their universal judgements. Readers of this text can only assume that genealogy posits choices in history and asserts preferences. But choices and preferences, if they are true choices and preferences, can only be made by subjects or individuals.

For this writer such a view represents a call to reinscribe the subject. Foucault desires a historical perspective which is not void of passions and instinct, but manifests a will to knowledge. It is unfortunate indeed that he does not elaborate this most significant point, for it is one of the issues most vital for a discussion of women's autobiography. Women have had little confidence in their passions and instincts, little sense of entitlement to choice or preference, little sense of "self". For them especially the assertion of choice is an issue both for daily life and for autobiography, personal history.

Women do benefit from an anti-teleological, anti-idealist historical perspective both on history and on their own lives, but it is of the utmost importance that they do not relinquish the concepts of "self" or the authenticity of experience in so doing. Conceptualizing a *dispersed* subject may be necessary for women — and genealogists who wish to avoid hierarchies — if they are to liberate the subject, any subject at any time, from universals. But the concept of "self" is essential if we are not to remain fatalistic and without a sense of choice. At the last minute even the French "positiviste désespéré" reinstated hope when he reinserted the subject.

The question of course remains, how to transfer these theoretical considerations to textual analysis. Dilthey considered only the relationship of an individual to the historical totality, and the degree to which that individual expressed and furthered it. While he sought to *understand* the particular, he always measured it against his concept of the totality. Although he insisted on the individual, he continually undercut himself by subsuming any individual into the totality. As those more recent scholars of German autobiography have perceived, his models fail sufficiently to recognize the difference of class. They also fail to account for gender. For all his efforts to avoid abstract systems not rooted in reality, he assumed an insufficiently differentiated (dispersed) totality. The dialectical nature of the relationship of subject and community needs to be reestablished.

Like Dilthey, Schleiermacher emphasized the individual. He saw a continual reciprocal relation between the individual and the community, the particular and the universal. For him, however, the universal did not subsume and thereby cancel the individual. Schleiermacher did not sleight individual experience for the sake of logical coherence, and as a post-Kantian he also maintained that thoughts, as representations of reality, were distinct from "the real". However, while for him they failed to correlate absolutely with reality, they were not out of all relation to it![9]

In continually jostling back and forth between historical script and individual experience, between tradition and innovation a reader may hope to dis/close some truth about autobiographies and about women in nineteenth-century Germany. Barthes has warned: "To give a text an Author is to impose a limit on that text, to furnish it with a final signified, to close the writing." (147) Just that should be avoided. In order to do that the discontinuities and incoherences in a life cannot be "resolved". They must be allowed to remain.

At the same time one must recognize the individual in the active spirit of innovative autobiographical forms. Schleiermacher maintained: "Was aus der Menschen gemeinschaftlichem Handeln hervorgehen kann, soll alles an mir vorüber ziehen, mich regen und bewegen um von mir wieder bewegt zu werden, und in der Art wie ichs aufnehme und behandle will ich immer meine Freiheit finden, und äussernd bilden meine Eigenthümlichkeit."[20]) It is his recognition of the interaction of individual and social which is of interest for this study.

If one considers a life as a living out of a script that determines partially, and in no small way, the content and form of that life, writing autobiography becomes a complex and multilayered task. Both the text one has lived, and continues to live, as well as the text one writes have predetermined forms. There are both literary and social discourses which an autobiography must satisfy. An autobiographer must attempt to fashion one into the other. As always, however, there are a range of texts from which to choose, both in life and in literary form, and precisely those choices as well as the innovations on standard texts do *express* something of the condition and inclination of the author.

1

THE CASES OF BALDINGER, ENGEL, AND WALLENRODT

If a study such as this is to succeed it requires a firm understanding of the social as well as formal parameters in which women wrote, in particular, the social ramifications of the formal parameters. In the case of Germany around 1800 autobiography of the period has been well researched. With what is perhaps a characteristically encyclopedic approach combined with broad historical perspectives, German scholars have extensively documented the autobiographical traditions of this period (with the notable exception, of course, of works by women).

Among German historians of the genre there is now a consensus that autobiographical form evolved quickly at the end of the eighteenth century, simultaneously with the novel in Germany and linked with the new sense of individual worth gradually articulated by the middle classes. Misch had exalted Goethe's *Dichtung und Wahrheit* to the pinnacle of individual human consciousness and the achievement of near total self-awareness. As noted in the previous chapter, however, more recently the tendency has been to associate the development of the genre with bourgeois individualism, viewing it either as the triumph of that individualist spirit, as Neumann is inclined to see it, or as a manifestation of the struggle to achieve a sense of self vis-a-vis established powers against which one is largely helpless, as Müller in inclined to do.[2] In either case this process of evolution produced standards which would define the worth attributed to individual lives, standards by which members of the middle class could affirm their own worth.

To demonstrate both the difficulties confronting women who attempted to adapt to male models and the relative adequacy or inadequacy of various forms as vehicles for the portrayal of their lives, it will be useful to approach the problem with categories established by Günter Niggl. If I have chosen Günter Niggl's *Die deutsche Autobiographie im 18. Jahrhundert* as a starting point, it is surely not to single out his work as a particularly gross example of male myopia.[3] If anything his work represents some of the most careful and thorough analyses of the eighteenth-century forms and their development. Indeed just because he is so careful, his categories of autobiography in the eighteenth century reveal especially well the problems of

1

women writing then and the hazards for historians of the genre of neglecting women's lives as they lived and wrote them.

Niggl distinguishes three traditions of autobiographical writings in the eighteenth century. They are 1) the religious confession, 2) the autobiography of profession (*"Berufsautobiographie"*), and 3) the autobiography of adventure (*"abenteuerliche Autobiographie"*). In terms of sheer numbers confessions may have outweighed the others. With its emphasis on the emotional commitment of the individual soul rather than commitment to dogma; Pietism, like Quakerism in England, fostered confessional writing. Within Pietist communities the members were called upon to give testimony and admonished to keep diaries of their innermost feelings. The summary explanation of the history of one's rebirth would then be derived from journal entries. One early collection of confessionals, Johann Henrich Reitz' *Historie der Wiedergebohrnen* (1701), demonstrates their strong uniformity. In the second half of the eighteenth century the communities themselves began to publish these testimonies for their brothers and sisters elsewhere. Yet originally these testimonies were intended only for the immediate Pietist community and the diary, which was to be a dialogue with one's soul, was considered the primary form.

Regardless of the particular community of religious friends, German Pietist confessions were modeled for the most part after August Hermann Francke's *Lebenslauff* (1690/91). In turn, its structure of recognition of sins, fear, religious doubts, desire for salvation, intensive prayer, sudden awakening, and certainty of faith reflected the Augustinian tradition. Yet, beginning even with Francke, this form rarely retained a purely religious nature. For instance, in order to portray the sinful quality of his earlier life Francke incorporated the extensive pre-history to his conversion. While this allowed him to trace his early childhood development and education, the story often seems to find its own raison d'etre when Francke opines on the proper methods of child raising, lists all his teachers and disputation themes and provides excursive defenses of his earlier positions. Similarly Johann Wilhelm Petersen's *Lebensbeschreibung* (1717) recounts how he shut out the world in favor of God's service and then elaborates his difficulties facing the world as a devout believer. Worldly intrigues, debates, and theological positions come to the fore. In both Francke's and Petersen's cases the autobiography of profession had infiltrated and revised a more purely interior history of the soul. Only, it seems, among women Pietists did this infiltration fail to occur.

Both the autobiography of profession and the autobiography of adventure derive from a common source: domestic and family chronicles (*"Haus-und Familienchroniken"*) familiar since the end of the fifteenth century. Although originally written for family use, extant copies of early autobiographies of profession suggest a form closely related to the more public eulogy: biography, characteristics, list of works. The biography would normally include a list of ancestors; the circumstance of the author's birth and baptism; a brief description of childhood, focusing on misfortunes; education at home and in school; travels for study or business, including facts and details about business transactions; marriage, births, illnesses, misfortunes, and deaths. Following this chronicle there would be a description of the author's character in either psychological or moral terms. A bibliography of works, often annotated, concludes the autobiography. Thus the autobiography of profession focuses more strongly on external worldly experiences and receives its structure from those. Although such works had been published since the middle of the sixteenth century, an excuse to do so was usually found to be necessary. Initially such an apology would refer to religious or theological disputes, but by mid-century it might also refer to philosophical, scientific, or political debates. Early eighteenth-century lexica of intellectuals collected such autobiographies of profession.

The autobiography of adventure, differing initially from that of profession only in its content, soon developed a new form precisely because of that content. Due to the popular appeal of adventure no apology was deemed necessary, and these works focused increasingly on the individual. Indeed Niggl distinguishes between those autobiographies of adventure which focus on objective or practical purposes, such as providing geographical, anthropological, or business information, and those which tend to focus more on the biography of the individual. The latter was generally not published until the mid-nineteenth century and, like the autobiography of profession, intended for family use. The former were published much earlier. In form they differed only slightly from autobiographies of profession. There was a summary description of childhood and education before the narration of travel adventures as pilgrim, businessperson, craftsperson, or soldier. This central, most important and elaborate part was concluded by eventual marriage or discovery of a profession.

Investigating contemporary novels of adventure, Niggl proposes that after 1720 and the publication of *Robinson Crusoe* in German this type of novel came more and more to resemble narrative forms of actual travelogues and autobiographies of adventure in its unrestrained accumulation of experienced events and episodically introduced biographies of other characters. Simultaneously, novelistic techniques gradually enlivened the autobiography of adventure. Burlesque and erotic motifs began to appear; lovers' escapades, duels, robberies, exotic travels, and war experiences often elaborated or embroidered autobiographies of this type in the later eighteenth century. Niggl demonstrates that this overlapping of genres actually accorded with aesthetic programs formulated in the mid-eighteenth century to mix the formerly separate categories of novel and history.[4]

Since it increasingly influenced the form of the other two traditions, Niggl holds the autobiography of profession to be the most important autobiographical form in the eighteenth century. This, he maintains, reveals a stengthened sense of self at least among professionals and adventurers. Clearly the relationship of women to profession and adventure was not that of men, and that difference inevitably affects the nature of the autobiographies women write. But how? What might be expected of women with professional or adventurous ambitions in the eighteenth century?

To be sure, generally speaking, women were not in a historical position to take advantage of the new vitality displayed by these autobiographical traditions, but the eighteenth century did witness occasional examples of female professionals and adventurers. Encouraged by reports from Bologna where Laura Bassi had earned degrees in philosophy and medicine in 1732, two German women dared take similar steps.[5] Dorothea Christiana Erxleben (1715-1762) had grown up helping her doctor father. When her application for formal study in Halle was rejected on account of her sex she wrote a treatise on the right and ability of women to study (*Ursachen, die das weibliche Geschlecht vom Studieren abhalten* (1742)). After her appeal to the newly crowned Frederick II, however, the University of Halle was obliged to admit its first female candidate for a degree in medicine. After some years of interruption (she married and had four children) she submitted her dissertation and was awarded a medical degree in 1754. The case was famous, and the poeticizing mathemetician Abraham Gotthelf Kästner (1719-1800) wrote a satirical verse about her—the same Güttinger Kästner that Frederike Baldinger would claim as a friend:

Zusatz zu der Frau Doctorinn***Inauguraldisputation
Da man bey Curen oft sich gütig übereilt,
Läßt sich, Frau Doctorinn, dir noch ein Beyspiel sagen:
Da dein Geschlecht oft von gewissen Plagen
Zwar schnell und angenehm, doch nicht gar sicher heilt.[6]

The condescension and ridicule apparent in this satiric verse was undoubtedly a mild reaction for the times. Erxleben may be referred to as the "German Bassi", but her case remained unique in eighteenth-century German medical history.

Dorothea Schlözer (1770-1825) also acquired much of her learning at the knee of her famous professor father. At the age of 17, attired in bride-like white and with flowers in her hair, she was examined by Göttingen professors and awarded a master's and doctor of philosophy, the first German woman to be so honored. The same mathematician Kästner, one of her examiners, admitted his astonishment at Schlözer's adroitness in answering her last question, a problem that a long-since reknowned candidate had not been able to solve.[8] The poet Friedrich Schiller called the whole thing an "erbärmliche Farce", but Schlözer's image was nevertheless etched and silhouetted and sold far and wide. She clearly remained an exotic exception, while other women were allowed to languish for want of education. What was to become of such a woman? Could she earn her own living? Schlözer was not the woman to assert herself in the consequences of her accomplishments. She married a Senator in Lübeck, bore him three children and for a while headed a house that received domestic and international poets and intellects. The Napoleonic wars destroyed her family's wealth and health. Schlözer died at age 55, raising the question in many people's minds of the use of educating women when they were not to apply their knowledge in a systematic way.

Women, then, did pursue professions or adventures. Erxleben continued practicing medicine. Although Schlözer made no use of her formally recognized education, Luise Gottsched — not formally granted a degree — did use her learning. Like Erxleben and Schlözer, she too, had a demanding, highly educated father. She married and aided her husband in his translations, dramas, and poetics. She, too, was famed throughout Germany for her learning, but, although she authored several plays herself, she was and is known for the work she did in the service of her husband's career.

There were adventurers, too. According to song, legend and historical report the eighteenth century witnessed examples of women adventurers. Some women cross dressed in order to take out to sea or to soldier. But numerically speaking, most of these women adventurers were wives of sea captains or soldiers or female servants.[9] Might not women of this type, breaking with difficulty the limitations put on their lives, write autobiographies displaying pride in their accomplishment and a new sense of confidence — as had their male counterparts?

Certainly conditions mediated against women publishing autobiographies at all, but we do have some. And just because it must have been so difficult to publish these accounts, we might assume we have those autobiographies of the most bold. In examining a few of the ones we do have, the picture of their struggles with the limitations both of their positions and of the autobiographical forms becomes more vivid. In 1783 Frederika Baldinger intended to record the history of her intellect in *Versuch über meine Verstandeserziehung*,[10] thereby setting herself the same task that scholars and intellectuals had for centuries when writing autobiographies of profession. Certainly not as well known as Luise Gottsched or Dorothea Schlözer, she does seem to have possessed a modicum of fame for her learning. For reasons we shall come to understand, however, Baldinger herself never published this work. Instead Sophie von la Roche edited it in 1791. La Roche was, by then, a well-known novelist in her own right, having achieved fame with the publication of an epistolary novel of sentimental education, *Die Geschichte des Fräuleins von Sternheim*, in 1771. She hoped the *Versuch* and the reknown Madame Baldinger enjoyed among learned persons would encourage women to use every opportunity available to improve and enrich their minds. The work appeared therefore in an enlightened, even polemical, spirit for the education and betterment of the position of women.

If the lessons women might learn from this work are disconcerting today, they were dubious even in the eighteenth century, for Baldinger expresses doubts about her abilities even in the opening sentence: "Die Geschichte meines Verstandes soll ich aufzeichnen? Als ob ich so viel Verstand hätte, dass es der Mühe verlohnte seinen Gang nachzuspähen." (17) Even closing the *Versuch* she seems to doubt that the learnedness for which she is known can be credited to herself: "Ob ich mir nun was darauf zugute thun soll, wenn mich Freunde meines Verstandes wegen ehren, weis ich nicht. Gehen Sie stufenweise mit mir bis zu der Höhe, wo auch Kästner und Lichtenberg meine Freunde wurden, ich glaube, auch der dummste Mensch würde, in Absicht auf Verstand, bei beiden gewinnen. Verdient das wohl ihre Bewunderung wenn ich durch so gute Gesellschaft erträglich geworden bin."(38) To be sure Kästner and Lichtenberg were major figures in the German Enlightenment, but her very admirable virtue of giving credit to others is carried to a vice when she refuses even to give herself credit for attracting friends such as these. The accomplishments others admire in her, she minimizes by considering herself barely adequate. The *Versuch* is thus framed by Baldinger's painfully self-deprecatory remarks.

One wonders why she did go to the effort to record her story. Her own answer appears vaguely in the letter to her husband which La Roche placed as a preface. Apparently she hoped only to please her husband on his birthday, i.e., it was to be a domestic record. And yet she had, slyly, had her eye on publication. In the letter Baldinger stated she had not known if her husband would like to be surprised by first reading her published dedication to him and so revised her original plans of publishing it without his knowledge. After all she was "ein viel zu unbedeutendes Ding,...als dass [sie] verlangen sollte, man möge [ihre] Verstandes Erziehung gedruckt lesen."(15) She surely knew that of the standard apologies given for writing the history of one's intellect she possessed none: no publications, no theological, philosophical, historical, or political positions to defend. Her claim to fame was that famous men like Kästner and Lichtenberg, whom she mentions only the one time, enjoyed talking to her and admired her intelligence. She is at a loss for the traditional apology and so claims to write in obedience to her husband's wishes. Such apologies, however, may tell us less about the author than the perceived social expectations, for it is certainly also possible to see her modesty as a pose, masking what she imagines others would have considered immodest and unfeminine behavior. In her letter she wrote: "Wenig Weiber sind ihren Männern so viel schuldig als ich Dir schuldig bin. Dies mögen meine Leser beherzigen, wenn sie gehorsam gegen Dich, als Eitelkeit von meiner Seite auslegen wollten."(16) Her excruciating self-belittlement seems intended to counteract those who would think her too bold. And yet, insofar as such a thing is possible, the pose must also be considered genuine and absolutely mandatory, for we would not have the manuscript at all had her husband not given it to Sophie von la Roche. Ultimately she entrusted her entire pride to her husband for his decision regarding publication. She maintained the pose — and died without seeing her autobiography published. The role was as authentic as her self-pride.

Circumspection with regard to herself and her abilities characterizes the autobiography. Baldinger reassures her reader (in the first place, her husband) that she is happy to be the wife of a learned and wise man and finds the intellect of men and their books useful in women's domestic duties. She explicitly supports women's learning but subordinates it to a man's life. Such subordination is consistent with Rousseau's philosophy and with her own accompanying letter. She dedicates her talents, her learning and her reason solely to her husband and her domestic duties. And just this is precisely the problematic issue: the priority she must still give her domestic role. Such a critique of Baldinger's circuitous support for women's education is likely to be considered unhistorical, especially since Mary Wollstonecraft had not yet even argued on similar grounds in favor of women's education. From this point of view Baldinger therefore appears quite progressive. But if we look harder at the *Versuch* itself Baldinger's own compromises become painfully apparent. Indeed this work would be far less interesting if awe-stricken humility were the only glimpse of the author we received.

The very stance of the adult narrator clashes with her own self-portrait of herself as a spunky, defiant girl who had the loftiest goals for herself. As a young girl she had noticed that learned men were honored in journals as though they were kings and emperors and desired nothing less that the same respect for herself. Astonishingly little female modesty in these goals. The values were formed early; the humility evolved later. Although admonished for laziness and warned that no man would want a bookish woman, reading became her primary occupation and passion: "Meine Liebe zu den Wissenschaften wuchs je mehr ich mit ihnen bekannt wurde."(36) She clearly devoured books in her childhood for their own sakes and not for the benefit of any future husband or domestic responsibility. As a girl she had not even wanted to marry, since the dichotomy between domesticity and learnedness had been made so clear to her. She had had a tendency to poke fun at everything and a desire "immer frey und von der ganzen Welt unabhängig zu seyn."(26)

She reserved all her veneration for learning and for the intellect. Indeed, these became the primary basis for her estimation of people. She is therefore for instance somewhat harsh in her treatment of women. Of her mother she wrote: "[Sie] war die rechtschaffenste Frau, die ich je gekannt habe. Aber in allem Verstande *Frau*, die sich weiter durch nichts auszeichnete."(18) Although she is far from unaware of the social forces at work—she excuses an aunt since "sie hatte aber niemals etwas kluges gelesen und die Zeiten in welchen sie jung gewesen war, waren noch nicht die vortheilhaftesten für die weibliche Erziehung."(20)—she becomes, through her love of learning, something of a misogynist.

By necessity it was men who helped her learn and to whom she is grateful for whatever knowledge she has acquired. As a young girl non-learned men had failed to interest her in the slightest and she was unable to comprehend why men had all the power. "Ich hatte mir in den Kopf gesetzt: die Männer müssten schlechterdings alle klüger seyn wie die Weiber, weil sie sich das Regiment über uns anmassen, ich fand bei den wenigsten, dass sie aus Ueberlegenheit des Verstandes, ein Recht dazu hätten. Dies machte mich gegen ein ganzes Geschlecht feindselig."(27) Although she thus admits to a childhood anger at the irrationality of male dominance in society, and in consequence at a whole sex, she now considers such an opinion "unbeson-nen"(27). Must we assume that she has since been persuaded of the vast su-periority of male reason and learning and therefore accepts their domination? Or did her perception change as a result of concrete pressures? That the attitude she espouses in her narration caused hostility toward her own sex does not seem to concern her. She knows that her sex excluded her from the possibility of becoming a scholar, but she never questions the "providence" which ordained her for the kitchen and not the school. Bluntly stated, she comes to admire men because of their privilege. Sophie von la Roche also emulates this perspective when she praises Baldinger's mascu-line intellect and character in the preface and admires in both the worthy friend of Kästner and Lichtenberg. The sentence which concludes the *Versuch* sums up this sentiment: "Als Frau bin ich erträglich geworden, wie klein würde ich doch als Mann seyn."(38) The awe impressed on her of male tra-ditions approaches a kind of psychological terrorism, one which necessar-ily produces a sense of a self at odds with itself.

What the reader learns about the intellectual development of the author is her ultimate acceptance of male domination, but precisely this story is not told. We are only allowed a glimpse of the real story by contrasting nar-rator and protagonist. But who is the "Author" of this text, as it is written? The narrator? The protagonist? The only possible answer is that she is all and none. As an autobiography of profession this work is a failure. Bal-dinger's unresolved childhood dreams of respect and power reflect her earli-est desires and remain unfulfilled. Her sole intellectual accomplishment is the friendship of two famous men, and that is not quite an accepted stan-dard for "profession".

In most male autobiographies of intellectual development one learns about the content of that learning, how philosophical positions were ar-rived at. Even another social outsider like Solomon Maimon described his development in this manner in his *Lebensgeschichte* (1792/3). Baldinger, however, conveys nothing of the content of her learning, only its fact, and her struggle to acquire it. She had learned to compromise and it is here that our critique must not be unhistorical, indeed must see history. Baldinger's compromise is a weaker position than the one she held as a youth and in that sense she accommodates herself. As a child she had not needed the ideo-logical justifications of usefulness in domestic activities to buttress her de-sire to learn or acquire respect. Her compromise represents a rationalization she, and possibly Wollstonecraft, had to make to get the notion of educa-tion for women accepted at all. There were few opportunities for unmarried women to pursue goals of scholarship or support themselves, as Baldinger would have needed to do. Women's desire for learning did not change with the advance of history. There was not suddenly a new conscious-ness. Moreover, not only does that desire have a history, it has also been expressed by women like Baldinger.

One statement toward the end of Baldinger's *Versuch* almost symbolizes the difficulty. As a child she had separated domesticity from learning. The avid child reader "hatte alle Anlage zu einer Heiligen, [sie] war fromm, und eine Vestalin, schwärmte auch."(32) If she had to choose, she would choose the mind. Even in her marriage she did not seem to respond well to sexual advances of her husband: "Da meine oberen Seelenkräfte immer das Übergewicht für allen Niedern behalten haben; so weis ich nicht, ob [mein Mann] sich (sic), als Frau betrachtet, bei mir allemal nach seinen Wünschen gestanden hat [. . .]. Ich suchte meine Fehler zu verbessern, dass ich meinen Kopf mehr anbauete; setzte Freundschaft an die Stelle thierischer Liebe."(35) Not only is she able to emphasize her continuing interest in the intellect with this statement, such an image corresponded well with sentimental, Rousseauian notions about marriage and the nature of women as asexual beings.

But her sex life could not have been as negligible as she would lead us to believe, for she reports the fact of many pregnancies. While these experiences represent perhaps the core of domesticity, and from that point of view for Baldinger the antithesis to learning, it was only in this way that she was able to read at all. Only during the six weeks lying-in period did she have the time to devote to books. Thus, in a peculiar fashion, the requirements of domesticity actually provided the only chance for a woman of her background to pursue any intellectual occupation at all.

Baldinger's experience and the uncertainty with which she approached the form has stamped the form of her *Versuch*. Her education was sporadic and undirected and she therefore fails to show the traditional lines of intellectual development. In fact she relates more about the people who helped her to learn and those who did not than the development of her intellect and her beliefs as such. Her struggle for permission to read and learn is really the content of her autobiography. But this very experience she felt unable to describe explicitly. She fails to show the transition of childhood to maturity; she shows only the discrepancy. In addition (or as a consequence) the paragraphing is awkward and the narration often disconnected. She makes syntactic and grammatical mistakes which Sophie von la Roche did not correct. Her difficulty in speaking and her lack of practice in writing make themselves felt in the content, form, style, and spelling. Accepting the traditional form of male autobiogrpahies without critical consideration for her own real experience has produced a very painful work to read.

The autobiography of profession had highlighted the acquisition of a life's calling or learned position. Since she had not been permitted to become a professional or a learned person, Baldinger's accomplishments appear small when measured by those standards and inappropriate for the form. To highlight her interrupted struggle to learn and her incomplete progress would require a different form, perhaps even an autobiography in a descending line. Despite that her determination, industry, and intelligence merit the pride which is masked, and even denied, for the sake of public appearances.

Baldinger's inability ever to feel comfortable acknowledging her achievements and talents suggests the very different attitude toward profession, namely the possession of a profession was not a source of unambivalent pride or self-confidence for women. It was an attitude which not only kept many women from attempting to learn a profession, but which also made their relationship to the form, autobiography of profession, necessarily more complex than for men. The life scripts available to ambitious women were woefully limited; but the dominant autobiographical scripts were also woefully inadequate to express the reality of their lives. Neither Erxleben, Schlözer, nor Gottsched wrote autobiographies, but it seems reasonable to assume that had they attempted to shape their experience into the traditional professional life story they would have encountered similar contradictions. In all likelihood they would not have dealt with them any more creatively than Baldinger. This form, which Niggl claims to be the most productive and influential in the evolution of modern autobiography, was utterly inappropriate for the expression of women's experience.

Not only was there no place in society for Baldinger to realize her dreams, there was no room in the autobiographical tradition either to express straightforward pride in her achievements or frustration at the limitations confronting her. The adventurous lives of Regula Engel, the Swiss Amazon, and of Isabella von Wallenrodt tell us even more about the constraints on women in traditional autobiogaphical forms. The widow of a Swiss General in Napoleon's army Regula Engel (1761-1853) first published her memoirs under the title *Lebensbeschreibung der Wittwe des Obrist Florian Engel* in 1821![11] They became so popular that a second edition appeared in 1825 bearing the much more sensational title, *Die schweizerische Amazone*. While she engaged in battle on two occasions, that title is nevertheless somewhat misleading as fighting was certainly not her profession. If at all, her feats were amazonian in a very different sense. She accompanied her husband on Napoleon's campaigns, traversing most of Europe and the Near East. As a widow she traveled to North America. By themselves these experiences were surely trying enough for a woman in the early nineteenth century, but in addition she amply fulfilled her domestic responsibilities in as far as she bore, in the course of her travels, 21 children in 36 years of marriage. (She eased the task of caring for so many children somewhat by leaving all but the youngest child with friends.) Engel had followed her husband's bidding to share his joy and sorrow, but if love and obedience provided a rationale, Engel also distinctly relishes her adventures and even preens herself on her bravery and acquired wisdom. This form of autobiography offered the opportunity to display her experiences.

The *Lebensbeschreibung* follows typical patterns of the autobiography of adventure. Engel narrates her childhood cursorily. The story of her parent's adventurous union precedes that of her childhood in which the most monumental event was her parents' divorce. Episodes with a mean stepmother are followed by her adventures when she runs away. Her real mother teaches her to sew, but it is a profession to which she will not take recourse. The chapters devoted to her life with Florian Engel are filled with reminiscences of military campaigns. Napoleon bestows many favors on the couple, and in gratitude they follow him into exile on Elba. After Florian Engel's death at Waterloo her requests for a pension from the new French government are, perhaps understandably, denied. Without income she sets out to find her five remaining children hoping for a source of support in her old age. Her travels to America and Italy prove fruitless. Destitute and thrown on the mercy of friends she resolves to earn money by writing her memoirs. Thus her primary admitted motivation was financial. In addition to the sale of books moreover it seems likely that she thought the tale would advance her appeal for a pension. Apparently Engel felt no compulsion to invent an apology for a woman presenting her memoirs to the public. Indeed, as Niggl has indicated, an autobiography of adventure usually needed none, since adventures themselves guaranteed pleasure and interest. Barely six years after Waterloo a work such as Engel's could be assured of finding readers.

Soldiers and statesmen usually told the kinds of insider stories Engel relates about the Napoleonic campaigns. Learned or professional men most often describe their travels to exotic places like North America. Engel enjoys her unusual status as a female memoir writer, and she shows herself to be well aware of her tradition. The form requires, for instance, that only those events involving the narrator be told; otherwise it would invade the territory of historical writing. While Regula Engel may have witnessed the campaigns as a whole, she did not generally participate in the battles or the politics. So she describes forts being erected around Cairo or winds that prevented Napoleon from landing in England and appears careful to observe formal limits: "Doch ich schreibe nicht Kriegsgeschichte und darf von diesen Vorfällen nur so viel anführen, als mich etwa besonders berührt. . . (.)"(34) and elsewhere: "Ich bitte um Entschuldigung wenn ich hier ein wenig zu politisieren anfange, ich verspreche dafür nur so zu erzählen, wie ich es gehört habe. . . (.)"(59) As these passages themselves suggest however she had some difficulty staying within those limits, and she seems to prefer explaining things like why the Emperor made his brother King of Naples. Moreover she seems either to recognize that the association with Napoleon will draw readers or to feel that this experience was truly her most exciting, for she embroiders her relationship to him with suspicious personal details. Claims that twins she bore and named after the Emperor followed him to St. Helena cannot be verified.(271) Her attempts to visit them later, then, must not have occurred in reality. The scene in which Napoleon seems to notice her sturdy Swiss legs and to offer her coffee appears only in the second edition. It is easier to explain why she may have added this anecdote than why she omitted it the first time. But if we cannot totally trust her veracity in all respects, surely it is not the first time an adventurer has enlivened a tale, and it can be no accident that the enlargements concerned the figure of Napoleon.

As a traveler to North America, after the death of her husband, her attention turns to customs and manners. Without the catalyst of the Napoleonic army major historical events no longer present themselves to her for description. At the same time she emerges more clearly as a personality. With her husband she had followed Napoleon's fates; now she must make her own. She must find money, make friends, and look for her children. Earlier she had merely idolized Napoleon (she refers to him as "mein Herr Gevatter" (151)), but now her own, progressive opinions surface. She admires a utopian community in Ohio, the Constitution of the United States, the freedom, and the ability to move upward through hard work.

Her broad travels surely qualified her as an observer of customs, and yet she comments with exaggerated modesty (though still nothing approaching Baldinger's humility): "Da ich jetzt von meiner grosser Reise auf dem Continent Nord-Amerikas zu erzählen beginne, muss ich meine Leser zu voraus erinnern, dass ich weder als Naturforscher, noch als Staatsmann oder merkantilischer Spekulant reise. . .Was ich indessen von den Sitten und der

Lebensart der Einwohner dieser Länder beobachtet habe, das will ich in meiner Einfalt, wie ich's gesehen, mittheilen . . . (.)"(110) As her person asserts itself more fully as the focus she becomes somewhat uncertain of her narrative authority. Any number of reasons suggest themselves. She had lost her husband; she was now virtually a charity case; her subject matter was not as sensationally historical. Any or all of these might account for a loss of narrative self-confidence, which is curiously recouped toward the end of the volume as she reports her return to Europe and her trip to Italy in search of a daughter. She relates numerous individual episodes with various personages. Her good reception and the general respect and interest accorded her for her experiences on the campaigns, and her many hardships surely aided her decision, made at the end of the volume, to record her memoirs. The interest has shifted to her as a person. For the first time Regula Engel becomes the focus of the memoir, even though it is as if by proxy for the interest first in Napoleon and second in America.

As characteristic as this phenomenon may appear to be of the lack of legitimacy accorded women's lives, it actually does little to illuminate the constraints on women narrating their life stories. Autobiographies of adventure often leaned toward the form of memoir and tended to focus on public events rather than the narrator. Indeed Niggl had distinguished two types: those concentrating on external events and those concentrating on the author. It is not so much in narrative self-effacement then that the limits on women's autobiographies of adventure can be observed. Rather, the most significant feature about the content of Engel's memoirs is perhaps the least surprising.

Engel had had difficulty with the narration and the requirements of the form itself insofar as she wished to narrate continuously events in which she, as a woman, could not have participated: battles and politics. She had also had difficulty in finding her authority when not discussing world events. She felt the limits of her knowledge and her person in her description of America. Yet those events in which she actively participated or on which her authority would be unquestioned, activities more typical for women, are rarely included. The life in a military camp with only few other women, the difficulties of childbirth under such circumstances, the lives of women in countries she visits, the financial problems of widows; none of these experiences — fraught though they surely were with adventure — are addressed directly or significantly. She need not have focused on herself to call upon her authority. If she thought of it at all she must have suspected that there would be no readers for reminiscences of domestic situations. She knew instinctively, if not consciously, that the narration of female experience would not draw readers. The culture was assumed to be uninterested in the adventures of women's lives, at least in autobiographical forms. Had the comparison of women's experience in childbirth (especially under those circumstances) with that of men in battle been familiar to her, perhaps Engel would have discussed her numerous confinements in more than the subordinate clauses to which she usually relegates them.

While she thus keeps the expectations of the form clearly in mind, the tension on it from the direction of her daily life is poignantly felt. Though her bravery and love of adventure appear genuine, occasionally another side of her life forces itself upon the attention of the reader: her family, domestic, and emotive life. True to chronicle form she does not tarry by announcements of births or deaths. In particular her description of the battle of Waterloo is chilling in its distanced objectivity: "Unser vierter Sohn, Florian...war wahrscheinlich schon tod, als ich meinen lieben Mann fallen sah...(.) Mein jüngster Sohn Joseph, erst zehn Jahr alt, focht an meiner Seite, sein Kopf ward von einer Kugel zerschmettert, ich sah das eine Aug' und sein Gehirn gerade vor mir verspritzen."(87) There is no description of her feelings at this point. She merely notes that she began to attack a British cavalryman, was shot through the neck, and bayonetted through the side. Only after emphasizing that no other woman was ever admitted to the hospital Hotel Dieu or endured so strict a cure does she return to the deaths she witnessed commenting again dryly, "Der Verlust meines geliebten Gatten war schon Stoff genug zum stillen Nachdenken über mich und meine durchlaufenden Schicksale und...mein künftiges Fortkommen...(.)"(89) It is reasonable to assume that Regula Engel experienced some very strong emotions during the time this passage describes. Just what they might have been however we cannot know precisesly. As much as she claims to have loved her husband, the loss of a means of financial support was also a serious matter and undoubtedly entered into if it did not dominate her reflections.

Once before she had thought her husband dead. At that time she recorded no emotions, only her unsuccessful attempt to establish a business. Later, after all her efforts to find her children have failed and she depends totally on charity, she throws herself on her husband's grave and wants to die; but it is the sympathetic reader rather than Engel who assembles these isolated causes for what seems to be a rather sudden misery. She had filled pages with her impressions of America and, to be sure, had noted her unhappiness at finding her son three days before his death: but as she did not generally alert the reader to her state of mind her own wish to die remains unprepared. The rhythms and accents of Engel's life—important births, deaths, turning points—do not correspond to those of the form, the adventure of military engagement and travel. Underneath her narrative of adventures is another life seething with unexpressed feeling and experience, which seems to have felt inappropriate to the form. The turning point in her life which the death of her husband occasioned was critical—for financial as well as any supposed emotional reasons. And yet it plays an insignificant role structurally. Early in the work she had described the emotional effect of her parents' divorce on her and then excused herself: "der liebe Leser verzeihe mir hier an dieser Stelle den kleinen Erguss meiner Empfindungen...(.)"(9) Another life, an unwritten autobiography peers through the restrictions of the traditional form, a life which cannot be expressed given the expectations of that form.

The publication and success of the two editions of her memoirs raised Engel's self image. In 1828 she published a sequel in which she allows herself to come forward more clearly. Book sales still motivate her. Although the first part had been well received, her income from it had been modest. In the second part she describes the renewal of her petition to the French government. More importantly she explains, "Das allgemeine Zutrauen, das ich von allen ächten Geschichtskundigen, ja von allen geneigten Lesern und Wahrheitsfreunden, durch die Ausgabe des ersten Theiles meiner Lebensgeschichte erwarb, der Drang nach diesen Begebenheiten, ja das persönliche Ansuchen veranlasste mich nun, zu einem zweyten Bruchstück oder vielmehr zur Fortsetzung meiner Lebensgeschichte."(191) She now has no great historical events or exotic lands to describe, but seems to believe that interest in her person is sufficiently high to attract readers.

After rejection of her petition for a pension she returns to her home town of Zürich where she expects to be introduced into social circles of "berühmten und gewichtigen Personen in Gastfreundschaft"(238). She is rudely disappointed when her compatriots neglect to accord her these honors and permit her to settle only in Langwies, her husband's birthplace and a village she considers dismal. She resents this decision as she feels herself clearly "ausgezeichnet (ich getraue es mir zu sagen, und der meine Lebensgeschichte gelesen, wird es nicht bezweifeln) unter allen Frauen, nicht nur in Zürich, sondern im übrigen Theile der Schweiz und selbst ausser dessen Grenzen; mit dem Gepräge mitgefochtener Schlachten und mit meinen 21 Kindern umgeben, da diese unsere Namen in unverwesliche Felsen Frankreichs eingehauen...(.)" (238) Although her only education has been her experience, she records for the first time that she misses educated society and desires to return to it. When passing royalty finally take her in and are eager to hear her tales she feels appropriately recognized. In her new self-confidence she closes her memoirs imparting words of wisdom to her female readers. They should not give in to contemporary notions about feminity which restrict their movements and turn them into weeping, fainting, sentimental creatures. She points with pride to her own good health and longevity (she was 67 and would live another 25 years). As naive as her expectations for intellectual recognition may have been, the attention her *Lebensbeschreibung* had earned increased her self-esteem.

It is not surprising therefore that Engel's style changes. In the first part it had been hardy and spare. Now it is mannered and shows strains of her efforts to be literary. She attempts rather clicheed metaphors. Returning to Zürich: "Ich bin nun angelangen am Bord meiner sehnsuchtsvollen Laufbahn, eingewallt in die Ringmauern Zürichs meiner lieben Vater-, Geburts- und Erziehungsstadt, wovon ich über zwei Jahre von den stürmischen Wogen des ungewissen Sees, bald diesseits, bald jenseits, bald vor-, bald rückwärts, wie ein Schifflein, das ohne Steuermann von der wilden Wuth der Wellen umhergetrieben, abgeschnitten schmachtetete. Das Missgeschick platzte über mich wie Wassergüsse, obschon sich bisweilen die liebe Sonne wieder zeigte."(237) Never in the first part had she longed for anything (except to die on her husband's grave); nor had she ever expressed homesickness. The language seems to take control of the content. There is much involuntary humor in such awkward, high-flown style. She combines a baroque expression of emotion with occasional misuse of the language: "O! des Schmerzegefühles! gleich als ein Vorbothe meiner ehmaligen Schicksale, der alle Farben meines Missgeschicks darstellte. . .(.)"(195) or "O wie wehmütig durchwühlten Gedanken meinen Busen. . .(.)"(193) In the continuation however she is not ashamed, indeed she does not hesitate to express emotions. She even voices feelings about events in the first part as if that first account did not satisfy her. On the anniversary of the battle of Waterloo, for instance, she records: "O! welche Trauergefühle durchbohrten nicht meine Seele in diesen Stunden. Ich konnte nicht mehr weinen, mein Gemüth war gramvoll vor dem tödtenden Gedankenstrom. . .(.)"(218) At that later moment her feelings appear much stronger.

But Engel's stylistic awkwardness is once again a sign of her awkwardness with emotions in general. Her inept adaptation of high-flown, baroque literary style reveals her inability to express herself in a more genuine way. More than once she comments: "die Worte mangeln mir, Ihnen schätzbarste Leser!"(195) She has another person say what she must also have felt:

18

"O ich kann meine Lage nicht mit Worten mahlen, sinnbildlich machen...(.)"(233) Even when she attempts to portray her feelings Engel seeks out a tradition which is inadequate. She cannot find one which will express her experience. One is tempted simply to conclude, she chose the wrong form. And yet surely the choice of that form expresses the person of Regula Engel. She must be both that script and what she leaves unsaid.

In the works by Baldinger and Engel awareness of the discrepancy between the expectations of autobiographical forms and the actual life and/or feelings of the author, between available scripts and experience, appears to remain subliminal. In Isabella von Wallenrodt's memoirs it approaches hypocrisy. Niggl has demonstrated the cross-fertilization of autobiographical forms which enlivened the long static traditions in the mid-eighteenth century and the autobiography of Isabella von Wallenrodt (1740-1819) weaves elements of the three major traditions.[12] Her background had been pietist. The women in her family in particular had shown leanings in this direction and, had a relative not prevented it, her grandmother would have bequeathed her entire fortune to a pietist sect of Herrenhuter. Nevertheless impoverished, her widowed mother held the family together by learning husbandry on her sole remaining estate. She raised her daughter according to contemporary aristocratic standards with a little training in French and a little in music. However these skills were to be of little use to Johanna Isabella for, to her mother's chagrin, she spurned the hand of a wealthy Baron to marry a Prussian cavalry captain in 1762.

When the captain died in 1776 leaving her with five small children and very little money she was forced to fend for herself. Like Engel her repeated requests for a pension from the king yielded nothing, and her adventure into manufacturing proved disastrous. Ineptitude at finances and at worldly affairs in general soon brought her not only poverty but also disrepute. Only when she turned to writing was she able to support herself and her family even meagerly. Her adventurous, historical novels earned her a large readership, but no great fame. Critics agree her works exhibit extreme verbosity (although they inevitably fail to mention that she was paid by the page), a serious neglect of style and an exaggerated expression.[13] Even Chr. Touaillon, who considers the novels significant for their portraits of the fallen woman, objects to her moral turpitude. Critics of the time were no less harsh, so that, like her contemporary male autobiographers, she in fact had works and a life to defend when she published *Das Leben der Frau von Wallenrodt in Briefen an einen Freund* in 1797.

To do that credibly Wallenrodt vowed to narrate her story honestly, admitting her real errors and confessing "Wo und wie ich nur selbst soviel Schaden und nachteilige Beurtheilung zuzog."(I,8) Her self-defense would thus become confession and her subtitle, "ein Beitrag zur Seelenkunde und Weltkenntnis", suggests its intellectual origins in Pietism. In general the secularization of Pietist introspection merged with foreign influences, especially English, in shaping German sentimental literature (*Empfindsamkeit*). In particular "Seelenkunde", most literally translated in its latinized form as psychology, was a secular outgrowth of the practice of Pietist introspection and Wallenrodt aimed to contribute to this young science – as well, apparently, to world knowledge. A prime example of autobiographical "Seelenkunde" is Karl Phillip Moritz' *Anton Reiser* for which the author distilled entries from his Pietist diaries.[14] Moritz published *Anton Reiser* in segments between 1785 and 1790 in his journal, *Gnothi Seauton*. Dedicated to such secular investigations of the soul, that journal moreover was indicative of a more general interest in autobiography in the late eighteenth century. In fact the strongest voice urging the writing of autobiographies was that of the reknown theologian Johann Gottfried Herder. In a broad sense he was like Moritz insofar as he pleaded for a more profound appreciation of individuals from all walks of life. He repeatedly encouraged morally instructive confessions in order to build a sense of national identity among those whom he considered productive laborers – from merchants to servants.[15]

Given Herder's reknown and respectability it is not surprising that Wallenrodt's alleged editor quoted him, albeit without giving credit. She wanted to be useful, to give "eine praktische Rechenschaft"(iv) of the way in which her character contributed to the sorrowful turn of her fate: "Die Welt, oder wenigstens ein Theil derselben, soll diese Briefe lesen; wie gut, wenn sie hier und da ein unbefangenes frohes Geschöpf, welches zur gehörigen Prüfung jeder Handlung zu lebhaft ist, in sich zurückführen, und ihm Vorsichtigkeit lehren!"(I,546)

Although she secularized the moral aims of pietist confessions, as Herder and Moritz encouraged and many others practiced as well, she still attributed direct responsibility for her life to divine guidance: "die Vorsehung [läßt] keins ihrer Geschöpfe aus den Augen und hat mit allen unsern Schicksalen den Zweck zu unserm Besten verwebt . . . (.)"(II,35; see also II,491) Indeed Wallenrodt professed to interpret her secular life from this perspective. As such this, too, was not unusual. Johann Heinrich Jung (Jung-Stilling), for instance had interpreted his medical successes to prove God's benign and just intervention in his life. But Wallenrodt's besieged position in society

left much for her to desire and so she had to unearth various sins to account
for the evil turn of fate at God's inevitably just hand. And this proved a problem since almost everything in her rebelled against accepting blame for her
condition. Her situation is complicated: "Wie sehr wünsche ich, dass diese
offenherzige Bekenntnisse, der mir selbst verursachten Nachtheile, die mir
seit mehr als 18 Jahren so viele schlaflose Nächte, und den nagenste Küm-
mer verursachte, so viel — wahrlich — unverdiente schlimme Urtheile
zugezogenhaben, jungen und lebhaften Leute zur Warnung sein
möchte!"(II,599) Her disrepute was not earned and yet she accepts responsibility for it. Can such a contradictory confession be heartfelt?

Wallenrodt records the character flaws, or sins, to which she credits her
bad social situation. Examining these however reveals just how unrepen-
tant she remained, while seeking to gain the sympathy of the reader. Among
her sins she listed some traditionally Christian ones: vanity (I, 408ff; I, 160f.);
temper (I, 144); and pride (I, 145). However by far the majority of her transgressions are incured by virtue of "faults" which are curious amendments
of the normal Christian ones: her generosity in financial affairs and her
open-heartedness in personal affairs. Having accepted room and board from
her impoverished mother, for instance, she paid her some rent. To protect
her mother's reputation with her husband she intentionally led him to believe that she had lost the large sum of money he left with her. She thus earns
a reputation for being careless with money. Against her husband's certain
censure she pawned household items to loan her gambler-brother money.
When the brother is unable to repay it she is found out and scolded by her
husband for her irresponsibility. As a widow she moves into town, against
the advice of friends who then withdraw their charitable support. She spends
too much on her daughter's schooling and causes herself and her children
bankruptcy. When she befriends women who had lovers, but whom she held
to be honorable, she is ostracized and gossiped about. These confessed transgressions, of course, inevitably reveal defiance of marital, social, or practical order, but eminently respectible motives. Each time she "sins" therefore,
she becomes a misunderstood martyr on a thorny pilgrimage(II, 512). She
accepts blame for her social situation, but she is not nearly as humble as
she pretends. With her logical contortions it is the best of Chritian virtues
which occasion her ill repute and impoverishment and perversely demonstrate God's justice in punishing her.

Having admitted faults such as these, it is no wonder her advice to others,
the "practical accounting", is equally contorted. She suggests parents should
avoid letting their children fall into dissolute ways: "Einem Kinde, das alles

willig hingiebt, sollte man lehren, seinen kleinen Habseligkeiten für sich selbst aufzunehmen, weil es sonst in Mangel gerathen würde; wenn es überall weichen will, sollte man ihm vorstellen, dass dieses nur mit Bedingung Tugend ist . . . (.)"(I,140) Similarly although hers was a love match she now advises young girls to marry for money. And she recommends that only women who are financially independent befriend socially questionable women. She did not intend her lessons to destroy anyone's goodness of heart, she claims, but only to render these virtues harmless. Hers is not the morality of a Christian as much as one of a social pragmatist. Without irony Wallenrodt exposed what Brecht, much later, revealed as the hypocrisy of bourgeois morality: if one is generous, one is left with nothing. A Karl Phillip Moritz might imply criticism of the charitableness of his compatriots in his autobiography, but an Isabella von Wallenrodt avoids all social criticism and adopts a posture of humble accommodation. Unlike Baldinger, she masks bitterly critical insights with statements affirming accommodation which at least border on hypocrisy.

Ultimately that disingenuous pose undermines credence in her promised confessional attitude and suggests more pragmatic concerns which in fact also surface if the larger structural moments of *Das Leben* are considered. The work is comprised of two parts. Her husband's death marks the end of the first volume, where Wallenrodt asserts that up until then readers will be able to praise her behavior; whereas in the second part they will scold her.(I, 604; see also II, 597) Although this parallel to a Christian loss of grace reverses the order of traditional pietist confessions it might convey traditional messages if she really were to confess irreligious feelings or immoral behavior. But as we have seen such is not the case; she admits to errors because society has reprimanded her for them. In reality they remain Christian virtues. How then are we to interpret her projection of what amounts to a fall from grace?

By clearly structuring her autobiography around her husband's death Wallenrodt accords it the pivotal significance it merits in her life. She shapes the form of the autobiography to that of her life. Engel had not treated her husband's death so strategically, although her life had been similarly affected. An autobiography of adventure accommodates personal tragedy poorly. Wallenrodt made this event the center and peripetie, or turning point, of her autobiography.

In much sentimental literature, although not only sentimental literature, marriage is a major structural element. But the importance of Wallenrodt's marriage does not imply the sentimental significance it will for other female autobiographers. Wallenrodt had described eagerly and fully the events of her courtship. The moment of her marriage however is barely accorded significance. Rather than focusing on sentiment Wallenrodt had elaborated the adventures and intrigues necessary for her to marry the man she loved instead of the one with money. Moreover in the total scheme of things this courtship period, so idyllic in some literature, has less importance for her than the later period of her marriage, which she called her "shining hour"(I, 382). But this, too, was not because of a concept of domestic bliss; indeed her passing praise of such a concept at the birth of her first son does not oblige her to dwell on it or to portray each of the numerous other child-births (or deaths) in her family. Instead she emphasizes the pragmatic side of raising children: the cost of childbirths and education. Her married life was framed in gold for her because they kept a large household and enter-tained often. It was the more public function of marriage which actually crowned her existence, rather than the intimate details of private domes-ticity or sentimental affects. It is not callousness. The ideology of mother-hood and family simply had not yet affected her as it would women only a few years younger than herself. Her attitude harkens back to an older aristocratic tradition of representation in which the entire family occupied a more public function. It is an attitude which we will find also expressed by the step-mother of Elise von der Recke.

It is not necessary to denounce Wallenrodt's claims of love and devotion to her husband and family as misrepresentations in order to accept the more complex constellation of the factors at work on her life and to see the mate-rial loss that women suffered when their husbands died and they were thrown on the financial mercy of others. For nothing less than money reveals itself to be the hidden pivot of this autobiography. Wallenrodt finds it is also the factor by which her readers will unequivocally know that this is an autobi-ography and not a novel. They will know her story is true because no novel would concern itself with the petty, financial details of daily life.(II,207) Furthermore it is the real basis of Wallenrodt's assumption of grace or guilt, for apart from her marital status it is only her financial situation that changes from the first to the second volume. If entertaining lavishly had been the zenith of her life's course, then financial ruin must surely have represented the nadir.

That this perspective of decline is not brought about by her unmarried state is perhaps best illustrated by her mature opinions about her marriage after the death of her husband. She refuses to marry again even though mar-riage would mean financial security. To be sure her motives are expressed in terms of her children's likely disadvantage with a step-father, still she proclaims she does not want any more children at all. It is the same excuse her mother had used after the death of her own husband. More convincing perhaps is the fact that Wallenrodt finds her new independence "ungemein süss" (I, 595) and while reassuring her readers that she had fulfilled her marital duties gladly, nevertheless reports that it was natural "dass ich's. . . fühlte, es sei eine Last, die ich trüge, und wer ermüdet nicht endlich dabei?"(I, 595) She calls her marriage a yoke and herself a slave in it. (I, 597) Her husband had been honest, faithful, and kind: "Ich schätzte den, dessen Ketten ich trug. . . aber den Druck fühlte ich doch."(I, 597) The importance of money over sentiment is perhaps best illustrated when the reader learns of her husband's former mistress. The author is disturbed not because this earlier relationship represents a prior attachment, but rather because he had settled the majority of his fortune on the mistress that she might marry well, thus seriously jeopardizing the financial position of his eventual family.

Wallenrodt has been much maligned for her verbosity ("Weitschweifigkeit"). But Niggl has already asserted that numerous digressions were typical of the structure of autobiographies of adventure. Many of Wallenrodt's digressions moreover bear significance for her own life, as they are short biographical sketches of family members: her mother, because her fate affected her own life (I, 36lf.): her husband, because it will interest her children and grandchildren (I, 568): her son, because she will absolve herself of guilt for his debt-ridden misfortune (II, 318). With some regularity however women and their relation to money reveal themselves to be the hidden theme of many of these digressions, as it is of the autobiography as a whole. Her parents had lost their wealth saved from the Herrenhuter because her father gambled. Her brother-in-law cheated her mother out of the remainder of her estate so that she died totally impoverished. Wallenrodt's husband, who was tight with her household budget, had not only given his fortune to his mistress, but of the remainder, he spent a great deal on fine hunting dogs, maintaining a hunter, hiring musicians (rather than the promised music teacher for her), and grand entertaining. Her own brother was a gambler, whose fairly wealthy wife feared to let her fortune into his hands. Irresponsible men repeatedly jeopardize women's social position in her autobiography without Wallenrodt ever drawing the obvious conclusion explicitly. Moreover except for her brother-in-law, she never once criticizes these men. She merely narrates the incidents. It would seem to transgress a social code to suggest criticsm of a blood-related male or husband. This circumspec-

24

tion, too, would seem to form a limitation to women's narration of autobiography.

The first volume contains many incidents involving her financial difficulties and differences with her husband over finances. She had hated asking
her husband for money. But since she was relatively poor after his death
she had to continue to beg for it — the only way she had learned to acquire
money. She petitioned the king for a pension. Only after many years of hard-
ship did she become more active and try to found a factory, but like Regula
Engel inexperience prevented success in the business world. Her children
were grown by the time she began to write for a living. Self-sufficiency must
have been very important for Wallenrodt, who continually complained of
being a burden to others and longed for the day when she could redeem her
pride and shower gifts on those who had helped her. The practical advice
she has on this score however is minimal. As correctives to her alleged inability to spend money wisely, she suggests that her mother might have given
her an allowance as a child, that her husband might have given her control
of the entire purse during their marriage. She never fully thematizes the importance of financial self-sufficiency for women, although she had learned
it bitterly.

Wallenrodt's false humility clearly did not keep her from seeing social
injustices. And her accommodating narrative pose did not keep her from
presenting what she saw. As a child she had been particularly clever and
sharp to criticize but just this had caused her trouble: "Andere (Menschen)
hatte ich vielleicht durch ein wenig Satire oder durch den Beweis, dass ich
sah, hörte, und unterscheiden konnte, aufgebracht, sie mussten nach ihrer
Sinnesart mich durch alles was sie ersinnen konnten, aufs tiefste herabwür-
digen."(I,6) Defiance and rebelliousness out of clear insight (which the reader
has seen circuitously) had a long history with Wallenrodt. But her spirit,
like Baldinger's, seems to have been broken. She had insisted on a love match
for herself, but her experiences taught her to recommend considering
finances first. She flaunted society's rules by associating with women who
had lovers, but she advised others guardedness in choosing friends. When
first married she once danced ahead of her husband on a walk and was
quickly reprimanded for behavior unbecoming a married woman. And although she claimed not to be one of "those" women who want to govern,
she very quickly learned that if she wanted anything in her marriage she
had to manipulate her husband for it: "so bald ich wollte, hatte (mein Wille)
die erste Stimme, aber um diesen Vortheil zu behaupten, musste ich mich
doch sehr nach ihm richten, und ohne dass es aussah, als thät ich mir Zwang

an."(I, 596) Her narrative posture of smiling accommodation manifests the same desire to manipulate. It is a posture masking a very different attitude and ultimately a much more rebellious story. But precisely that story is not told.

Modified, but plainly apparent, in this alleged confession are elements of the autobiography of profession. In combining and modifying elements of all traditions Wallenrodt also testifies to the renewed vitality of the form in the late eighteenth century. Rather than following her biography with a character description, she has interspersed portraits ("Gemälde") throughout the entire work. There she discusses her personal virtues and faults, gives stationary portraits of her soul. Concluding the autobiography she lists and defends her individual works. In connection with this defense she returns quite naturally to the theme of her education, and here she is far more direct in her social criticsm and her self-defense. She even seems quite incisive and far-sighted.

She defends herself: Had she been born a man, she, too would have become a scholar. Had she been born a woman in an earlier time she would have become one of those famous learned women, who do not abound anymore.(II,6ll) She bemoans the state of education for women in general and identifies with those earlier, unnamed models. She claims that whatever education she was able to acquire was broken off, especially her education in languages: "Als ich verheirathet war, sollte italiänsche (sic), englisch und sogar noch lateinisch gelernt werden; aber alles das kam nie über den Anfang hinweg. Viele Wochenbette, Hausgeschäft und gesellschaftliche Zerstreuungen unterbrachen alles."(II,612) Since she finds foreign languages necessary for a good education, indeed for a sensitivity to language in general, her stylistic ineptitude is blamed on her impoverished education. Her style in all her works would have been only the best "wenn [sie] mehr Aufmerksamkeit und Musse aufs Zierliche hätte verwenden und mehr hätte lesen können, wenn [ihr] mit hunderterlei Unannehmlichkeiten angefüllter Kopf der Präzision, die [sie] doch so sehr liebte, immer fähig gewesen wäre; diese aber zeigt sich nur in den Werken eines längstgeübten Schriftstellers, der nichts als seinen Stoff im Sinn hat, und sich mit der dahin gehörigen Gedankenfolge nicht durch tausend fatale Nebenideen krümmen muss."(II,615f.) Repeatedly she claims she is not insensitive to style and her own "Übereilung und Mangel der Feile" (II,648), but she never fails to mention the lack of peace and time to polish her prose (II, 614,615,616,629,639) or the fact that she is poor and paid by the page. Hers is, ultimately against its will, a materialist autobiography and not at all a sentimental or psychological one.

If she has beaten around the bush in other parts of her autobiography, she clearly defends herself with social criticism in this last segment. It appears to have been socially acceptable for someone as slavish as Wallenrodt to suggest general improvements in the education of women, but not in their financial or marital situations. There she remains coy and reminds us of Baldinger. On the most personal and most threatening issues she was not silent but not explicit either. She did not explicate; she hinted and allowed the reader to see. Her defense of her works is somewhat unusual in the tradition in that it is not a defense of their intellectual or literary value, but of herself and her life. It becomes, in fact, rather explicit social criticism from the point of view of a woman. She saw many of the same phenomena upon which Virginia Woolf would expound over a century later in *A Room of One's Own*.

If Wallenrodt had aimed to instruct her readers, she also explicitly aimed to entertain them. Here her practice as a novelist of adventure and intrigue makes itself felt. According to Niggl this was not unique among autobiographies in the late eighteenth century. And Klaus-Detlef Müller has also carefully shown the mutual effects of contemporary novels and autobiographies. Wallenrodt thus does not exceed contemporary innovations when she occasionally raises the reader's expectations of adventure: "Jetzt bereiten Sie sich, die letzte und unterhaltendste Begebenheit meines unverheirateten Standes zu vernehmen"(I, 161); or explicitly tells stories for their amusement value or for a change of pace (I, 418). Amorous caprices, narrow escapes, secret correspondences, and besieged but triumphant virtue enliven the text. Her tutor intrigues to keep her from confirmation in order to punish her impudence; gossips prevent marriage plans; and court personages prevent her from getting her pension or the capital for her factory from the king. Novelistic elements like these allow her to realize, to some measure at least, her youthful desire to play the heroine in a novel. (I,102)

However it is not only the adventurous elements which suggest traits of the novel. The autobiography is structured in chapters called "letters" and in this way the work suggests that epistolary form of the sentimental novel which was intended to reveal more closely the innermost feelings of the character. It is appropriate, in Wallenrodt's case, that the epistolary form remains as superficial to the text as the sentimental influence in general.

According to the author the "letters" which compose *Das Leben der Isabella von Wallenrodt* were not originally planned for publication, but rather expanded upon recommendation of the unnamed editor for public consumption. Since the letters are numbered and form units which build on each other and since no addressee or editor is named, we can only assume that these were not originally conceived as letters. On the contrary the author seems fully aware of writing a longer work since she takes pains that adventurous digressions divert and amuse the reader periodically. Wallenrodt has probably simply extended this conventional fictional device from her novels to her autobiography with no profound consequence for the narration of the text. This will not be true for other women autobiographers.

The particular combination of romantic and adventurous intrigue and self defense through alleged confession are reminiscent of Rousseau's *Confessions*, of which Wallenrodt may certainly have been aware. However, where Rousseau assaulted conventional morality and retained his livelihood, Wallenrodt's flaunting of convention caused her financial ruin. Women simply could not afford the same state of rebelliousness. Moreover unlike Rousseau Wallenrodt repeatedly professes her virtue and innocence, succumbing all the while to the disastrous and undeserved consequences of it. Thus this work clearly illustrates the prevailing double standard of morality — which has severe financial effects on her life. Despite that vague similarity with Rousseau it is interesting to note that Wallenrodt may have been influenced by Rousseau's narrator, but not by his sentimental ideology of women as they are portrayed in *Emile* or *La nouvelle Héloïse*. If she identified with anything it was Rousseau's narrative position in his *Confessions* and not the position of women as he portrayed it. That image would influence women only slightly younger, as we shall see, and have somewhat surprising results.

Regardless of their varied backgrounds in one way or another all of these authors expressed their admiration for learning and their desire to be respected by learned men. They tried to enter that world and its life scripts — sometimes in their lives, but inevitably with their autobiographies. Baldinger, probably the best read, published nothing but prided herself on maintaining intellectual friendships. After Engel became known for her adventurous memoirs she wanted to be the equal of historians. Wallenrodt tried to redeem a reputation based on novels labeled inferior. Ultimately their struggle for acceptance by the world of letters paralleled their struggle with autobiographical forms. Their lack of education, of certain male experiences and of money made their attempts appear awkward. Where their works are most glaringly contradictory it is because they failed to acknowledge that, for historical and social reasons, the life patterns of women were different

28

from those of men. They failed to insist on the authenticity of their own experience, on the authority of their own selves, and accepted all too willingly the life scripts available to them in traditional (male) forms. If Wallenrodt had not wanted — or financially needed — that acceptance so much she might have written a very different autobiography. Of the three she most clearly saw the powerlessness and second rate status of women in that culture. But she was dependent on that very culture for the sale of her novels and her income.

And it was not a favorable climate. For despite examples of educated and professional women in the eighteenth century, the wave of interest in education in Germany which followed the appearance of Rousseau's *Emile* (1762) failed to affect women's lives. Erxleben, Schlözer, Gottsched — and Baldinger, or even Wallenrodt — remained exotic exceptions. Johann Bernhard Basedow (1724-1790) whose *Philanthropinum* in Dessau provided a model for the new pedagogy to gently unfold a child's innate talents, disputed the intellectual ability of women. He believed: "Die ganze Erziehung der Töchter muß ihre Absicht auf das männliche Geschlecht haben. Den Männern gefallen und nützen, sich ihre Liebe und Hochachtung erhalten, sie verpflegen, ihnen raten sie trösten, ihnen das Leben annehmlich und süß machen, das sind zu allen Zeiten die Pflichten des weiblichen Geschlechts, diese muß man dasselbe von Jugend auf lehren."[16] While the fathers of exceptions like Erxleben, Schlözer, and Gottsched clearly possessed faith in women's learning, some of the most enlightened men of the period upheld quite unenlightened attitudes regarding women. Immanuel Kant (1724-1804) professed that enlightenment signified humanity leaving its self-imposed immaturity. But women's immaturity, apparently, was innate and not self-imposed. Nor was their education necessarily desirable: "[Frauen brauchen] ihre Bücher etwa so wie [sie] ihre Uhr brauchen, bloß um sie zu tragen, damit sie gesehen werden, obschon sie meist stille steht oder doch nicht nach der Sonne richtig gestellt ist."[17] The famous pedagogue Johann Heinrich Pestalozzi (1746-1827) boasted that the graduates of his school were no "snivelers" or "yea-sayers" ("Kriecher" or "Jasager"), but he refused to educate women.[18]

Whatever impulses there may have been to educate women in the earlier part of the century were undermined in the latter. And for all their fame professional or educated women were not likely to be the source of social prestige, rather more likely the opposite. Despite the admiration (or bewonderment) expressed for the learning of Luise Adelgunde Gottsched (1713-1762), few women felt they wanted to emulate her. Johanna Schopenhauer, later a well-known author — and mother of the misogynist philoso-pher Arthur Schopenhauer — had even viewed her as a negative model in childhood. Similarly Dorothea Schlözer's learning made her an anathema to the young Caroline Michaelis, later the Caroline Schlegel-Schelling, so controversial for her own singularly independent and unconventional life. Is it a wonder that the confidence men gained by their participation in profes-sions did not accrue to women in similar circumstances? The self-confidence required to write an autobiography from the authority of experience would have to come from a different source for women.

Even if women did achieve a profession or learning, then, they still lived in a patriarchal family situation. The acquisition of learning or the prac-tice of hard-won knowledge was restricted by family considerations. Whether one regards the existence of these considerations positively or negatively, such a situation is not conducive to the type of autobiography described by Niggl as autobiography of profession, or even autobiography of adven-ture. Family concerns enter into a woman's biography in material way, one alien to male biographies — and autobiographies. The hindrances to Bal-dinger's learning may be a biographical issue, but her deference to her hus-band and her narrative self-effacement become elements of autobiography. Wallenrodt's devious evasions of criticism of male members of her family suggest further restraints, not merely on her life, but on its telling as well. Sons may rebel in order to acquire learning and a new place in society, daugh-ters can seldom escape the financial pressures to conform. A woman who explains why she defied her family naturally risks the support of that fa-mily (usually materially necessary to her in a way it is not to a man), but she also risks public censure and ostracism as well. Wallenrodt's contor-tions illustrate the possible effects on narration of this need to adapt.

But family concerns enter in matters of content as well. Engel knew that family issues would not sell her autobiography. They were not considered worthy or appropriate to disclose. They seemed to contain no public interest. The one form in which such matters were discussed was the novel. Here domestic life, indeed adventures by women, were in fact an appropriate sub-ject matter and here dissatisfactions with families could be concealed — and denied — in fiction. For women's autobiography it was not novels of adventure which were the major impetus, but sentimental novels of family struggles.

The generally admitted sources of autobiographical impulses are miss-ing for women, and indeed few professional and adventurous women have left us records of their life histories. The confidence which provided the autobiographical impulse for women had to have a different source, and it could not depend on external interest and support. It had to rely on inner strength and conviction. It had to predicate the importance of the soul or its secular counterpart, the self. Neither the autobiography of profession nor that of adventure was the major form employed by women. Only the confessional form corresponded to the discovery of inner strength in the face of external opposition.

2

THE CASES OF RECKE AND STÄGEMANN

The difficulties Baldinger, Engel, and Wallenrodt encountered in trying to shape their experience within the traditional structure of autobiographies of profession and adventure reflected the real social censure of professional and adventurous women. They had each led lives that did not conform neatly to the "normative" female ideal of the period. Whether as intellectual companion, camp follower, or bread-earner, each had in some way passed over the stricter boundaries of the domestic sphere and hazarded a step into the broader, more public one. None found an appropriate and ready form in which to relate her unusual life, and all had tried to conform to extant traditions. Standard autobiographical forms proved inadequate to express the particularities of women's experience. However these authors were not as innovative as others in shaping the genre to their own needs.

For reasons that seem evident, but must still be examined, those female autobiographies from this period who confront the specific experience of women more directly were not published at the time. Not only did they reveal experience alien to most "scripts" available to women, they did so in forms alien to those available generally in the market place. For the most part these works manifest a closer relationship to the tradition of confession, rather than that of profession and adventure. That means they examine the desires and evolution of a "self". And they are quite innovative in the structures they evolve. However, precisely because they were so innovative, they have not even been recognized as autobiography and have not been drawn into the corpus of works normally studied. Whether any of these facts can be construed as an admission that women did not participate fully in the formation of the modern form of the genre remains a matter of formal/historical destinctions. For the issue of gender in autobiography raises serious questions of genre theory. These need to be made explicit.

The "model" autobiography, in the German tradition, integrates private and public experience (as in fact is implicit in Niggl's formulation of the genesis of the genre). The relationship of the author to society, the degree to which s/he was influenced by it and influenced it is bound to the inner development of the author. Generally speaking, a pattern of inner struggle and growth provides the structure of autobiographies. The historical period which has favored the development of such autobiography has been the modern one (in Germany from the mid-eighteenth century), with its focus on the individual and its belief in the ideas of historical progress and organic evolution.

Studying various German autobiographies of the nineteenth century Bernd Neumann observed their tendency to become memoirs (descriptions of external events without reference to internal growth) at that point in the author's life when a social role was assumed! Intellectual growth becomes an intellectual position to be defended against others. Emotional growth finds a perspective from which to view events and to act upon them. Spiritual growth becomes commitment to a set of beliefs which causes one either to suffer social isolation or to act in their behalf. It is usually the acquisition of a profession or social position which occasions such a shift in generic qualities within one given work. Whether acquired by choice or compulsion a defined social role would seem to inhibit personal growth. On the basis of his research Neumann is able to posit a fundamental antithesis between the development of self or identity and the acquisition of social role, one which played itself out in the very structure of autobiographies.

The hypotheses concerning the evolution of a life as well as those concerning the distinction between memoirs and autobiography were tested on and extracted from a body of works which failed to raise questions of gender. The moment women's life writings are considered, however, the pertinence of these genre distinctions becomes dubious — although they will be helpful to us in locating the theoretical challenge of women's life stories. For, if we assume that women's (inevitable) "social" role was that of wife and mother, then some questions remain to be raised and answered by genre theory. Are issues of family relations — women's social role — appropriate to a memoir form in the same or different ways in which, say, courtly relations are? Isabella von Wallenrodt might have answered that they were the same. And yet the very strangeness of the question makes us realize the extent to which we expect family affairs to belong to the sphere of inner experiences, to the province of autobiography. We expect a family woman's life story to be appropriate only to autobiography, or the story of inner affairs. In fact, we expect her identity to be congruent with her social role. Although some critics might find a certain social harmony in this supposed integration of "identity" and social role, that expectation necessarily contradicts the conclusions of Neumann's study of male autobiography that "identity" and social role are, to some degree, antithetical. It is precisely in undercutting the traditional notion of "identity" that French theorists can be helpful in the analysis of women's autobiography.

Another troubling question presents itself, however. If we believe that women's life stories inherently manifest the material of autobiography (rather than memoir) we may want to look at the issue of inner growth — intellectual, emotional, and/or spiritual — and its relation to a young girl's assumption of her destined role. Do women portray themselves growing emotionally until they are ready to assume their domestic responsibilities? Does that emotional maturation represent the conclusion of personal growth? Or do men become, while women are? Perhaps by very definition women's autobiography will not manifest inner growth — a prerequisite for inclusion within the genre category.

In the last chapter we observed that male forms of autobiography were inadequate to express the reality of women's existence, even if the authors led unconventional lives bearing some external resemblances to those of men. What happens when women's autobiographies focus on the domestic role? Do the authors identify with it from childhood? Do they portray themselves as growing into it? The answers to these questions, asked of history and of women's experience, bear consequences for the shape of autobiography.

One thing is certain, male versions of female lives, in fiction, were equally inadequate to express the reality of women's domestic lives. But, because these ideas about women's lives belonged to the dominant ideology, they naturally influenced the way women thought about themselves. They formed women's "ready-formed dictionary" (to recall Barthes) in terms of which they might try to describe themselves. The more important question is, what did women add to these dictionaries? What were the connections between their innovative discourse and their real experience, subjectivity? They may not have succeeded in presenting pure and "coherent identities", as is doubtful anyone might, but they did engage in unique autobiographical experiments. We have observed women trying to describe their lives on essentially male terrain, in terms of male dictionaries. What of women who described their own experienced reality on female terrain, the domestic front? What of women who ammended those dictionaries, who did not necessarily replace them, but added their own vocabulary? Are their innovations to be credited to the mysterious, unidentified "instance saying *I*" or to their actual experience?

In so far as it is possible, let us first be clear about the female ideal constructed by the emerging middle-class ideology, which dominated literary production and the imaginations of most who read. In large measure that ideal in Germany had derived from Rousseau; it projected women's personal identity with her domestic role. Like the hero of Johann Wolfgang von Goethe's (1749-1832) *Sorrows of Young Werther* (1774/1787) for instance its heroine Lotte is full of sentimental admiration for the poet Friedrich Gottlieb Klopstock (1724-1804). The scene in which they stand at a window in a storm, moved beyond expression as she reverently utters the poet's sacred name, has impressed itself on the memory of many readers. Although this scene affirmed the mutual attraction of their souls (*Seelengemeinschaft*), it is actually another attribute which initiates Werther's devotion. He had first been attracted to Lotte when he saw her cutting bread for her young wards as they gathered eagerly about her. Lotte possesses natural ease in her maternal roles caring for children, for the sick and for the old. It is this motherly image rather than the one of Lotte as reader of great poets which dominates the book. Precisely those maternal qualities settle her in the symbolic realm, associated with Nature, which speaks to and echoes Werther's innermost being, his private longings. When social convention both prevents him from assuming the place in society to which his innate talents entitle him and prohibits his union with Lotte, he exercises the only real freedom he feels he has: the freedom to end his life. Even in Werther's death the author grants this lone hero of epistolary novels more freedom than the standard heroines — Clarissa or Julie — who either pine away or otherwise bear no active responsibility for their deaths.

Although characters like Lotte are intended as positive representations, they articulate very little of women's actual experience. Certainly they fail to suggest the reality of women in situations like Engel's or Wallenrodt's. This is not a consequence of Goethe's lack of interest in realistic characterization. In his conversations with Eckermann Goethe unabashedly admitted that he had drawn his male characters from life, but that his female characters had been created inside himself — and were always better than the real women he knew.[2] Better they might have been, but compared to the real lives that women were living, characters like Lotte are, frankly, rather dull. Goethe's "Werther" was highly autobiographical and drawn from life, but his method of character portrayal reveals a double standard and a lack of interest in the lives of women. If Lotte's character were taken for what it was — a male projection and a male fantasy, as Goethe himself admitted — one might not complain. But real men and real women (as we shall see) took "Lotte" as a real model.

Lotte may be understood as an example of the sentimental heroine whose characteristics were drawn from Rousseau and who represented so clearly the domestic image of women. But two other works have long held the reputation of being particularly progressive with regard to their ability to imagine new social roles, new "scripts", for women: Goethe's classical play, *Iphigenie auf Tauris* (1786) and Friedrich Schlegel's romantic novel, *Lucinde* (1799). In Goethe's play Orest's arrival on the island of Tauris occasions Iphigenie's release from her enforced role as priestess of Diana. This is accomplished neither by invoking deities nor by turning to violence. Rather Iphigenie, demonstrating the power of inner harmony and restraint, pleas for her freedom from the tyrant Thoas. She argues the commonality of their feeling. Her noble thoughtfulness and dignified commitment to humane values seem to offer a model of generosity and gentleness to the barbarian (as he is portrayed) as much as to her brother, Orest. As truly admirable as she appears, however, we may be permitted to note that she is only able to achieve her pacifistic goals by simultaneously insisting on her integrity and submitting her fate to the will of the "tyrant".[3] Submission to his decision is a *sine qua non* of her brand of pacifism. Moreover her very desire to leave includes turning her back on that enforced public role of priestess and returning to her family. Fortunately, Iphigenie found an educable tyrant.

The eighteenth century was fond of the analogy between sovereign and husband. The husband's position in the home was thought to parallel that of the sovereign in his country. If we pursue this rhetorical figure and transfer Iphigenie's pacifist tactic to the private sphere, we are left with a model of questionable value for women trapped in forced marriages. Appeal to humane values and dignified resistance to violence was not a model that moved Elise von der Recke's household tyrant to humane understanding. We shall see what alternative she found in reality.

Friedrich Schlegel's *Lucinde* shocked his contemporaries with its portraits of free love and supposed ideal of androgyny. The hero's womanly ideal, Lucinde, is a painter of some natural talent, but without training. She is described as living in her own world, fully free and independent. Julius and she not only share interests, their very souls commune with each other. They form a free and harmonious union. Through this relationship he is able to order his life. She too blossoms, but in her own way. For it is not a fully androgynous idyll. Schlegel carefully records that Lucinde paints not for a living or for art's sake, but for her own pleasure. Not she, but he becomes the successful painter and makes trips away. She creates sociality (*Geselligkeit*) for her loved ones and friends, thus restricting her activity and creativity to the domestic sphere.

Lucinde may represent a feminine ideal, but if there is any example of a truly independent woman in the novel, it is Julius' paramour, Lisette. She is a prostitute, although as a very cultured and sensitive woman, she might more appropriately be referred to as a hetaera. Julius appreciates Lisette's character and refined taste, but she is described as too worldly and practical for him. In order not to plague him with requests for money, for instance, she breaks her vow of fidelity and soon thereafter becomes pregnant. When he leaves her, she kills herself — a dubious choice of action for one portrayed as so worldly. Apparently even the most worldly woman cannot live without the man she loves and no woman can earn a living for herself without whoring and losing her man. At least that alternative is never suggested. Although she is intelligent, companiable, and sexual (something Julius seeks) Lisette is not motherly or domestic. That would seem to be her womanly flaw. Unlike Lucinde she has never had a child; indeed she kills herself while pregnant. Readers learn that Lucinde's son had died and that she has suffered in the past, but they never know if that is exclusively because of the loss of her son or if she experienced other hardships. Although the conclusion to Elisabeth Stägemann's autobiography contains parallels to Schlegel's idyllic union between Julius and Lucinde, the route by which she arrived there illuminates another, ultimately more unsettling, perspectve than Julius' undefined, melancholy state and aimless search.

This brief excursion into the literary limits which male authors prescribed for women's sense of self is not without import for women's autobiography and its structure. There can be no doubt that, around 1800, the only fully acceptable role for women was in the domestic sphere. Moreover, development of a self before or outside that role was of questionable value. Women were not to develop particular talents (save that of virtue) for fear they might not appeal to men or be compatible with their husbands. More importantly it was felt that women fulfilled their definition in that role, it *was* their identity. They were to merge with their domestic role. What then were women to do when even that private realm, which permitted men to develop their selves, represented *their* compulsory role. By what literary mechanisms might they effect a distinction between their *selves* and the domestic role, thought by men to represent the private sphere? Dared they announce that for them it was a role, frequently forced upon them? Could they afford it financially and/or emotionally?

Not illogically that form of autobiography was most important to the development of women's autobiography which was most personal: the religious confession. But in ways which created structures not hitherto recognized by scholars of the genre. The conflict between social demands and real desires worked fissures in the autobiographies of Baldinger, Engel, and Wallenrodt; but that conflict was bound to erupt into a new form. When it exploded in real life the conflict marginalized dissenters in society. When literary forms were found to express these eruptions, they too became marginalized by literary historians. The autobiographies of Elise von der Recke and Elisabeth Stägemann represent one phase or possibility for this form. Those of Rahel Varnhagen and Bettina von Arnim demonstrate another.

The dissident content of the autobiographies under investigation in these two chapters found expression in radical formal choices on the part of the authors. With its emphasis on truthful examinations of the soul and on the implicit value of all souls, secularized pietist values permitted extraordinary autobiographies by women. Wallenrodt's telling of her life story had manifested only a superficial acquisition of that movement's practices and beliefs, but Elisa von der Recke's and Elisabeth Stägemann's suggest what a profound source of integrity that religious movement could be and the extent to which its tradition of close scrutiny of the "self" could produce powerful, and, in the case of these authors, highly innovative autobiography.

Elisa von der Recke (1756-1833) was born into a family of landed Prussian aristocrats. She was best known in her own day, and down to the present, for her religious poetry and her 1787 exposure of the adventurer and spiritualist, Alexander Count Cagliostro (1743-1795) (actually Giuseppe Balsamo). Publicly recounting her own mental seduction by the feats of Cagliostro and her gradual perception of his trickery ultimately ruined Cagliostro's adventures, established her association with rationalist thinkers gathered around Freidrich Nicolai (1733-1811) in Berlin, dissolved her friendship with the pious Johann Kaspar Lavater (1741-1801), and persuaded some that women were rational creatures. Catherine the Great of Russia, reportedly impressed with Recke's intelligence and grateful for her revelations, offered her a sizeable pension, which she refused. After the appearance of her denunciation of Cagliostro, Recke travelled throughout Germany to make the acquaintance of learned men. It was a trip of the sort young men often undertook before they launched their careers. However Recke settled in a somewhat remote town to live out her life, generally admired.

Even though they were written only shortly after her pamphlet on Cagliostro, the unpleasantly vivid recollections of her early marriage and divorce waited until long after her death for publication. Two separately written manuscripts come into consideration: one, dated 1795, relates her childhood until her betrothal in 1771; and the earlier one, dated 1793, the story

38

of her marriage and divorce. While the 1795 manuscript was bequeathed to the *Königliche Bibliothek* in Berlin with the request that it be published after her death, the more daring manuscript of 1793 was left to the *Königliche Bibliothek* in Dresden with no instructions of any sort. The explicit wishes regarding the 1795 manuscript were not immediately heeded, and neither autobiographical fragment was published until 1902 when Paul Rachel edited both and ordered them chronologically according to her biography.[4]

In the first segment Recke's secularization of the pietist confessional manifests itself in the structure of her childhood history. She echoes pietist sentiments in the introduction to that manuscript when she hopes that her sad experiences will be of worldly benefit to other sensitive souls and when she intends to lay bare her errors, but also her virtues. To be sure Wallenrodt had promised the same, but pietist leanings clearly inform Recke's entire account on a far more profound, albeit secular level. While Wallenrodt for instance introduced readers to a socially broad spectrum of characters and remained psychologically superficial, Recke focuses almost exclusively on her immediate family and her own psychological development.

As noted above, secular versions of pietist confessions often substituted the evolution of one's natural abilities for the evolution of faith; and self-fulfillment in a career for religious rebirth. For a woman at this time such secularization might be re-interpreted as education for a role as wife and mother, a role which purportedly satisfied the soul of any individual woman in the same degree as religion or a profession might have for a man. Since it was deemed to be their nature, that role might be portrayed as the fulfillment of their "identity". And indeed Recke consistently demonstrates the steps in her training for marriage. Nevertheless the structure of the narration ultimately exposes the intrinsic contradiction in the application of this teleological paradigm to women whose social role (here, telos) was afterall predetermined, and not internally evolved.

Specifically, the situation is as follows. Since Recke's mother had died in childbirth, Charlotte, as she was called as a girl, lived first with her grandmother. There she was educated for marriage in aristocratic society; reading, writing, arithmetic (not too much), and a little French sufficed. Her family destined her for a role as a decorative possession. She learned discipline in movement by standing absolutely still several hours a day and nurtured a pale complexion by avoiding any window through which sun shone. Charlotte detested this hot-house cultivation, which was even then slightly out of date.

When she was twelve her step-mother rescued her by taking her home with her. Somewhat more up to date, the step-mother read novels and plays with her, helped her overcome her fear of learning, allowed her to walk in the garden and encouraged her to take dancing lessons. It was the cultivation of more natural graces and of the sentiments in general. Body and soul received their nourishment; and, as her talents and interests blossomed, Charlotte became utterly devoted to the woman who had opened these new spheres for her. Yet even this, more modern education (perhaps influenced by the writings of Rousseau) aimed to prepare her for a marriage in which she was expected merely to amuse others: "die Wissenschaft, zu der ich erzogen wurde, bestand darin, die Anwesenden mit Bescheidenheit zu unterhalten und in Gesellschaft zu glänzen."(105) Such an insightful and critical statement is almost surely the result of later reflection. Throughout her childhood reminiscences she focuses on her acquisition of talents and the possession of physical qualities which make her attractive to men. She also highlights her feelings towards them and her expectations of them. She would thus superficially seem to concur that her nature and inclination destined her for marriage and a family. She seemed to have accepted without distance the "script" available to her.

The conflict between her prescribed destiny and her nature might not have emerged as violently as it ultimately did, if explicit and implicit promises to her had not been broken. In exchange for her confidences and a friendship which Charlotte trusted, the step-mother explicitly promised she would not be forced to marry anyone against her will. She also promised Charlotte would not marry before her twentieth birthday. When, toward the conclusion of this segment of her autobiography, and the culmination of her education, Georg Recke proposed marriage, Charlotte was 16. The pressure for her to marry him (because of his vast estates and her lack of dowry—it having been given to her brother) came primarily from her stepmother. There was only the appearance of allowing her to make up her own mind. Her confidence had actually been used to manipulate her, and her gratitude exploited.

Even more importantly, the implicit promises of her education were not kept. When talents and tastes are cultivated there is usually the assumption that they will be either useful or enjoyed at some later point in time. On her husband's estate, however, Recke would not be able to engage in her favorite pasttime: dance. She would be mocked for reading, even forbidden to do so. When she spoke with guests at dinner she would be ridiculed. Instead of finding her education and talents useful in fulfilling her role, she found she was expected to perform tasks for which she had neither training nor interest: overseeing a large estate, including the care of livestock. Although most of these contradictions became apparent only later, her knowledge of them casts a shadow on her opinion of her education, which she considers inappropriate. And indeed since she had been raised with fairly modern assumptions, but then forced to live under more traditional circumstance, the conflict was bound to arise.

As disjointing as this conflict between promise and fulfillment was, however, it was not even on this level that the real struggle for her identity took place. The struggle for self-affirmation and self-evolution which scholars take to be both the form and the content of autobiography is a sporadic and at first ill-conceived theme in this first segment of Recke's life story. Only toward the end does she begin to characterize herself as a "self" attempting to define itself — but then she is only 16 at the end of this segment. Readers become aware of the struggle in reported conversations between her step-mother and herself on the topic of marriage. While the step-mother represented a philosophy of marriage which may have been more modern than Charlotte's grandmother, it was not as modern as Charlotte's. She desired a marriage based on mutual respect and affection — an internal bond. Partly on the basis of her own experience, the step-mother had advised Charlotte strongly against marrying anyone for whom she felt great affection (73). She tried to teach her not to be empathetic (*mitempfindend*), recommending instead cold unsentimentality (*kalte Unempfindsamkeit*) (84). Only in this way would she be able to achieve her will in marriage (72). Recke observes, for instance, that although her step-mother never contradicted her husband, she always got her way. She would appear to have manipulated in much the same servile manner as Wallenrodt. And she recommended such behavior, if Charlotte were not to be helpless in her marriage. Such frank instruction made it clear that Charlotte should not think of developing her talents or personality in marriage or even of expecting respect from her husband. Thus, as a young girl Charlotte comes gradually to disagree with her step-mother's philosophy.

Charlotte's positions are upheld with the strength derived from a belief in the right of the soul to its integrity, no matter what its sex. Hofrat Schwander, a friend of the family's, was the first to make young Charlotte aware of these rightful expectations. He pointed out to her the difference between living for the sake of appearance and being true to oneself. Gradually she began to consider that her step-mother was educating her to maintain the appearance of devotion in marriage, where in fact there was merely manipulation. Just this was to offend her sentiments as she began to desire a marriage built on mutual respect and consideration. Georg Recke, whom Charlotte abhorred from the beginning, possessed "durchaus nichts Mildes und Gefälliges in seinem Wesen"(127). Yet the step-mother pressured her to accept him, all the while knowing "inniger Herzensbund unter guten, gleichgestimmten Seelen war früh das Bedürfnis [ihres] Herzens, die Freude [ihres] Lebens"(88). Ultimately the step-mother's demands ran counter to Charlotte's character (284), but at the conclusion of the first manuscript Recke loses the battle for her right to establish herself in a way consonant with her beliefs and desires. She is coerced into marrying a man she loathes. The fragile self which made its briefly defiant appearance just before her capitulation had been unable to withstand the siege of her step-mother. This manuscript ends not with the achievement or fulfillment of any identity, but unresolved and confused, reflecting Recke's own youthful confusion at her betrayal.

Not only was the domestic role one which did not always represent the telos toward which any given woman might strive, the personality of an individual woman could easily also clash violently with that of her husband. Despite one statement to the effect that she would rather not marry at all, Charlotte seems to have been willing to accept a domestic destiny. As autobiographer Recke focuses on her acquisition of talents and the possession of physical qualities which make her attractive to men as well as her feelings towards them and her expectations from them. Only at the end of this segment, when the unattractive and coursely mannered Recke appears, does the conflict of personalities surface. At this point she simply ends the narration. Nothing is resolved, but she exposes the terrible gulf between her expectations and the future she faces. For any teleological structure this was an impossible situation.

Up until this point Recke's narrative, although far more psychological (sentimental and pietist) than Engel's, Wallenrodt's, or Baldinger's, still largely bears witness merely to the inadequacy of male forms of autobiography to convey the realities of a woman's life. It is the second manuscript, the one actually written earlier and left without any instructions regarding publication, which breaks with autobiographical traditions. Not coincidentally it is also the manuscript in which Recke describes her break with her domestic role.

The solution to Recke's domestic dilemma — an anathema to her training, to the concept of teleological development, and to social expectations — proved to be a divorce and a refusal to remarry. The form she chose to narrate these unconventional acts is one which permits the author to concen trate on the well-being of her soul and to uphold her integrity, even though she comes into conflict with all of society. As such it is a form deeply indebted to pietist practices and pietist confessions.

In the introduction to the 1793 manuscript, Recke claims that after the death of her friend, Caroline Stolz, she received packets containing approximately 1500 letters she had written during her six-year marriage to Georg Recke. She claims to have burned 1388 of these, and that the remainder compose the manuscript which she eventually bequeathed to the *Königliche Bibliothek* in Dresden in 1842 with no instructions regarding its disposal. The second segment of these autobiographical writings is therefore epistolary.

While neither the original editor nor anyone else has questioned Recke's assertions about the origins of these letters, to judge by their content and style they are suspect as authentic letters. They focus too exclusively on the continued narration of the story of Recke's marriage. There are no gaps; no part of the action is left unexplained for the reader. This seems highly unlikely for letters, since Stolz, the family nursemaid, lived with Recke's parents during this time and would already be acquainted with many details communicated in the letters. Moreover even though the epistles are nearly all from Recke to Stolz, material not relevant to the history of the marriage is omitted. There are no references to Stolz' daily existence or expression of concern for her well-being wich one might expect in a genuine and unedited correspondence. Only when Stolz becomes suspect as a manipulator in the destruction of Recke's marriage, does information about her creep into the text.

Were it not for their style, one might assume that the letters had merely been carefully edited. However a comparison of these with authentic letters written by Recke to her brother Friedrich reveals a very different format. Since she felt close to Freidrich who shared her dislike of Georg Recke, one could reasonably expect a similarity of style. Yet those letters tend to be more abstract, describing feelings without describing the scenes which occasioned them in such detail. Occasionally she also discusses philosophical questions, something which does not happen in the autobiographical segment. She includes more pertaining to their relationship in the letters to her brother; more about him, less minute information about her own daily affairs or feelings. She has a stylistic tendency to pile up sentences with dashes and exclamation marks. The style is more conversational and less descriptive. She tends not to repeat dialogue to the extent she does in the story of her marriage.

In addition to stylistic discrepancies it seems doubtful that Recke would have poured out her soul to her friend and nursemaid Caroline Stolz. In the introduction to her diaries (1789-1790) she wrote, "Ich verbarg es jedem, wie unglücklich meine Ehe war; nur dem Prediger auf dem Gute meiner Eltern, einem höchst verehrungswürdigen und zugleich weltklugen Geistlichen entdeckte ich meine ganze Lage und die trübe Stimmung meiner Seele, der dies irdische Leben eine Last zu werden begann."(278) Moreover when, in later diaries, she was reunited with Stolz, who became her housekeeper in Mitau, she referred to her merely as "the good Stolz", "once again, Stolz". There is no indication of the kind of intimacy which would have been the precondition for these letters.

It is simply impossible to assume as the editor Paul Rachel has, that these are authentic letters: "ob in vollem Umfange und genauem Wortlaute oder in abgekürzter und veränderter Form läßt sich nicht entscheiden; doch ist eher jenes, als dieses, anzunehmen."(viii) And rather than enlightening us, the physical properties of the original manuscript actually obscure the issue. Rachel stated that the manuscript on which he based the 1902 edition had been copied into a single volume by a hand other than Recke's. He also claimed that the manuscript from which it had been copied was one that Recke herself had copied *in toto* (rather than individual letters). No editor has ever seen original letters.

Nevertheless it seems unlikely that Recke wrote the story of her marriage in such detail from memory. And here the original manuscript does offer a clue, for it was labelled "Tagebuch der Elisa von der Recke, geb. Reichsgräfin von Medem". Rachel dismisses the notion that this might be a diary in a footnote stating, "Späterer Eintrag von anderer Hand, dem Inhalt des Bandes nicht entsprechend."(I, 159) In fact however it is far more likely that diaries formed the basis of this manuscript. A stylistic comparison reveals their resemblance to other diaries more than to her letters. In her diaries Recke was exceptionally descriptive, noting details of dress not rendered in letters, but found in the autobiography. She frequently repeated conversation or at least used direct speech. Attractions to men were elaborated upon, reflected upon as they are in the autobiographical texts.

To be sure the diaries, like her actual letters, cover a wider range of topics than the autobiography; that is, they are not as focused on a particular story. However a later edition of other of her diaries offers a plausible explananation. In 1927 Johannes Werner published Recke's diaries from 1791 and 1793 to 1795.[5] Of the notebooks which were the basis of this edition he wrote that they bore evidence not only that Recke had read them repeatedly, but also that she had reworked them repeatedly. Many, variously dated comments filled the margins and longer passages were often crossed out. Several pages had even been cut out. All of this suggests a continued active interest in her diaries.

While there is no specific reference to diaries kept during her marriage, after the death of her friend Sophie Becker in 1790 she wrote, "Um nun jetzt, da ich Sopien nicht mehr habe, dennoch immer hell über den Zustand meines Herzens urtheilen zu können, so stellte ich heut diese Selbstprüfung in meinem Tagebuche auf und werde auch ferner ebenso offenherzig in diesen Blättern die geheimsten Gefühle und Gedanken meiner Seele entwickeln, so wie es vormahls in den seligen Stunden der innigsten Seelenergießungen mit meiner Sophie geschah."(II, 313) And she seeks "Zuflucht zu [ihrem] Tagebuch".(II,331)

It is not difficult to imagine Recke taking refuge in her diaries during those difficult, isolated years of her marriage. Pietists traditionally explored the corners of their souls in that form. Moreover in using pietist diaries as the basis for autobiography she had at least one precedent. Niggl has argued convincingly that Karl Philipp Moritz relied extensively on his diaries when writing his autobiography *Anton Reiser*.[6] While Moritz theoretically narrates his life from one perspective, however, Recke chose the epistolary form.

Significantly, it is also likely that Recke had ravaged childhood diaries when writing the more teleological manuscript of 1795. As in *Anton Reiser*, Recke's childhood narration often lacks the unifying perspective one expects in a work written at one point in time. For instance nowhere does Recke prepare her readers for the duplicity of her step-mother. Her role in manipulating Charlotte's betrothal against her innermost wishes surprises the reader as much as it must have surprised Charlotte. Her initial devotion to this woman remains fresh and untarnished by later events. The daily perspective of diaries (or letters) would permit the reconstruction of such pure affection, but an autobiography totally conceived only after the deception rarely would.

What interests us particularly in the second segment of Recke's autobiographical writings is the conscious choice of the epistolary form. As startling as the choice may be for autobiography, it is not at all startling for fictional narrations of women's lives. Nor would it have been thought unusual that a woman should pour out her soul in letters. In electing this form to relate this portion of her life Recke drew on an especially strong female traditon: letters and/or epistolary novels.

By the end of the eighteenth century it was a commonplace that women, whose style was considered unpretentious because it was unschooled in the mannered courtly fashion, wrote better letters; letters closer to the heart and in a more natural style. Indeed like autobiography, the new aesthetics of letter-writing developed midst a distinctly anti-aristocratic sentiment. Although the ideal of an unpretentious epistolary style was not uncommon before the 1740s, it was Christian Fürchtegott Gellert's (1715-1769) primer on letter writing, *Gedanken von einem guten deutschen Briefe* (1742), which radically popularized it. This preceptor of bourgeois morality in Germany maintained that the untrained pen of a woman who misspelled, mispunctuated, and constructed sentences awkwardly, was preferable in its heartfelt style to all the learnedness of men. The domestic intimacy of the private sphere began to be taken as a radical alternative to over-structured, hypocritical hierarchies, and women were encouraged to write letters when they were not encouraged to write anything else.

Since the epistolary form was so closely identified with women and what was closest to the heart, letters were the appropriate genre in which to relate domestic events or sentimental affairs. In Germany poetry and drama were elevated forms, vehicles for the expression of religious or philosophical issues. Personal affairs, that is mundane affairs of the home and heart, were not appropriate material for such genres. Prose and novels became associated with these everyday events; and it was logical that the modern psychological novel, in contradistinction to the courtly, chivalrous, or adventurous novel, should develop in the wake of eighteenth-century epistolary forms. In fact, it was through such novels in Germany that women entered the literary profession. This was the case for instance with Sophie von la Roche's famous *Geschichte des Fräuleins von Sternheim* (1771). If prosaic and domestic affairs were not appropriate material for poetry or drama—or autobiography, for that matter; by 1793 there was a tradition of relating such events in epistolary form.

Examining early British epistolary novels Ruth Perry describes some of their most important characteristics.[7] In their early forms these novels most frequently portrayed tests of virtue.(22) The heroine finds herself in a precarious position—alone, with no personal power or resources. She is often cut off from parents or surrounded by people who do not understand/value her. Letter writing becomes a helpless response to a bad situation, but it is also a means of getting at the secret information buried in the heroine's soul—the test of her virtue. The plots usually involve sexual intrigues and the villains have designs for either marriage or intercourse. As they are tests of virtue, these plots rarely portray maturing characters. Rather the heroine is defined, her true value brought to light, and her constancy rewarded.

Her isolation reinforces the personal struggle, emphasizes the tension of two states of mind: the pull of consciousness and that of oblivion, quiescence. Finally and importantly, these plots are often attempts to violate not so much the physical person, as her very identity. As Perry interprets them they are power struggles over the complete, i.e. also psychological capitulation of the woman to her domestic role.(129) They portray attempts to violate her very identity by demanding her private-most consciousness or feeling, love, in addition to (and sometimes masked as) her physical submission.

The epistolary novel was one obvious model for women writing about their experiences in the domestic role. The form itself would permit a woman, if she desired, to distinguish her identity from the role. For the material of Recke's life, inappropriate for traditionally narrated autobiography, epistolary autobiography proved an expressive vehicle. Indeed she was obviously conscious of two particular epistolary novels while writing this segment of her autobiography. Interestingly, she rejects — as a personal model for herself — the character of Goethe's "Lotte" and exclaims over the superior virtues of Sophie von la Roche's "Sophie von Sternheim".

Goethe's *The Sorrows of Young Werther* had appeared during the years of her unhappy marriage and although she draws parallels between events in her life and the novel, its impact on her self image was relatively small compared to la Roche's *Sternheim*. Isolated with her insensitive husband at his rural estate Neuenburg Recke was understandably receptive to the attractions of the sensitive young poet, Gottlob David Hartmann (1752-1775) when he became their guest. It was Hartmann who brought Goethe's *Werther* with him. Together he and Charlotte read it, stunned by it as intensely as Werther and Lotte had been by Klopstock. In letters to Lavater Hartmann acknowledged having read the work ten times and explicitly compared his situation at Neuenburg to Werther's. He probably saw in Elise von der Recke the same womanly ideal Goethe had embodied in Lotte, for when he observed her in her role as doting mother he was so emotionally overcome he had to leave the room — or so Recke records in her autobiography.

While Recke may also have envisioned herself as maternal, she maintains a more virtuous attitude than Lotte. She corrects through her own life what she considered the major flaw in Goethe's heroine. After their first reading of *Werther* she commented that Lotte, once aware of Werther's love for her, should not have allowed Werther in her presence. True virtue, for her, lay in not letting others confess an impossible love (279). Some critics have speculated that Recke's disapproval of "Lotte" induced her to substitute

"Elise" for "Charlotte" as her own first name. In real life Recke sent Hartmann away when she became aware of their mutual attraction. Almost as
if to underscore the degree to which life imitated art, Hartmann soon became ill and died.

In May of 1772 Recke had raved about la Roche's *Sternheim* which had
just appeared in 1771. In that novel the heroine, Sophie (carefully raised
by loving parents) is orphaned at a young age. When she moves to the city
to relatives, they plot to install her for their own advantage as the local au-
tocrat's mistress. Sophie resists, but falls prey to other court intrigues so
that a possible alliance with the virtuous Lord Seymour is ruined and the
wicked Lord Derby has a friend imitating a priest marry them. When he
tires of this "metaphysical" and "moralistic" lover he informs her their marriage had been a fraud. Discovering the truth Sophie recovers splendidly
and establishes a school for young women in the countryside. Following
an invitation of Lady Summer to England, however, she is soon abducted
by Lord Derby, who has since married Lady Summer's niece. When Sophie
refuses further advances on his part he incarcerates her and leaves her to
die. Not long thereafter he himself is struck deadly ill, soon repents, and
sends a search party to find Sophie (who had been rescued anyway by Derby's
servant). Sophie finally marries Lord Seymour, but an equally eligible and
enamoured Lord Rich chooses to live near the couple to be near Sophie and
the three share an idyllic and virtuous life together.

Explicitly comparing herself to the plucky heroine Recke wrote in her autobiography: "O! die Sternheim war viel besser, viel liebenswürdiger und
viel unglücklicher, als ich."(230) She vowed to imitate her virtues though
she knew she would never be as happy in the end. Indeed twenty years after
that reading she would integrate characteristics of that fictional heroine into
her own self-portrait.[8] Sternheim poured out her innermost feelings in letters to her intimate friend. Like Recke, she too was the victim of jealousy
and family intrigue. Forced to marry a man she could not love she took refuge
in books, as had Sternheim. She also found comfort in knowing that her
own heart was pure and her behavior beyond reproach. In fact, her soul becomes so noble that "the evil one" no longer dares to approach her (232).
In an oppressive situation resembling Sternheim's, Recke prided herself on
her own virtue and knew how to value herself in her behavior toward the
coarse Georg Recke. This belief in her self-worth gave her the integrity with
which to expect the respect of those closest to her. Adherence to the principles of virtue and the sense of self-worth, traits of Sophie von Sternheim,
were a means to distance herself from an uncomfortable situation and as-

sert her intrinsic dignity. Virtue becomes a means of protecting one's dignity, and what might otherwise be thought of as Recke's prudish criticism of Lotte appears, in the light of *Sternheim*, as a refusal to sacrifice her integrity for anyone.[9]

Recke's ability to value her personal integrity and moral stance in the face of external assault is undoubtedly a secular version of a trait that the pietist tradition would have encouraged. In particular the figure of the quietist mystic Mme. de la Motte Guyon needs to be mentioned. Even though her name never falls in Recke's autobiography, her influence is powerfully felt. It extends, I believe, to more than Recke's sense of integrity.

If it was not traditional in male autobiographies to narrate simple domestic affairs it was even less traditional to relate intimate marital experience. The level of intimacy to which Recke exposes her readers is unique for autobiographical writing of the period, although parallels may be found in novels. Hers are among the most frank admissions made in the eighteenth and even nineteenth centuries, certainly for women. She acknowledges adolescent sexual attractions and portrays her parents concern about her sexual awakening. In her intimate relations with her husband she describes her repugnance at the thought of kissing him on the lips, her manoevers to evade sexual contact, and pressure from her entire family to have a child. We might have had even more intimate details had Paul Rachel not censured certain passages. One reviewer of the 1902 edition gratefully acknowledged Rachel's intervention when he noted that at least Recke and her husband were not followed beyond the bedroom door.[10] Even a century later Recke's revelations were deemed too daring to appear in print.

Far from being merely scurilous however such intimate detail was vital for her text, for only through it could she explain how she arrived in her predicament and why she defied her husband, family, and society. Without knowing that Georg Recke was capable of petty cruelty like killing her pet cat or abused her when she bore him a daughter, rather than a son, it would be difficult for readers to comprehend her decision to avoid sexual relations with him until he had treated her humanely for two years. Without knowing how he ranted at this display of self-respect and rallied her family against her it would be difficult for readers to sympathize with her socially unacceptable defiance of her entire family and her ultimate decision to divorce her husband and never remarry. The dignified and pacifist composure of Goethe's "Iphigenie" was without effect here. Iphigenie's appeal to reason and humane values would have fallen on deaf ears if her tyranical sovereign had been Georg von der Recke. Fortunately Elise had an alternative in this case, difficult though it was and requiring as it did an unusual reserve of integrity.

When women possess no other respectable source of financial support than their families, the strength required to defy them so thoroughly should not be underestimated. But whatever strength of character Recke may have been born with, it seems unlikely that it would ever have shown itself had it not received assistance from some direction. To be sure Recke had internalized many of the virtues of sentimental heroines, especially ones Rousseau liked to find in women: nature affects her greatly; she describes herself as sensitive, but not sensual; she appears as a careful and adoring mother, who would have been happy to fulfill her domestic responsibilities in accordance with the ideal. However part of that same ideal consisted in the mutual respect and admiration of marriage partners. Willing to uphold her part of the image, she also demanded respect from her husband. In the refusal to remain passive in her fate Recke subverts the ideal.

The confessions of the mystic, Jean Marie Bouvier de la Motte Guyon (1648-1717), had been published in 1720.[1] Their influence on Recke, along with that of von la Roche, suggests the importance of a distinctly female tradition of shared experience. Guyon's confessions had become common reading fare for many pietists, incuding the young Karl Philipp Moritz. Recke not only would have been able to read the French original, this friend of Lavater and Jung-Stilling, well-known through his own autobiographical writings, would also have found a sympathetic nature in Guyon. Recke fails to explore in any detail her increasing involvement with mysticism while she was married to Georg von der Recke. Yet we know from other sources that it was then that her mind took the turn of direction which allowed her to fall prey to the machinations of the conjuror, Cagliostro. Still, she does report reading Schwedenborg and once feeling spirits about her. As she was also an avid reader it seems highly likely that she read the memoirs of this French mystic, even while at Neuenburg.

Born almost a century apart and raised in different cultures these women nevertheless shared certain experiences. Episodes in Guyon's childhood find counterparts in Recke's. Jealousy causes young playmates to treat them badly. Other children whip them for not telling the demanded falsehoods. Although they then receive the blame for misdeeds committed by others, each is too scared of reprisals to expose the lie. Had these false comrades not interfered, they would have been good children, for they both possessed the proper inclination. As soon as the young Guyon came under the positive influence of an elder half-sister she began to discover qualities in her-

50

self that God had placed there and wanted to develop. Recke's talents unfolded rapidly after she entered her step-mother's care.

In particular the marital situations of these women parallel each other. Neither wanted to marry: Guyon wanted to enter the convent, Recke to go on the stage. Guyon was betrothed without her consent, Recke's consent was coerced. For both marriage meant relative loss of freedom as their behavior and movement was restricted. Neither could voice her opinion without being either intimidated or mocked. These unfortunate marriages were made intolerable by the intrigues, slander, and misunderstanding of other relatives. Both women view their lives, and in particular their marriages, as schools where patience and virtue were learned. Recke frequently comments, "durch Leiden werden die Kräfte der Seele geübt."(281) She claims too that her faith in life after death strengthened because on earth she had received so unsuitable a position (162) and notes: "der Gedanke, daß selige Geister mich umschweben, da diese in meinem Herzen leben, der giebt mir Muth, heiter zu bleiben, wenn ich mich von dem verkannt und verachtet sehe, dessen Leben ich so gern erheitern möchte."(224) Guyon's turn to mysticism had followed immediately upon a painful pregnancy and allowed her to withdraw somewhat from her husband. After Recke gave birth to a daughter her husband became so abusive that she refused sexual encounters with him.

Although mistreated by their husbands and families, each woman was aware that she enjoyed social admiration in general, a situation which led to a certain amount of self-assurance. More than this, however, it would seem that the pietist tradition with its emphasis on the equality of souls provided these women with enough belief in the importance of their own worth and dignity to expect treatment commensurate with it. Recke waged a continual fight with her husband and relatives in order to be allowed to read, commenting on their supposed belief that women ought not to read, "als hätten wir keine Seele und nur ein Stück Fleisch." (213)

Since social attitudes traditionally held women to be chattel such similarities in experience seem inevitable (despite the difference in time and country). But the extent to which Recke actually chose to relate these similarites is the astonishing aspect of this parallel experience and, under the circumstances, probably not accidental. We recall the great pains Wallenrodt had taken not to criticize her husband, her family, or the king. Although no effort to conceal hostility to near relations is apparent, neither Baldinger nor Engel reveal any. To do so would have transgressed a social code. In the face of the absence of such criticism from other autobiographers, at least two of whom had stated their marriages were the equivalent of slavery, the willingness of Recke to criticize her family requires some explanation.

Both Recke and Guyon were extremely careful in real life to maintain the appearance of a satisfactory marriage, and Guyon notes: "Und wie verschieden war das, was ich ihnen äusserlich zeigte, von dem was innerlich Statt fand."(81) Although Guyon and Recke both reveal in writing what they consider culpable behavior in their families neither "betrays" her family without great pangs of conscience. Guyon must attribute her descriptions of her family's behavior to the fact that her spiritual advisor instructed her not to leave holes in her story. She also attempts to recommend virtues of her relatives in order to counteract the effect of her negative comments. At first Recke does not seem to mind demonizing her aunt and cousins, but she is careful not to vilify her father or step-mother in the first segment. In the second she repeatedly asks her correspondent to destroy her letters so that no one will find out how painful her situation was, especially her daughter. Guyon's confessions and Recke's autobiographical writings never appeared during their lifetimes. Recke allowed the publication of her childhood memoirs only after the deaths of all the people mentioned, and she left the particularly devastating history of her marriage with no explicit request for publication. Precisely the tenacity of this resistance to exposing familial cruelty, along with the large number of parallels, suggests Recke was probably specifically encouraged by Guyon's example. This connection would seem to be one of the many silenced fragments of a female tradition.

Neither Guyon nor Recke submitted to the daily horror of their marriages, and the source for their strength to resist came from some inner voice. Guyon interpreted it as the voice of God. Because she believed it to be imbued with God's presence she was able to demand respect for the untameable portion of her character. She declared that voice independent of social or church requirements, and asserted the sovereign right of her divine passions. Her most true self belonged to God, no true sentiment or intimation could exist except as it was God's. The voice of reason (or social reason) held no sway here. She found within her own self something unnameable which rejected everything evil and approved what was good. She harkened more to that which arose from the depths of her soul than to that which passed through her head. And it was this that required her to write as she did. She considered herself anything but willful and rebellious. She followed only the inner divine voice, her songbirds, and became a martyr. And if love of herself was demanded as love of God, then boundless love for all of God's creation also resulted from this mystical identity of innermost self with divine Being. This was not a selfish conjuring of individual rights.

It will not surprise us that Rahel Varnhagen included Guyon among the women she most admired. For she too loved and respected her own soul as part of a universal Being. She too wanted to write from the depths of that soul so that there would be no traces of a dead order or narrow morality, in love and care for the particularity of every living thing. Even at the turn of the next century Marie von Ebner-Eschenbach will bear witness to the strength of this mystical tradition among women. Whatever other attractions it holds for them it also validates an inner voice in opposition to confining social convention. Recke's narration of her life story has already evidenced the implications of such a faith for women's secular lives.

If pietism influenced Recke's autobiography more profoundly than Wallenrodt's, one major character trait binds Recke more closely with her than with the French mystic. According to Guyon all her trials and misfortunes represented the direct intervention of God, whose aim it was to test and strengthen her and to lead her, like Job, through pain to absolute trust in the divinity. Her youth and marriage are an earthly prison and the pain others willfully inflict finds its only explanation in that superior being. No other answer could give meaning to the senselessness of her pain and she refashions that suffering into gratitude to God. For Guyon the only socially acceptable escape from the earthly prison of her marriage was mysticism.

Despite her mystical inclinations Elise von der Recke had the courage to make a very real decision to divorce her husband. Although references to God seeing into her soul and recognizing her innocence appear several times, her explanation of her situation remains essentially secular. Like Wallenrodt she claimed to want to show divine providence at work, but undercut this claim with secular explanations. To be sure she accepts her suffering as education, but a worldly one. The tensions between herself and her husband, she explains, arose because of difference in temperament. She admits having made mistakes in her marriage and explains that Recke wanted her to be something she was not, "eine feurige Liebe" ("a passionate lover'). Everything could have been different if she had been older and her relatives had not interfered. Her suffering was not necessary to God's plan and she no longer seeks divine excuses either for her own behavior or for that of others. The secularization of her experience means that her grandmother's sternness and her aunt's jealousy remain just that and are not rationalized as originating in a divine plan. Her resentment of her step-mother for "selling" her to Recke remains personal. Her attitude toward Recke himself waivers ambivalently between pain and anger at his callousness on the one hand and sympathy for someone caught in a role he does not want to play on the other. Recke directs her anger at real sources.

Guyon had asked her spiritual advisor to read her confessions in a particular way: "Sehen Sie die Dinge nicht von der Seite der Natur an, weil Ihnen sonst die Personen tadelnswerther scheinen würden, als sie waren. Alles muß in Gott angesehen werden, der solche Dinge erlaubte, damit mein Heil befördert würde, und ich nicht in Verderben geriet(72). Recke refuses to provide such an apology for her family, which is viewed from the perspective of nature. She asks God to forgive those who destroy our happiness and health so unfeelingly (403), but they bear the blame and responsibility. Her autobiography thereby acquires a more critical political stance than that of Guyon, albeit in a limited sphere.

Recently it has become popular to note that women, especially bourgeois women, traditionally have been relegated to the private sphere alone. This autobiography suggests that the issue was not that simple, especially for women restricted to domestic roles. In a non-parallel fashion women, too, experienced life as divided into a public and a private sphere. In this case anyway, "public" was for Recke what "private" was for her husband. That does not mean that her domestic role was the equivalent of a man's public role. It does suggest that the arena in which one's "identity" might evolve was a different one for women, than for men. And for autobiography it meant that an author had to find a different place from which to speak. Recke found that necessarily very interior place in letters.

The contradictions in Wallenrodt's narration of her life were as obvious as her refusal to admit her rage and frustration at her treatment not only by society, but by her husband as well. To be sure, she had chosen an epistolary form, but somewhat disingenuously. She did not reveal attitudes contrary to social expectations, but then she published her autobiography during her lifetime. In Recke's narration of her marriage the epistolary form acquires a profound function. It is a form and a tradition which permitted her to express — and apparently consider at least the posthumous publication of — her personal non-identification with the social role that had been imposed on her, rather than internally evolved.

Historically Recke's defense of her "self" occurs simultaneously with the assertion of "identity" in male autobiography. No doubt it derives from the same pietist sources. Like male autobiographers she used that conceptualization to confront expected role patterns and demand certain respectful treatment, rights. Only the assumption of a "self" gave her the strength to

54

expect that respectful treatment. It seems unlikely to have been coincidental that the two adopted "scripts" by means of which she gained the strength
to resist her entire family were written by women. La Roche's epistolary novel
and Guyon's narrative autobiography provided her with the necessary
models of an alternative "self". In part this is, of course, merely a new fiction; it is the creation of a "self" according to someone else's model. However, it is hardly necessary to assert the absolutely unique nature of any
individual, in order to assert the existence of a "self". Indeed Recke's ability to combine and manipulate the content and form of these works for her
own ends gives evidence of the activity of a "self". It was her decision —
and her need — to narrate "real" experience in epistolary fashion.

To some extent Recke does not exploit the epistolary form as she might.
Although this intimate form seems justified by the revelations of deep, dark
secrets and by her social isolation, in another way the narration of her marriage is less radical in its structure than some others. It is composed almost
exclusively of letters written by her, and suggests a single "identity" in conflict with external social pressures. Elisabeth Stägemann's autobiography
takes this form another radical step further.

Like Recke's that of Elisabeth Stägemann (1761-1835) was only cautiously
intended for publication. Completed in 1804 this remarkable work was first
published by Wilhelm Dorow in 1846 under the title *Erinnerungen für Edle
Frauen.*[12] It encompasses only a fragment of the author's life, the period
just prior to her first marriage until shortly after her remarriage. Although
she had given Dorow the manuscript in 1827 for publication after both her
death and that of her husband, she had at least contemplated publishing
it herself in 1810. To that end she wrote a false introduction in the style of
an epistolary novel. The fictional editor claims to have received this document from a dear friend on her death bed. The woman whose story it is
(Stägemann) also writes an introduction, however, and here she admits that
these letters are not authentic in the sense of having been sent between two
real persons. Rather they are letters she wrote in a period of semi-isolation
to clarify for herself the direction of her life. It is a dialogue in which she
wrote both parts. Her imagination created the friend she had never had,
the friend to whom she could communicate her innermost feelings and
thoughts: "Ich suchte Dichtung und Wahrheit, so gut sich's thun ließ, in
der Unterhaltung mit ihr zu verschmelzen, und fand eine sonderbare
Befriedigung darin, über meine Gefühle mich aussprechen zu können, ohne
von mir selbst zu reden."(7)

This "strange satisfaction" is worth noting, for it arose from the expression of feelings which she wished not to claim directly and fully as her final views. It alone was not to be considered her "self". In her reluctance to identify herself completely with them she created two persons to represent two sides of her "self". The characterization of the self is thus not self-identical and these letters are nothing less than a dialogue between her two halves. One correspondent is the ideal friend she never had: "[Ich] ließ die Freundin, welche meine Phantasie sich schuf, oft die Stimme der Vernunft führen, während ich mich ganz den Eingebungen und Ergießungen meines Herzens überließ."(8). This imagined friend, whom she named "Meta", acts as her more rational side, a kind of super-ego with a view of the larger perspective, the "Meta-Elisabeth". The other correspondent, whom she named "Elisabeth", is allowed to express her socially unacceptable desires. The two sides of the conflict between role and "self" are internalized and anthropomorphized. The real struggle takes place within the psyche itself.

Johanna Elisabeth von Stägemann, born and raised in Königsberg, had married Justizrath Graun in 1780. She bore him a son and a daughter; and when he was transferred to Berlin in 1787 she remained in Königsberg, living with her mother and caring for her children. Otherwise the social life to which she had been accustomed, as center of a salon, was abandoned. In 1795 she went to Berlin, where for uncertain reasons, she decided to divorce her husband. After returning to Königsberg she married Friedrich August von Stägemann in 1796. In 1809 the Stägemanns moved permanently to Berlin where she again became the center of a prestigious salon. She bore Stägemann one son and one daughter as well. These facts carry a certain import since Stägemann took some liberties with her material. Indeed her introduction admits the combination of fiction and reality presented in her reminiscences.

Stägemann's alterations will be significant, but the autobiographical intent must be stressed. Having admitted to her readers that certain facets of her autobiography are fictionalized, she nevertheless emphasizes its autobiographical nature. Not only does she tell Dorow the real names of persons disguised therein, but she also allows him to publish diverse real letters along with the manuscript. It is an autobiography à clef, deciphered by Stägemann herself. In accord with eighteenth-century novel techniques she referred to people by initials. Johann Friedrich Reichart was named simply "H."; Friedrich von Gentz, "G."; the Warrendorfs were friends in reality, not relatives; Herzog von Holstein-Beck was named Graf Werdenberg (also "W.", "Leopold"); Friedrich August Stägemann was named "Gerson"; and so on. Moreover, as if to underscore her autobiographical intent, she emphasizes that the letters represent "den treuen Druck meines Ichs".(10)

Stägemann carefully structured her autobiography into three parts corresponding to stages in her life conflict: duty, freedom, and harmonious resolution. In the first part Elisabeth arrives in B-lin (Berlin) to live with her father who plans to marry her off well. That father and the narrow, unattractive streets of Berlin are contrasted to her circle of friends and the natural beauty of Stägemann's imaginary "Grünthal" which she had left. There she had enjoyed the bounty of the country, living in harmony with her mother; her friend, Meta; another close friend; and count Werdenberg. That lost idyll is preferred to Berlin, as her mother is to her father. The father, as well as her eventual husband, embody those unsentimental, disciplined souls of the rising merchant class. In Berlin Elisabeth feels caged, since she cannot go out without a chaperone, does not enjoy society, and even loses interest in her beloved painting. Like Recke she agrees finally and under pressure to marry a man whom she dislikes from the beginning. Only later does she learn the financial motivation for her father's urgent pressure. Like Recke she compares this marriage to slavery (I, 184) and is compelled to live a lie (I, 192,231). She longs simply to be free enough to arrange the furniture as she pleases (I, 193). As if to prove the failure of her marriage, the daughter born to her, the only joyful thing in her life, suddenly dies. Elisabeth distracts herself by becoming the star of an active social life in K-g (Königsberg) where they now live. Quickly and suddenly her husband also falls ill and dies.

Many of these details are fictitious. The most significant alterations of reality are transforming her actual divorce into the death of her husband and obscuring the fact that two children from this marriage grew into adulthood. The first she may have altered either because of the difficulty of writing about such a socially unacceptable step in 1804 or because she did not want to seem to justify such an action for other women. The second distortion served literary purposes: the representation of her marriage as emotionally barren. It also made acceptable her later consideration to pursue an artistic career.

Despite the apparent absence of any discussion of her divorce, there may be a disguised narration of the real events leading to it. In the explanation of her parents' separation one may choose to see the explanation of her own real action. Certainly external circumstances seem similar. After a separation of some years (in the autobiography due to the mother's health) the mother had joined her husband in B-lin, much as Stägemann, who had remained in Königsberg when her husband moved to Berlin, later joined him there. In reality Stägemann soon returned to Königsberg to divorce her husband. In the autobiography Elisabeth's mother finds a housekeeper-relative in full control of the house in Berlin, and this further strains an already difficult marital relationship. Rather than unsettle that authority she merely returns to "Grünthal". Since the physical actions are so similar it does not seem unlikely that Stägemann transposed the experiences leading to her own divorce onto the autobiographical mother. However this necessarily remains speculation.

The second part of the autobiography begins with Elisabeth's new-found freedom. Like Wallenrodt and Recke she chooses not to remarry and cannot imagine ever finding a man who would make the sacrifice seem justified. She enjoys her freedom, occupies herself again with her painting and other pleasures she had neglected during her marriage. This is a relatively carefree time for Elisabeth who finds herself surrounded by admirers. In particular Count Werdenberg, her childhood friend, and Gerson, Meta's cousin, vie for her affections. Indeed the Count, neglecting social distinctions, proposes marriage to this bourgeoise, who has come to consider him her ideal (I, 96, 197).

In the third part Elisabeth learns, as Wallenrodt had, that society mistrusts a woman living alone, especially when it is by choice. Gossip about her and the Count threatens to ruin her reputation. Moreover the thought of the Count's attachment to someone beneath his standing distresses his family. Elisabeth had thought she could withstand social pressure, but learns that her pleasure is dependent upon the blessing of society (I, 235; II,3,21). More than that, in trying to evade his family's desires, Werdenberg assumes hypocritical stances and this disillusions Elisabeth about her ideal. After all it was just this forced hypocrisy that she had resented in her own posture vis-à-vis her first husband.

Elisabeth also learns that the greatest pleasure in life comes not from pleasing merely oneself, in being "ein abgesondertes Ich"(II, 95), but rather in accepting a purpose beyond oneself by engaging in purposeful activity (I, 75, 129; II,30). With considerable cost to her own happiness Elisabeth refuses to see Werdenberg until he is betrothed to the woman his family has chosen for him, a woman in every way admirable and agreeable. Moreover, Elisabeth's adored mother had recommended — on her death bed — a life of activity and justice, had dismissed as nothing the suffering incurred by the noble act of resigning oneself to one's duty. All our efforts to please, she asserted, come to nothing if they distract us from our duty (I, 72). And so marriage becomes Elisabeth's duty and profession. Meta advises: "Und die Ehe... ist trotz allen Ungemächlichkeiten, denen wir uns dabei unterziehen, doch immer die zweckmäßigste Einrichtung in der bürgerlichen Welt, unsere Ruhe und Sicherheit und selbst den Frieden unseres Herzens zu schützen."(II,32)

Although he did not initially excite her passions, or precisely because he did not, Gerson turns out to be the right choice. Elisabeth had considered him her best friend and had not wanted to sacrifice that friendship to marriage. But he has won her affections. Just this tender affection makes him the more appropriate mate. He is gentle, loving, and thoughtful. The final scene in the autobiography is a domestic portrait of the Werdenbergs and Gersons enjoying a harmonious evening together.

In this unusual autobiography the central conflict is the classical one between free will and necessity (II, 16ff). That conflict, which had been responsible for the contradictions in other women's autobiography, becomes the explicit theme of Stägemann's. The promise of bourgeois society for the free development of each individual was impossible in the face of the predetermination of women's roles. In her introduction Stägemann had outlined the shape of her life: In her first marriage she tortured herself "in einem vergeblichen Streit [ihrer] Kräfte und Neigungen, und sehnte [sich] nicht weniger nach Wahrheit, als auch der Vollendung in irgend einem Theil [ihres] Wesens. Die Gewalt der Umstände entschied endlich, denn das praktische Leben ward durch [ihre] herzliche Liebe fär die [ihrigen] nach und nach so ganz in [ihr] Interesse verflochten, da jede Wahl verschwand."(8) Rather than representing the telos of her personal evolution, Stägemann clearly represents her marriage as interrupting the natural course of her development. Even when her life takes a more positive turn and she finds a suitable husband she records: "Ich mußte den zweiten Theil meines Lebens für Andere leben, wie ich bisher für mich gelebt... als könnte ich nichts von dem, was ich einst liebte, was ich mit so unsäglichem Fleiß geübt, auf die zweite Hälfte meines Lebens übertragen.—Wie das abgetrennte Glied einer Kette, lag das Vergangene hinter mir... (.)"(9)

Since she seriously contemplated moving to Dresden to care for an elderly aunt in order to be able to devote herself to her beloved painting, any real reconciliation with her fate can only occur when she adopts a totally different view of art. She learns that: "nicht die praktische Übung der Kunst es sei, was uns vorzüglich beglückte, sondern die läuternde, erhebende, Alles verschönernde Kraft, durch die sie uns auch dann noch beseligt, wenn wir ihrem Altar kein anderes Opfer mehr bringen, als das, welches, durch Glaube, Liebe und Anbetung angefacht, in unserm Innersten in ewiger Reinigkeit fort lodert."(9) She must therefore resign herself to a passive stance with regard to her formerly energetic pursuit of painting. She significantly altered her expectations for herself. The teleology of her development was halted by her domestic activity and the role society assigned her; and yet she presents her solution as a more perfect ideal: the true profession of women (I, 67f). Women are happiest, she asserts, when they can combine personal ambitions with domestic responsibility. Moreover passionate love is also rejected as an ideal. A flaming passion only consumes and destroys while a love which is tender infuses each daily activity and informs one's entire being thereby providing real happiness. Clearly the dangers of strong individual goals and passions must be overcome through accommodation if one is to find harmony.

Radical readers might label this accommodation resignation. Indeed, when Gustav Kühne reintroduced the book to the public in 1858, he claimed it was a good example of women's natural ability to suffer!13 Pragmatic readers might call it idealism. For Stägemann it was both ideal and pragmatic. And perhaps she felt comfortable articulating the conflict for women so clearly just because she believed she had found a response to it that challenged society without totally rejecting traditional female values. For if Elisabeth ultimately accepts a domestic role, it is only because she found the kind of man that would make it possible for her. She does not simply succumb. Stägemann makes her own demands. In stressing the importance of the right kind of man, she establishes an ideal which challenged the traditional image of men and with it the nature of an industrializing society.

Stägemann's criticism of the mercantilist, rational culture of the burgeoing middle-classes, with its emphasis on work, is associated more directly with men. Indeed men and women sometimes appear, as Rahel Varnhagen would once state, to be two different nations. Elisabeth's father and first husband are both businessmen and portrayed as distant, matter-of-fact, non-sentimental, and without the ability to empathize. The two of them are overly concerned with time and rationality (27). Her father's library contains only books relevant to his business (21). Her father assumes she is vain and brings her baubles for which she has no interest (21). In general men encage their women and isolate them from one another: Elisabeth must leave Meta and her mother when she moves to Berlin; Meta's husband is frequently the reason she cannot visit Elisabeth, and he distracts her from writing letters to Elisabeth with his own demands. Men cannot endure contradictions (230). Men love selfishly (II,7). Her first husband approaches her lustfully with no consideration for her feelings. Often, Elisabeth reflects, their love and

dependence is the need to treat women as domestic appliances and the secret desire that nothing shall occupy their thoughts or please them that does
not have the closest connection to the male ego (I, 230). As long as she lives
with her father or her first husband she has little desire to paint. These men
manipulate women for their own purposes, much as they manipulate their
businesses. Her criticism of them is also a criticism of the mercantilist repression of love, fantasy, and art.

Of women she maintains that they have a talent and a taste for living with
refinement. They are inherently able to emphathize with others and to beau-
tify life by imbuing it with culture and education (*Bildung*) (II, 34). In this
Meta saw the more privileged lot of women. She extols the art of beautify-
ing daily life more than the art of a painter, and she advises Elisabeth not
to move to Dresden and devote herself to painting. At first Elisabeth rebels
against social necessity: "O Meta, kann ich dafür, daß die Empfindung der
natürlichen Freiheit, welche jedem Menschen heilig sein sollte, eben durch
mein Mißgeschichk angefacht ist, da sie bei hundert Andern dadurch er-
stickt sein würde? – Ist dieses Gefühl nicht mit der Ausbildung meines Verstandes erwacht – und müssen wir erst dumm und stumpf werden, um
glücklich zu sein und Andere glücklich zu machen?"(II,40) She abhors the
role of a woman who is consumed totally by the requirements of daily life –
sewing and lacemaking. She also abhors the deceptive role many women
accept, the pretense of the most lovable of female characteristics: devotion
and sacrifice, etc.

Elisabeth's refusal to accept just any marriage by no means indicates that
she rejects in principle the role society expects her to play. Indeed she recognizes nobility in that role, so long as it is properly defined. Like Recke she
will not relinguish her integrity. She honors the destiny of her sex to perform even the most lowly of services for the man "der mein Versorger, mein
Freund in der genausten und engsten Bedeutung des Wortes wäre. . . (.)"(II,
41) Until that man appears, however, she intends to guard herself from any
new servitude. With Gerson her role as wife and mother becomes the noblest:
"Ich träumte von Ungebundenheit und lerne, daß das Weib ihre wahre Unabhängigkeit, das heißt, den schönsten und freiesten Gebrauch ihrer Kräfte,
nur in einem geordneten Leben, selbst unter den beschwerlichsten Pflichten
findet. Was sonst als Schwäche unserer Natur erscheint, wird hier geheiligt.
Verleugnung und Hingebung kämpfen hier nicht länger gegen den Stolz des
weiblichen Herzens. Die Unterwerfung unter einen andern Willen, die meinen Blick sonst zu Boden schlug, der meine Eitelkeit sich gewaltsam einst
entziehen wollte, ist unter dem Gesetz der Ordnung mein Triumph gewor-

den. (...) Unter dem dichten Laubgewölbe, das [die Zufriedenheit] um meinen Wirkungskreis gezogen, dringt weder der brennende Strahl der zu lebhaften Fröhlichkeit noch der zerstörende Sturm des Leidens auf mich ein."(II, 103f.) (Kühne should have taken note of this passage.) Perhaps Baldinger, too, had resigned herself to the domestic role so convincingly. The difference is that Stägemann permits apprehension of the process and the choices she made.

If the lost paradise of "Grünthal" was composed mainly of women: Elisabeth, Meta, another girlfriend, and Elisabeth's mother, with Count Werdenberg as the token male; then the paradise regained at the end also centers on women. The domestic scene, described as one would a genre painting, occurs in the inner sanctum of Countess Werdenberg. This room is "ein Heiligthum, das nur selten und nur von Wenigen betreten wird. Hier steht zwischen hohen Blumenbüschen ihre Harmonika; hier hangen ihre liebsten Gemälde und Zeichnungen, und unter ihnen ein Madonna, die ich einst für den Grafen gemalt."(II, 105) The scene occurs in the moonlight, the participants sit in a semi-circle with children playing at their feet. Elisabeth's little girl sits on the lap of the countess. In the distance the moon illuminates a ruined fortress and throws shadows against the wall. Elisabeth is asked to sing and the countess joins her. The two men shake hands in friendship and the Count unites the hands of the two women. Women's art is appreciated and the individuals are united in an expression of heartfelt tenderness. It is a "small paradise" against a romantic background evoking the past glories of a decaying aristocracy. In terms of upholding class distinctions the final scene seems to express a subtle longing for a more hierarchical society. From the point of view of imagining a society which incorporates generosity, aesthetic values, and caring this image suggests a clearly utopian vision. Possible contradictions do not concern Stägemann.

Although the harmony of this nearly androgynous scene is reminiscent of Schlegel's *Lucinde*, there are several important differences. Schlegel had not felt obliged to explain his hero's choices in terms of the dichotomy marriage or freedom. For Julius the choice was one of hypocritical or genuine human relationships. He does not relinquish his freedom in his relationship with Lucinde. But the difference in the portraits of women's lives is the more important distinction. As already noted Stägemann has shown us the process by which a woman may decide to relinguish more general human claims to the individualistic development of her innate abilities. Schlegel's "Lucinde" remains something of a mystery. Perhaps we should not expect him to portray the history of this ideal woman, but then neither

62

should we take it for granted that "Lucinde's" social and familial role was her natural destiny. At least as important a benefit of knowing Stägemann's history is knowing that this final harmony is only possible, is only chosen, because Gerson has proven himself to be so sensitive and nearly feminine. Stägemann has insisted on her own terms.

Somewhat atypically, for instance, Gerson had had a female guardian and Elisabeth praises his continued deference to her (I, 167). When he argues with his friend, G. (Gentz), Gerson allows his emotions to surface. In what is characteristically thought to be female behavior, he complains of a headache and lies down on the sofa in the next room. He can speak of his feelings with clarity and ease, and he also occasionally breaks into tears (II, 67-71). He is thoughtful and generous in his love. If Elisabeth's first marriage was a purgatory her second is a "ein Vorgeschmack des Himmels"(I, 187).

As Stägemann resolved her conflict with society the two sides of her own personality seem to have lost their need to engage in dialogue. Meta had always advised sensibly, urging her to be "reasonable", to marry her first husband if her only objection was that he was not her ideal (I, 59), to accept the role society had chosen for her. A child would fill her empty heart, she advised, when she observed Elisabeth's unhappiness in her marriage (I, 119). She encourages her not to expect, or even desire, an "ideal", flaming love; to wait for her husband's regard; and to accept the fact that he will never understand her (I, 123). Meta's is the voice of reason (I, 124), Elisabeth's mentor (I, 16, 173), and the voice of her conscience (I, 190). She reassures her when she is innocent (II, 30, 60). She predicts early that Gerson, her own cousin, will be the "right" husband for Elisabeth. She has a more firm psychological constitution and can adapt to daily life more easily (I, 49), she is more domestic and enjoys "stille Wirksamkeit"(I, 51).

But Meta is not totally self-satisfied either. She envies Elisabeth for not allowing herself to be consumed by mundane reality and suggests that she, Meta, will always be diverted from her own artistic endeavors, which she enjoys by her efforts to maintain "Ruhe und Ordnung in unserem Wirkungskreis".(I, 205) Meta claims Elisabeth is and was her own better self, corresponded to "der schönere geistige Genuß".(II, 84) If Meta is Elisabeth's meta-self and the voice of reason, then Elisabeth is Meta's more profound understanding (I, 25), her sentiments (I, 116), and her imagination (I, 35). Especially after the death of her husband Elisabeth repeatedly asserts (or longs to assert) her right to establish her own life, to pursue her own ideal, and to be involved in more than the humdrum of domestic chores. She longs to become part of a larger social entity. Elisabeth possesses "Sittlichkeit ohne Ziererei, Freimüthigkeit voll Selbstvertrauen".(I, 170) She is Werdenberg's ideal (I, 170) and writes once of herself: "Freilich hatte ich mir einst ein Ideal (von meiner selbst) gemacht, auch kann ich meinen Glauben daran nur mit dem besseren Theil meiner Existenz aufgeben."(I, 82) That would mean giving up Elisabeth herself and only permitting Meta to exist. Understanding, courageous in its confinement, strives for independence. Yet Elisabeth comes to learn that, like Meta, her heart must be bound in one place (II, 33).

Silences in this correspondence and dialogue are revealing. On the one hand Meta fails to write when Elisabeth is not in need of her conscience. Thus Elisabeth complains of Meta's silence after she has renounced Werdenberg (II, 65). On the other hand Elisabeth does not seek out her conscience when she enjoys unclouded freedom at no one's expense. Between her marriages she can blissfully pursue her own interests without depriving someone else of attention or care (I, 213). She also fails to make her presence felt when she becomes depressed after the death of her daughter, at which point Meta complains that she cannot bear living without hearing from Elisabeth, her imagination. In the final letter Elisabeth acknowledges that neither has written in a long time. Presumably her desires and her conscience are reconciled since she has married Gerson, Meta's cousin and the friend she had feared losing (II, 102). The two halves of her "self" are now wed and in daily communication.

The constellation of correspondents — one more adapted to social requirements and the other straining them — recalls Goethe's epistolary and semi-autobiographical *Sorrows of Young Werther*. There the distant friend, Wilhelm, tries to guide an artistic and idealistic Werther to a reconciliation with a too rigidly structured society and the fact that his ideal woman, Lotte, had been won and married by a representative of unsentimental rationality. However, while Werther despaired of becoming involved in social relationships, gave in to his solipsistic effusions, and committed suicide, Stägemann envisions a less violent resolution. If Recke's correction of *Werther* could be described as a victory for integrity, Stägemann's could be called utopian. The extent to which this is true becomes clear in another comparison.

Neither Werther nor Lotte can be said to have influenced Stägemann's self-portrait. But another heroine from eighteenth century epistolary fiction may have. At one point in the autobiography Gerson gives Elisabeth the complete works of Rousseau, and there are certain similarities in the character of Stägemann and the heroine of *La nouvelle Héloïse*. Julie is also a very sensitive, at first overly sentimental heroine who corresponds with her more rational, better adjusted cousin, revealingly named "Claire". Julie learns to control her passionate impulses — also for the benefit of the immutable laws of social hierarchy. She claims that obedience to her father was an emotional necessity for her, much as Stägemann does. Nevertheless, while the tyrannical and patriarchal society of Rousseau's novel may be "punished" by the "crime" of Julie's death, Stägemann, taking her life in her own hands, proposes no murder/suicide of any portion of herself, but rather the possibility of a true harmony of interests, a reconciliation of desire and reason. While Stägemann upholds the older class order by renouncing her claims on the Count, she and Gerson become the intimate friends of the Count and his admirable wife — a relationship founded on the kinship of souls rather than social hierarchy. While Stägemann upholds the sexual order by renouncing her desire to pursue her individual artistic ideal, the patriarchal order is broken, for her, insofar as Gerson is somewhat androgynous and insofar as their salon-like society centers on women's art and domesticity, rather than the mercantilist world of Elisabeth's first husband. Stägemann rejects the pessimistic outcomes of both Goethe and Rousseau.

If Stägemann identified with few character traits from Goethe's hero or heroine, aspects of the artistic crafting of this autobiography definitely recall *Werther*. For instance the lives of marginal characters are portrayed as parallel to or in contrast with that of Stägemann's ideal. The major story to contrast with her life is that of Baroness F. Unlike Elisabeth who married against her own sentiments and with her father's blessing, Baroness F. married for love and against her father's explicit wishes. The child she bore died just as Elisabeth's had, suggesting that this is also an unacceptable response to parental pressure. When Baroness F.'s father dies without having retracted the curse he pronounced on her, she becomes fully destraught at the fact of her defiance, takes ill, and nearly dies herself. The burden of guilt for disobeying the commands of fathers extracts a heavy toll.

Also in contrast is the story of Frau Warrendorf who had purchased her peace of mind by ignoring her husband's amorous escapades. She plays the perfect hypocrite, pretending not to be aware of them. It is the only way she can adapt to an intolerable situation. Elisabeth finds the hypocrisy forced on this woman by her marital situation highly unattractive. Meta's happy marriage stands as the positive example. She had married for love and although she must endure certain lack of attentiveness, sentiment, and even consideration on her husband's part, she remains essentially happy surrounded by an abundant family.

Isabella von Wallenrodt had inserted short biographies of relatives and they, too, illustrated her own experience insofar as they related parallel stories of other women deprived of their means of living through the death or action of some man. In Wallenrodt's case, however, the moral of these stories contradicted her assertion that she did not blame her husband for having squandered his fortune on his mistress and expensive entertaining, or for not allowing her to manage her own purse before she became a widow. Her criticism is not explicit or direct, but sly. Stägemann's artistic sensibilities and experience allowed her to buttress and clarify her position through the narration of other stories, as Goethe had. Rather than working against her text, these parallel stories enrich it.

Painting was the art in which both Werther and Elisabeth expressed their souls and Elisabeth judges the men in her life largely by their relationship to that art. Her first husband had not only forbidden her to participate in a home theater production before their marriage (I, 87), he also expressed the view that her painting was useless. By contrast, shortly after her engagement to that representative of the rational order, Elisabeth encounters Count Werdenberg in an art gallery as she admires a painting and he shares her admiration (I, 96). Recalling the scene in which Lotte and Werther share their rapture for Klopstock, the object of Stägemann's and Werdenberg's joint admiration is, significantly for this autobiography of reconciliation with the domestic role, a madonna by Raphael. Werdenberg also encourages her painting by sending her drawings to copy (I, 206,214).

Not only is painting a vital form of expression for Elisabeth, descriptions or references to paintings, music, literature are not accidental or casual. Rather they reflect, exemplify, and vary the emotions she feels. We understand her character when we learn of her taste in literature and art, much as Werther knew Lotte's heart when he heard her speak of the books she favored. Elisabeth had read *Clarissa* secretly, in fear someone would forbid her to do so (I, 18). She is familiar with one of Werther's favorites, *The Vicar of Wakefield* (I, 28); with *Faust* (I, 216); and with the writings of Wieland (I, 136). She also identifies readily with certain literary heroines. One stage character with whom she especially emphathizes is 'Astasia.' As an imprisoned young woman who must plea for her freedom from a tyrant, 'Astasia' bears at least a superficial resemblance to Goethe's 'Iphigenie' (I,30). However, like Georg von der Recke, neither Elisabeth's father nor her first husband are inclined to listen to her views. In addition to the Raphael Madonna, other pictures which Elisabeth describes represent her ideals. Af ter her period of unrestrained freedom she paints a picture of a mother nursing one child with another at her knee. In the background a ship lies ankered in a peaceful harbor (II, 4). Other paintings are not treated favorably. A genre picture of a family dining scene hung on Meta's wall and occasioned comments about how boring such events inevitably were in reality (II, 38).

If art often seems to illuminate and explain reality in this autbogioraphy, reality is also frequently viewed as art. Various episodes might be paintings. One day Elisabeth must wait with Gerson for an axel to be fixed. They are in the country and Gerson reads aloud to her beneath a willow. She sees a rural idyll. The final scene, the harmonious ending, is described as if it were a painting. Perhaps most telling in this regard, however, is Meta's suggestion that girls only learn of the world and of men through literature. They lack worldly experience and do not study history. This means their picture of men and of the world seldom corresponds to reality. Stägemann knows that perceptions of reality do not necessarily coincide with it, that fictions sometimes determine how we make our choices. Even Meta comments that marriage was somewhat disappointing (I, 57). And it is Meta who observes that she and Elisabeth have longed in vain for 'unsere Geßnerische Idyllenwelt.'(I, 94) Stägemann recognizes that literature does not help women understand the reality of the world in which they live. They are presented, by male authors, with false idylls. Stägemann attempts to correct the situation by presenting an idyll which she sees as both real and ideal.

There is little doubt that Stägemann's is a highly literary autobiography. Fact and fiction are inextricably woven. She goes a step further than Recke whose actions and descriptions of actions seem drawn from literary ideals. And she goes at least one step further than Wallenrodt who emphasized the novelistic adventures in her life in order to entertain the readers of her autobiography as much as she did the readers of her adventuristic fiction. Stägemann carefully structured her narration, integrating supportive parallel tales and using symbolic elements consistently. While her autobiographical intent is explicit, there can be no doubt that she also had literary ambitions. But more than that even she knew that the distinction between fact and fiction was not a strict one.

Niggl had perceived the mutual influence of novelistic and autobiographical modes of narration in the late eighteenth century, but Klaus-Detlef Müller has traced in detail the proximity of Blanckenburg's influential theory of the novel, expounded in *Versuch über den Roman* (1774), to the practice of autobiography in the same time period![4] Crucial for Müller in this interaction — indeed fusion — of forms is the tendency of autobiography to

avail itself of the epic mode of 'realizing' an event or emotion ('epische ver-
gegenwärtigende Darstellungs formen'); of presenting it, rather than merely
telling it. [15] His examples are Johann Heinrich Jung's *Henrich Stillings
Jugend* (1771), Karl Philipp Moritz' *Anton Reiser* (1786-89), Ulrich Bräker's
*Lebensgeschichte und Natürliche Ebentheuer des Armen Mannes in Tock-
enburg* (1788-89), Friedrich Christian Laukhard's *Leben und Schicksale von
ihm selbst beschrieben* (1792-1802), Carl Friedrich Barhdt's *Geschichte seines
Lebens, seiner Meinungen und Schicksale. Von ihm selbst geschrieben*
(1790-1), and Johann Wolfgang von Goethe's *Dichtung und Wahrheit*
(1811-31). Stägemann's deft juxtaposition of characters, inclusion of parallel stories, and consistent use of motifs like paintings make her autobiography another example of Müller's 'literary autobiography.'

Müller does not discuss manipulation or distortion of facts as an issue,
but in the face of his observations of Goethe's license with some of them
in order to enhance his 'realization' of events, Stägemann's appear no more
grievous. For instance, while in reality Goethe flirted with several women
in his student days in Leipzig, in *Dichtung und Wahrheit* he condensed these
into one episode, giving the whole experience more shape. Similarly, although
the Gretchen episode of Book 5 in *Dichtung und Wahrheit* ended in a court
case, there is no trace of such a hearing in any legal record of the city of
Frankfurt or in other family documents. Müller's analysis of Goethe's literary intentions make it at least plausible that he invented the story.

Two of the autobiographies classified as literary are narrated in the third
person and use names other than real ones (*Anton Reiser* and *Henrich Still-
ing*). Moritz even disguised his work by calling it a novel at first. While
historians of the novel traditionally refer to it as such, scholars of autobiography regularly include it among examples of that form. Clearly the definition of genres, like the distinction between fact and fiction, cannot be
strictly upheld in cases like this. Nor is it absolutely necessary or necessarily desirable to untangle these forms by means of further definition.

However, those interested in uncovering biographies of women from this
period will need to note the fusion and confusion of genres. While novelistic techniques, as well as autobiographical tradition, frequently shaped autobiographical content, there may also be untold numbers of narrations of
real experience masquerading behind the label, novel. Rahel Varnhagen's
friend, Regina Froberg, for instance, wrote an epistolary novel, *Maria, oder
die schweren Folgen des ersten Fehltritts* (1810), in which she describes the
secret and dangerous escape of a young women from her violent husband
and then her seduction and abandonment by her lover. Varnhagen's copy

of the novel contains Karl August Varnhagen's marginal notes on the true identities of the characters in this roman à clef.

While men and women alike availed themselves of fictional covers to narrate their lives, the temptation to do so may have been greater for women. Fear of exposing one's family to public scrutiny was probably greater for women. In addition, writing was one of the few professions more accessible and acceptable to women, since it could be done at home and kept secret. Inexperienced in worldly events as many indisputably were, women novelists may have drawn more frequently from events in their own lives in order to build plots. While novels may hide treasures of information about women's lives and beg for investigation, rarely will readers of today be fortunate enough to have sufficient information to distinguish fact from fiction. If it is to be done at all, however, familiarity with literary and autobiographical traditions of the period are essential.

Schlegel's *Lucinde* created such a scandal in part precisely because it was so autobiographical, and readers deciphered, without any help, the real identities of the main characters. Moreover, in that novel Lisette contemplates narrating her autobiography in such a manner that it would appear to be the life of someone else. To be sure, no historian of autobiography has examined *Lucinde*, but the explanation for this may be more complicated than hindrances posed by Schlegel's own designation of it as a novel and its fictional elements. Unlike an autobiography such as *Anton Reiser*, for instance, Schlegel elaborates very little on his childhood; and the central fragment, 'Lehrjahre der Männlichkeit', focuses primarily on amorous episodes as the content of his life. The form of the novel is also unusual in that it is not linear, but rather composed of dreams, letters, fantasies, essays. Quite apart from issues of fictionalization, then, and like women's autobiogarphy it does not fit standard assumptions about the structure of the genre.

The autobiographies of Recke and Stägemann differ from the literary autobiographies named by Müller in precisely those structural ways in which *Lucinde* also differs from literary autobiography: the period of life covered and a non-objective, non-integrative narration. To be sure, it is only the women's autobiographies which are thoroughly epistolary. To be an account of one's self—and hence an autobiography—according to Müller, narration of personal experience must record an entire life. 'Die innere Form der Autobiographie ist . . . zirkelhaft: vom sichtbar gemachten Erzählpunkt, der zugleich das (vorläufige) Ende des Lebens bezeichnet, wird erinnernd auf die Anfänge des eigenen Daseins zurückgegriffen und dann fortlaufend zu dem im existentiellen und erzähltechnischen Sinne vorgegebenen Ende hin erzählt, wobei sich im Erzählvorgang, der eine kontinuierliche Reduktion des Zeitabstandes bedeutet, fortlaufend die Identität von erzählendem und erzähltem Ich herstellt, indem sie aus den Inhalten des Lebens gewonnen wird."[16]

This intention can only be fulfilled by a complete narration of the author's life: "jede bewußt ausschnitthafte Schilderung kann auch bei konsequenter Ich-Perspektive die Vermittlung zwischen dem erzählenden und dem erzählten Ich nur ansatzweise leisten und tendiert zu epischen Emanzipation der geschilderten Vorgänge."[17] He mentions travelogues and war reminiscences as examples of this form. Where the intent to narrate a whole life is missing, according to Müller, only narrations of experience which do not have the self, the 'I' ('das Ich') as their subject can occur. Such narrations cease to be autobiography, since the author's 'self' is no longer the subject of narration. Reality is merely viewed through the perspective of subjective experience. Other critics would refer to this distinction as defining memoir as opposed to autobiography.

Now Stägemann clearly restricts herself to the few years of her first marriage and the events preceding her second marriage. However Recke also exhibits the tendency to focus on her marriage and divorce. Only later did she narrate in a more traditional manner the story of her childhood. And yet it would be difficult to say that either of these women did not intend to portray their 'selves' rather than objective reality as experienced subjectively. Indeed in both cases the authors focus on the struggle of the struggling or conflicted 'self.' Müller simply assumes the importance of childhood experience in that struggle, whereas for these women it occured most profoundly precisely in the years of their marriages. Whatever development of the 'I' may have occured in their girlhoods, both authors reveal that marriage interrupted a particular evolutionary direction in their lives. It meant a significant reordering of aims, interests, concerns, and even talents. For these women this period in their lives was distinct from childhood insofar as childhood had not prepared them for it. Their marriages were intense struggles to maintain their sense of 'self' in the face of social or marital demands. The absence of any teleological structure in such a fragmentary life seems absolutely appropriate, and their focus on that period represents the acknowledgement of distinctly female experience.

Similarly, the second distinction between these works and those cited by Müller, the epistolary form, acknowledges female tradition. Clearly epistolary novels were hardly written exclusively by one sex. Nevertheless this form *was* strongly associated with women, in particular the lives and domestic experience of women. Indeed *Werther* is one of the truly rare examples of an epistolary novel with a male protagonist. In autobiography this author is aware of only one attempt by a man to narrate his life in epistolary form; but Heinrich von Kleist's effort in this direction is apparently lost. (Perhaps it is no coincidence that he was a friend of Elisabeth Stägemann's.) Precisely this form of narration, however, proved to be the vehicle for women's expression of the 'selves' which did not comfortably fit the roles established for them. Not only did it encourage the interiority and provide the tradition of a domestic milieu necessary for women to narrate their experience, if the autobiographer chose, it also permitted a non-identical, non-objective, non-harmonizing understanding of that 'self.' This proved to be more the case for Stägemann than for Recke, but it was more definitively the case for two other women — even as this form of narration became all but extinct.

For popular epistolary novels gradually succumbed to newer, more objective narrative patterns. In Germany this trend had begun more than twenty years before either Recke or Stägemann wrote her autobiography; and they then wrote in a form already fading from the tradition. Insofar as the novel and autobiography manifest closely allied structures in this period it is possible to infer a rejection of epistolary autobiography from theoretical writings about the novel. In the very year in which Goethe's *Werther* appeared, Friedrich von Blanckenburg (1744-1796) published the first theoretical treatment of the novel in Germany (1774). In his attempt to elevate the novel to an aesthetically satisfying form, Blanckenburg scornfully noted the popularity and influence of what he considered trivial contemporary novels. He desired, in the future, to raise the form "zu einem sehr angenehmen, und sehr lehrreichen Zeitvertreib: und nicht etwa für müßiges Frauenzimmer, sondern auch für den denkenden Kopf."[18] He maintained that the contemporary novel lacked an all encompassing, objective perspective which would add meaning to the trivial events narrated in novels.[19] Because the epistolary form was narrated by persons in the midst of the action, he argued, it could not plausibly develop such a broad and objective narrative perspective. According to his supposition epistolary narration is too subjective (and the content too trivial). It lacks a more abstract level of significance because it lacks an objective narrator to perceive cause and effect and weigh events according to a larger scheme. (Naturally it is against the evolution of just such an 'objective' presentation that the modern French critics have reacted.)

The influential theologian Johann Gottfried Herder was the principal supporter and theoretician of autobiography in Germany at this time. Without mentioning, or probably even conceiving of, the possibility of epistolary autobiography, he harbored similar hopes for a more objective autobiography: autobiography which would include an understanding of one's life in relation to larger historical events or metaphysical concerns, an autobiography which explained cause and effect.[20] While Herder never explicitly expressed doubts about epistolary autobiography, the prejeudice of Blanckenburg and the general historical evolution of objective narrations in the novel would probably have extended to autobiographical forms.

Theoretical emphasis on the abstract and general tended to assert that women's lives as well as their epistolary autobiographies were irrelevant or trivial. Their lives simply did not conform to images of the dominant (objective) culture and were ignored in its abstract conceptions of reality. Clearly though, women ignored those ideological pressures and wrote autobiography against the current of the times. Modern scholars have tended to view the form too consistently through the optics of the dominant culture and have overlooked some significant works.

Elisabeth Stägemann seems to have been aware of prejudice against the epistolary form when, in her fictional introduction, she tells her fictional editor, "Welch ein gewagter Gedanke, meine Freundin, eine Briefsammlung, die ohne eigentlichen Zweck und Plan, ohne sorgsame Bearbeitung auf's Papier geworfen ward, einer kalten und fremden Beurtheilung Preise geben zu wollen."(4f.) As a disclaimer of literary intent, however, this statement is not persuasive. Stägemann's autobiography is obviously the crafted product of a single aesthetic purpose and such a remark can only be interpreted either as false modesty or as a plea not to be judged too harshly. When Baldinger disclaimed any desire for public recognition, she protested the unsuitability of her person. Stägemann, more certain of the validity of the content of her autobiography, only misleadingly intimates the insignificance of the subjective form she has chosen. Still, as innovative as Stägemann's autobiography is, the real credit for boldness in publishing unstructured correspondence as autobiography would more appropriately be accorded two contemporaries of Stägemann's: Rahel Varnhagen and Bettina von Arnim. For, despite the fact that epistolary narration was already 'officially' out of favor, other women would avail themselves of this form as well.

3

THE CASES OF VARNHAGEN AND ARNIM

When women attempted to pattern their autobiographies after men's, the contradictions between their lives and their autobiographical models broke open the form. There could be no closure. When they focused on their domestic lives, they created remarkably innovative, open forms appropriate to the complexity of their situations. But neither Recke, nor Stägemann was a "typical" housewife. Recke was famous for her exposure of Cagliostro and her religious lyrics. And she enjoyed a wide circle of intellectual friends. Stägemann was the center of two salons, first in Königsberg and later, the more famous one, in Berlin. The lives they led, which extended beyond the sphere of family relationships, are not contained or represented in their autobiographies. This is important for autobiography of the time, because it means that they omitted discussing a significant part of their lives and possible source of confidence and realm of influence.

However if they were not typical housewives, neither were Recke and Stägemann alone in the redefinition of women's roles in society. While some women, frustrated at the limited options for them, left family life behind and went to sea, others tried to expand the domestic sphere to make it more comfortable for them. Whether from sheer economic need, idleness, or uncontainable talent, for instance, more and more women began to write for publication in the late eighteenth century. Wallenrodt and Engel had both tried repeatedly to collect pensions from the government after the deaths of their military husbands. When these efforts failed Wallenrodt tried to establish a manufacturing enterprise before turning to writing novels for her daily sustenance. Engel turned to autobiography to help plead her case and earn some money. Surely their fates as widows were hardly unique or even unusual, and writing was defintely one of the more acceptable solutions for financial dilemmas. It was a source of income for which it was not necessary to expose oneself to public ridicule and censure. It could be done privately at home and one could publish anonymously or under a pseudonym. As writers women could escape public disgrace for having to earn money. It was a new "script", but obviously not one totally accepted by the "public".

When Sophie von la Roche's name became associated with her novel, *Die Geschichte des Fräuleins von Sternheim* (1771), she also announced in the introduction that after her daughter had left for boarding school she had become very lonely. On the advice of a spiritual counselor she filled her long, empty hours writing this novel of education for young ladies. However by stating she wrote only for her own pleasure and for the education of young women la Roche essentially disavowed intent of being taken seriously. Baldinger's fear lest she appear too vain if she published was thus ostensibly shared by this friend — and no doubt many others. Moreover la Roche's novel, which was a great critical success and influenced Goethe's *Leiden des jungen Werthers* (1774), did not particularly augment womens' reputation for the craft. It was thought to be largely the work of the famous poet Christoph Martin Wieland (1733-1813) since he had edited it, superintended its publication, and written an introduction for it as well.

Other women, even those whose works were favorably reviewed by prestigious authors, chose not to reveal their names to the public. In such cases their talent was usually attributed to men. Karoline von Wolzogen's (1763-1847) novel *Agnes von Lilien* (1796), was presumed by no less reknown critics than Friedrich and August Wilhelm Schlegel to have been written by Goethe himself. Caroline Schlegel's (1763-1809) significant contributions to the still admired Shakespeare translations were credited only to her husband August Wilhelm (1767-1845). As they masked their need or desire to write for public consumption these female authors allowed the blissfully domestic image of women to remain fully in tact.

Some women also challenged the domestic sphere on its own territory. Without necessarily venturing into the male domain, some of them made it clear they felt the conventional role too confined and that they, too, had needs they expected to be fulfilled. The lives of women like Caroline (Michaelis-Böhmer- Schlegel) Schelling and Dorothea (Mendelssohn-Veit) Schlegel (1763-1839), for instance, caused so much scandal precisely because they refused to accept traditional restrictions on their associations with men and had the audacity not only not to hide their affairs, but to find them morally acceptable. Their very lives told the story of their dissatisfaction with arranged or practical marriages. However these two women were never faced with the need to earn their own livings and could therefore afford to flaunt bourgeois social convention. Other women, like Wallenrodt, might have wanted to challenge society, but depended on it for their support. Indeed, most women who openly disdained the restrictions on their personal lives suffered social consequences. Rahel Varnhagen frequently admired the courage of her friend Pauline Wiesel (1779-1848) in this regard. The wife of a staid middle class businessman, Wiesel became the mistress of Prince Louis Ferdinand of Prussia. When he died in battle in 1806, Wiesel chose not to return to her former domestic life (which she might have done), but continued to lead a socially objectionable one, living alternately with men or women. She died alone and in poverty.

More acceptable, although also not without a certain notoriety, were the great Berlin salonieres at the turn of the century. They, too, ultimately challenged the traditional domestic image of women. To this group belong Rahel Varnhagen, Elisabeth Stägemann, Henriette Herz, Sarah Levy, and others. Somewhat later Bettina von Arnim would join their ranks. As a gathering place for disaffected aristocrats, bourgeois intellectuals, women in the disreputable profession of acting, and Jews the salon occupied a status on the periphery of society. As forums for new ideas on politics and literature some, like Rahel Varnhagen's, were also considered liberal and therefore politically suspect. While they received disapproval from some quarters, however, the salonieres were still not totally ostracized. Moreover such institutions gave women, who remained in their homes, an opportunity to participate in public dialogue with a limited amount of praise.

Subtly and even gingerly the lives of these writers, sexually free women, and salonieres manifest their restlessness or economic need. Although they wrote no treatises and led no political movements the dissatisfaction of increasing numbers of women with their domestic roles surfaces in attempts to find other, more or less acceptable alternatives. If they were usually prevented from leading the lives patterned in professional or adventurous autobiographies of middle-class men, many nevertheless rejected the idealistic images of women presented to them as models in contemporary popular culture.

Recke and Stägemann were clearly disaffected with conventional definitions of women's domestic roles. However, when they wrote about their lives, they focused courageously, but exclusively on that sphere. Although neither Varnhagen, nor Arnim divorced her husband, both were similarly disaffected with that narrow sphere of activity. When they wrote about their lives, they too chose the epistolary form, but without focusing on their domestic lives. In fact the choice of epistolary form was motivated by different aesthetic and philosophical principles, ones more closely related to the broader conception of their roles in society.

Normally of course literary historians are careful to distinguish autobiography from letters. They emphasize that the former is written from one point in time, while the latter are daily communication lacking a unifying perspective. For these historians the genre is actually defined by the narrative perspective proposed by Blanckenburg. However, epistolary autobiography not only implicitly challenges these genre distinctions, it can also radically challenge philosophical assumptions upon which the very idea of autobiography has been based: the superior truth of a unifying perspective and the very notion of what it means to be an individual.

Recke's reworked diaries and Stägemann's explicitly internal dialogue produce an epistolary form in which the author permits an otherwise unexposed, unexpressed side of herself to speak. Recke wrote first of all in the private form of a diary, rewriting for a public. The epistolary form was chosen as the literary convention which permitted public expression of private sentiments under the pretense that they were actually only expressed privately. It permitted the expression of a "self" at risk. Stägemann's self-dialogue was also presented as first of all a private affair, a means of coming to herself by herself. Later, so the traditional ruse, she decided to make these imagined letters public. She also presented her self as being at risk. And while Stägemann's narrative arrangement of the correspondents asserts the non-identity of that very self, at the end it also reconciles the discordant voices into one harmonious whole. Most importantly, though, in both cases they are attempts in the first instance at dialogue with the self. They are personal projects carried out in isolation.

Only at the end of Stägemann's autobiography, in the ideal harmony of a new society, is the manner of sociality suggested which shapes both the content and the form of the epistolary efforts of Varnhagen and Arnim. Both these correspondents explicitly questioned the superior truthfulness of unified and hierarchical forms of narration. They also implicitly, if not explicitly, asserted the fundamentally non-identical nature of the self. Their lives are chronicled for readers in a more radical epistolary form. For if, at one end of an imaginary scale, epistolary autobiography seems to merge with the novel, then at the other it seems to merge with historical documents, namely letters actually exchanged between real people.

Needless to say no historian of the genre has discussed the place of these correspondences in the development of autobiography. In the cases of Varnhagen and Arnim this failure is all the more revealing. For, in contrast to the works previously examined, the letters of these two women have been very familiar to literary historians. Several factors however argue in favor of viewing the correspondences of Varnhagen and Arnim decisively within this tradition. One lies in the historical context in which they were written:

both the existence (albeit unpublished) of Recke's and Stägemann's epistolary innovations on the genre, and their coincidence with Romantic philosophy. A second lies in the explicit comments by the correspondents which question narrative prose as opposed to more spontaneous forms. A third lies in suggestions, however subtle, that these authors in fact considered their correspondence to be autobiography.

Like Recke and Stägemann both Rahel Varnhagen (1771-1833) and Bettina von Arnim (1785-1859) wrote in the secular tradition of pietist examination of the soul. They took letters seriously as inner interrogations and as expressions of personal experience. However more than the idea of constructing the self in isolated meditation (like Recke and Stägemann), the letters of Varnhagen and Arnim illustrate that of constructing the self through the medium of others and emphasize the importance of sociality. Actual letters, rather than diaries form the basis for this consideration of autobiography.

The emphasis on sociality and the concept of the non-identity of the self betrays their share of German romantic philosophy. However the role these women accorded letters in their lives, though consonant with that philosophy, is perhaps more radical than that of their male counterparts. Like other early romantics they aligned themselves with those elements of emerging bourgeois culture which understood themselves to oppose conventional society and established hierarchies. Such a stance was not alien to the pietist tradition. For, like Quakers and Shakers, the pietists of the seventeenth and eighteenth centuries felt their communities to be beyond the authority of established secular or religious power. They not only felt their system of values to be fundametally opposed to those of the court, they also maintained communities with more egalitarian forms of government. In its beginnings bourgeois culture and society also evolved values and forms of organization which were similarly perceived as antagonistic to the established culture. The role of friendship and letters in this culture of opposition requires further explanation.

It was through the medium of pietism that the concept of sentimental friendship evolved. If at first the religious movement discouraged worldly friendships as threatening one's personal involvement with God, the very isolation imposed by such intensely private and immediate religious exertion eventually made soul friendships necessary.[2] One of the founders of the movement Philipp J. Spener (1635-1705) ultimately distinguished three orders of friendship: first, friendships founded merely on usefulness or pleasure; second, friendships founded on the communication of moral attitudes and virtue; and, third, friendships founded on a harmony of the spirit and the common effort for divine mercy. Obviously, the last of these ranked highest in his eyes. In such relationships the partners assisted each other along their path to salvation and to God.

Secular versions of such friendships manifested themselves in personal unions providing spiritual sustenance for the achievement of a higher secular goal. In Germany such friendships might be formed in common opposition to crass motives of court intrigants and to dominant social structures. Gellert's immensely popular novel, *Die schwedische Gräfin* (1747), asserts the advantage of the breadth and substance of character a person acquires not from engaging in worldly or state affairs or from pursuing otherworldly beliefs, but from opening the soul to a friend and exchanging inner wealth; indeed, the novel reaches its climax in a scene of friendship. The small society which gathers in a setting removed from the courts is described as one in which its members lived without giving orders and without obeying.[3]

Another of the influential prophets of friendship was the greatly admired poet, Klopstock. He had conceived and cultivated a circle of friends as an alliance, in which all might develop their individual talents and still belong to a common spirit. After his friends dispersed throughout Germany they continued their close support of each other — spiritually, through letters and, practically, by trying to find positions of each other.[4]

Devotion to such friendships of the soul could be viewed in different ways. Goethe was somewhat critical of the tendency in these cases to withdraw from public affairs. His epistolary novel *The Sorrows of Young Werther* (1774) portrayed all too vividly the dangers of the cult of sentimentality. In the tenth book of his autobiography he suggested that, as a reaction to their limited possibilities for worldly action, the poets of friendship had overemphasized the importance of intimate personal relationships. However, the dramatist and controversial essayist Gotthold Ephraim Lessing (1729-1781) would find such friendships a source of integrity in the face of authority, an alliance by means of which one could evade seduction by rigid, fundamentalist power.[5] For Lessing these chosen, open, and tolerant relationships carried political implications. By mutually nourishing the formation of free personalities they advanced the secular goal of a humane society.

It cannot be a coincidence that the mania for letters in bourgeois culture paralleled the importance of friendship. The general fascination, even obsession, with letters in the eighteenth century manifested itself not only in the countless novels and essays which assumed epistolary guise, but also in actual letter writing. Increasing numbers of primers on letter writing appeared throughout the century, providing models for how to write to anyone from the King to one's best friend. Gellert's influential primer urged correspondents to strive for naturalness of feeling and expression: a sentiment integral to the ideology of friendship. Just as that ideology of open and generous friendship was seen to offer an alternative to the social rigidity, hierarchiy, and artificiality of the aristocracy, so too was naturalness of style intended to correct the stilted, manipulative style of court language.

Nor should letters necessarily be viewed as private communications. While the readership for any given letter may not have been large, it was customary in the eighteenth century to share incoming news with members of one's family or circle. Despite growing numbers of newspapers and journals the information network of the mid- to late-eighteenth century was still relatively undeveloped, and letters often complemented printed matter in providing news. Correspondents regularly furnished information about events in distant places, travel descriptions, or even philosophical exegeses. Such letters were frequently read by more than one person, perhaps in a small circle of friends where they would be discussed afterward. Goethe described just such a series of scenes in the home of Sophie von la Roche, and Rahel Vanrhagen's and Bettina von Arnim's letters are full of statements assuming that others will read their letters. Indeed exceptional correspondents were not infrequently surprised to find their letters in print,[6] and newspapers, after all, regularly published letters from paid and unpaid "correspondents". Thus, although clearly not a mass-medium, neither were letters totally private. In the oppressive social situation of late eighteenth-century Germany, bonds of friendship sustained with both emotional and practical support burgeoning oppositional awareness. The particular model for friendship also provided a vision of an alternative social structure, and letters were the literary manifestation of this utopian vision.

For the creation of progressive middle-class thought in Germany at the turn of the eighteenth century institutions such as the salon functioned, like the English coffee houses, as informal catalysts of new intellectual movements. It should perhaps be noted that coffee houses were not as prevalent in Germany as in England, and that unlike older French forms of the salon, the German ones were not aristocratic. As stated previously these salons also fostered friendships across race and class barriers and, more than elsewhere, a person was valued for natural talents rather than high birth. Here the ideology of friendship found a concrete means of expression. Here one strove for a more generous, natural, and unrestrained atmosphere than existed at court.[7] Those attending were usually commited (at least theoretically) to natural and spontaneous conversation and to the notion of individual freedom acquired through a community. Unlike the English coffee houses, however, these salons were civil societies "governed" by women; miniature societies in which values attributed to women were integrated more fully than in society at large. Indeed, the utopian image of a new harmony which concluded Stägemann's autobiography undoubtedly owed much to the existence of salons at the end of the eighteenth century.

Rahel Varnhagen is best known in German literary history for the prestigious salon of which she was the center. Many notable figures gathered in her attic room for tea and for what was reputed to be the most scintillating conversation in Berlin. Indeed, with conversational participants like Heinrich Heine, Friedrich Schlegel, Alexander von Humboldt, Friedrich Gentz, Johann Gottlieb Fichte, and Leopold Ranke all orchestrated by Rahel Varnhagen the reputation was undoubtedly deserved. The most successful period in the life of this particular salon was 1789 to 1806. After Napoleon's conquest of Austria and Prussia (1805/6), the forced liberalization of many restictive Prussian laws produced a native backlash against foreign intervention in German affairs which extended to the liberalization itself.[8] Varnhagen's salon could not maintain itself in this more conservative atmosphere. When she re-established it in 1819, in the aftermath of the Napoleonic era, many former friends no longer frequented liberal houses or even homes of Jews. The era of friendship had been eclipsed by one of more entrenched prejudice.

Of course Rahel Varnhagen (born Rahel Levin, married to Karl August Varnhagen von Ense in 1814) never wrote an autobiography or even edited her letters as one. However just this fact remains of particular interest for the problematic of women and autobiography. Neither Elise von der Recke nor Elisabeth Stägemann had permitted her epistolary autobiography to be published during her lifetime. The prohibitions against women's self-expression which resulted in the conflicted published works of women like Frederike Baldinger, Regula Engel, and Isabella von Wallenrodt remained in tact. After all, roughly speaking, all of these women were contemporaries. And in these times when the discussions of female destinies were not conducted by men, they were carried on in disguised forms, such as novels, or not publicly at all, but in private. Or if one were daring in that semi-public, semi-private form: letters. The story of women's vast and profound *consciousness* of their own repression in this period has of course not been told. For it remained an "underground", private discussion. Yet it *was* discussed.

Rahel Varnhagen wrote volumes of letters. Three volumes of them were edited by her husband after her death. Love letters to various men were gradually published throughout the nineteenth century. Even so Hannah Arendt made use of many still unpublished ones in the 1920s when she researched her biography of Rahel Varnhagen.[9] Apart from a few fragments from her letters and diaries however Varnhagen herself published nothing during her life. That does not mean she did not intend to. On at least two occasions she had intended to publish lengthier portions of her correspondence, but those intentions must be understood against a background of her general theory of letter writing. And since she never wrote a treatise on the subject, her views on this form and on autobiography must be garnered from her letters themselves.

Rahel Varnhagen and Bettina von Arnim developed their own epistolary styles, replete with distinctive metaphors and themes. Among Rahel Varnhagen's metaphors many involve either economics or nature. Even in her earliest letters Varnhagen wrote about the "economy of the soul" in terms that disregarded principles basic to bourgeois economics. In the tradition of enlightened secular examinations of the soul, piety had meant not only turning inward, but also working on yourself, improving yourself according to an external standard. For Varnhagen, however, there was no external standard. Perfecting yourself, being pious or good, meant exploding rational constructs, saying what confused and what pained you. Only then could one's inner gardens flourish. The nerves, fibers, and desires of the soul were sacred and should not only be accepted, but revered as well, even if it led to the greatest bankruptcy.[10] Of necessity this would undermine the ration(aliz)ed order of the soul, "(die) auf das innerste sich beziehende konomie"(II,576), that constituted for her "eine todte Ordnung". Only when that well-managed, well-ordered economy was challenged could we do justice to the nature alive within us, eliminate the prejudices against our/selves. Energies invested in this undertaking would never have a particular goal in mind and would consequently not always be productive. When David Veit wonders if he should become a doctor Rahel Varnhagen responds that she cannot imagine him becoming anything specific. A class or profession is just as restricting as marriage (I, 120). Of women she wrote, not without irony, that they should be encouraged to write, for even if it had been proven for all time that they were incapable of expressing their thoughts, still it remained an obligation to make the attempt over and over again (III,10). One should care for inner selves, desires; and, like Stägemann, she perceived these internal interests in conflict with modern bourgeois requirements. Their cul-

tivation required unbudgeted time and leisure. Being good was a commitment not to common sense or to dollars and cents, but to the senses. It was
a fundamentally inefficient use of human resources, but it was humane and
hopeful and it strove to resist external authority.

For Varnhagen, constraints on the soul's economy could only be lifted
in dialogue — with one's self and with others. Truth lay in connections, in
relationships. She refused to define or to delimit. She wanted to hold possibilities open. Conversations and letters were important communication
because friends corresponded to and awakened various sides of herself. She
wrote Gustav Brinkmann that, were she to lose him, she would lose a part
of herself. Only he recognized that part and it needed to be recognized or
it would die (I, 198). Hers was therefore clearly not the classical notion of
a self-identical, harmonious subject whose life was a concatenation of causes
and effects or which unfolded itself teleologically. Hers was a multi-faceted,
de-centered self with unimagined potential.

Parsimony would not build the open exchanges necessary for the realization of that potential, and hoarding would not nourish inner gardens.
One could not be stingy with one's self. The only talent she valued in herself was precisely her talent for openness and friendship: "Welche Freundin haben Sie gewählt, gefunden! und empfunden! . . . [Ich] vermag es, wie
doppelt organisirt [einem Menschen] meine Seele zu leihen, und habe die
gewaltige Kraft, mich zu verdoppeln ohne mich zu verwirren."(I,265) Capitalist economies do not duplicate themselves without establishing hierarchies.

Moreover, since friendship held the soul sacred it became a secular religion. Mutual confessions undermined external hierarchies, papacies, and
subverted established orders. A protestant revolution of the psyche, in the
tradition of pietism. The self, truth blossoms in the warmth of friendship
and once in flower continues to diseminate truth. If dead orders were abol-
ished, "die schwere, dunkle, geduldige Erde (gäbe) Fülle her; sie brauchten
nicht zu kriegen, nicht zu lügen, und Proklamationen zur Rechtfertigung!"(II, 305). Holding the desires of the soul sacred, through friendship, would unleash a truth powerful enough to resist, even crumble
repressive orders.

Friendship was not only a religion, it was an art: "Ich bin so einzig, als
die größte Erscheinung dieser Erde. Der größte Künstler, Philosoph, oder
Dichter, ist nicht über mir. Wir sind vom selben Element, im selben Rang,
und gehören zusammen. . . (.) Mir aber war das Leben angewiesen."(I,266)
As a *Lebenskünstler*, an artist of life, life itself became her artistic metier,

and her mission was nothing less than to affect and perfect her immediate reality and through that the world.

Friendships become audible in conversation (as in the salon) and legible in letters: "Auch werde ich Ihnen solche Briefe schreiben; wo die Seele spazieren gehen soll, und nicht auf ausgefahrner staubiger Heerstraße eine Zweck- und besonders absichtsvolle Reise zu betreiben hat. Auf frischen, kleinen, abstrakten Wegen wollen wir gehen, die wir selbst noch nicht kannten: und auch dem Dunkel, wenn es reizt, nachziehen."(II,414f.) As mutual and leisurely exploration of inner landscapes and desires letters would be truth in praxis, both the means and end to the vision of a future which permits friendship and openness.

As art Varnhagen's letters were intended to capture the essence of moments and feelings normally ration(aliz)ed in more perfect forms: "Ich will nämlich ein Brief soll ein Portrait von dem Augenblick sein, in welchem er geschrieben ist: und getroffen soll es hauptsächlich sein, so hoch auch Kunstaufforderungen an ideele Veredlung lauten mögen...(.) Glücklich die schönen Gebilde eines lächelnden Naturmoments, die aller Menschenerfindung weit entrückt der kunstreichsten zu Vorbilde dienen können!"(III,55f.) Rooted in daily experience letters can become a momentary release from daily economy, a spontaneous image of unbounded inner nature. Glimpses of that nature exceed the potential of other art forms.

Varnhagen's letters communicated in "Form, Farbe, und Inhalt".(II,516) Her style, so admired by the progressive writers of the 1830s, is rich in metaphor, neologism, and syntactically eccentric. It fairly errupts with misplaced relative pronouns; postplaced modifiers; awkward, unbalanced phrasing; asyndeton; faulty punctuation, spelling, diction; frequent intrusions of French. Varnhagen often complained of never having learned German properly and of not writing beautifully balanced sentences, but one suspects that such comments are more an excuse than an explanation, because it is her eccentricities that lend her style the immediacy and spontaneity of a conversation, precisely the effect she strove to achieve. One suspects, in fact, that this disruption of rational discourse was a further intentional refusal to learn a "dead order". But it also seems a direct extension of Gellert's preference for heartfelt expression at the expense of a disciplined, schooled style.

Any conscious stylistic innovation was surely motivated by a deep respect for language as well as a belief in the inadequacy of all language. No language could express the essence of anything; nothing could be understood unless the listener/reader already understood what the speaker/writer meant:

"Wie kann man Unbeschreibliches beschreiben, höchstens! höchstens erzählen? höchstens? nein, gar nicht, ganz und gar nicht."(I,92) So she fashioned her own language: "Die Sprache steht mir aber nicht zu Gebote, die
deutsche, meine eigene nicht; unsere Sprache ist unser gelebtes Leben; ich
habe mir meines selbst erfunden, ich konnte also weniger Gebrauch, als viele
Andere, von den einmal fertigen Phrasen machen, darum sind meine oft
holperig und in allerlei Art fehlerhaft, aber immer ächt...(.)"[10] And although she refers to it as turpitude, it is probably not without some pride
that she reports Friedrich Gentz' appraisal of her letters: "[I]ch schriebe
Briefe, wo die Blüthen und Früchte drin liegen, mit samt den Wurzeln und
der Erde dran aus dem Boden gezogen. Und Würmchen."(I,574) She and
Pauline Wiesel even had their own language a "green" language (of nature).

Clearly no woman with pretensions to womanly modesty, Varnhagen knew
her letters aroused interest and planned publishing them on at least two occasions. For instance, she had once been engaged to marry an aristocrat,
Karl von Finckenstein. As his family strenuously objected to his marrying
a Jew, however, he broke the engagement, or rather Varnhagen allowed him
the opportunity to do so. After this affair and in the midst of her recovery
from it, she wrote a friend that she considered publishing their correspondence because it would make a good novel. Her plans shattered, apparently,
on his refusal to return the letters she had written him. Had she actually
succeeded in publishing such a "novel", we might have had a roman à clef,
perhaps under a pseudonym. Or we might have had a more explicitly autobiographical account in which case the focus on a relationship to a man,
although not her husband, would have yielded a work similar to the autobiographies of Recke and Stägemann. Unlike theirs, however, it would – in
all likelihood – have been based not on any self-dialogue, but rather on the
actual exchange of letters between the principal characters.

Collections of letters interested Varnhagen in general and not just when
they concerned amorous affairs. She was an avid reader of the published
correspondences of other people. In them the very process of history became clear for her: "Die Briefe des Mich Angelo, des Annibal Carucci
(sic)...versüßen mir meine jetzigen Tage. Ihre Plackereien sind in die Ferne
gerückt: ihr Bestreben, ihre Thätigkeit, ihre Wünsche, ihr Herz und Geist,
stehn klarer da: für mich ganz besonders, die aus den Briefen der Menschen
so unendlich viel von ihnen kennt. Von solcher Briefsammlung wird mir
die Historie und eine ganze Zeit klarer, als durch berühmte Geschichts-
schreiber."(II, 548) Varnhagen appreciated the "genealogical" value of letters. Like autobiographers, historians order information about history.

Letters not only do not predigest history, thereby permitting readers to view it as it unfolds, as Varnhagen read them a different sort of history became apparent. It was a subjective history and one which discovered hearts and desires, inner nerves and fibers.

Eagerly Varnhagen read the devout Swiss theologian Lavater. She praised his magnanimity, the immensity of a soul that could accept contradictions and was forced to bend with the times. She recommends the letters to her correspondent, Adolph Count Custine: "Lassen Sie sich nicht abschrecken von mancher präkautionirenden Weitläufigkeit in dem Buche, der arme Lavater mußte sich der damaligen Geistesepoche beugen; es war die der — vielleicht präsumtuosen — Aufklärung, er thut es mit Grazie, und Ungeduld: wir lernen jene Zeit und ihre Schwierigkeiten daraus kennen, und unsere tüchtiger auch schon als eine ehemalige beurtheilen, und sehen ihn flache Stüfchen mit großer Anmaßung betreten."(II,570) Drawing parallels between the letters of Lavater and Racine, she continues: "So hemmen die Begränzten die seltenen schönen Schwingen unserer Vornehmsten!" If correspondences are read this way, so that desires and longings and the very struggle with contemporary conventions become visible, then it is not merely a history of the period which emerges, but the biography of a life battle. To be sure, the reader must work harder and more actively engage in the text, but the insights into public and personal history are greater than if they had been censored by a single narrative perspective.

Varnhagen had wanted to tell her own biography: "Damit *ein* Bild die Existenz beschliet. Auch ist der Schmerz, wie ich ihn kenne, auch ein Leben; und ich denke, ich bin eins von den Gebilden, die die Menschheit werfen soll, und dann nicht mehr braucht, und nicht mehr kann."(I,266) She knows her feeling, itself, possesses human value and relevance. Significant deeds, adventure, or a profession are not necessary for a life to be significant. It took such audacity — and confidence in the value of sentiment — for women to write of their experience. Unlike those in the tradition of the enlightened perfectibility of the soul, who felt others might be able to learn from their mistakes, Varnhagen never thought they could or should learn from particular things she did. It was her struggle itself which was important.

In December of 1809, the year in which Goethe began to outline *Dichtung und Wahrheit*, rumors reached her that Karl August planned to publish their correspondence. She writes that she trusts him too much for him to do that and reminds him she is in possession of their correspondence. If her letters appear, she wants to edit them herself. In February of 1810 she acknowledges they both desire nothing more than that her honest life be made accessible to honest people and expresses confidence that one finds them when one prints anything. "Ich weiß, welche Freude, welches Behagen mir ein Fünkchen Wahrheit in einer Schrift aufbewahrt macht! Nur davon bekömmt die Vergangenheit Leben, die Gegenwart Festigkeit; und einen künstlerischen Standpunkt, betrachtet zu werden; nur Empfindungen, Betrachtungen durch eine Historie erregt, schaffen Muße, Götterzeit, und Freiheit; wo sonst nur allein Stoßen und Dringen und Drängen, und schwindliches Sehen und Thun möglich ist; im wirklichen Leben des bedingten beschränkten Tages, wie er vor uns steht! Nicht weil es mein Leben ist, aber weil es ein wahres ist; weil ich auch vieles um mich her oft, mit kleinen unbeabsichtigten Zügen, für Forscher, wie z.E. ich einer bin, wahr, und sogar geschicht-ergänzend aussprach. Und endlich weil ich ein Kraftstück der Natur bin, ein Eckmensch in ihrem Gebilde der Menschheit, weil sie mich hinwarf, nicht legte, zum grimmigen Kampf mit dem, was das Schicksal nur konnte verabfolgen lassen; jeder Kampfgesell der Natur, der größern Geschichte, ist in einem Thiergefecht in der Arene; glückliche Veteranen, wirken weiter, zu ihrem und der Menschen Bewußtsein; unglückliche, zerschellen; mich trugen Gedanken und Unschuld, als ich zerschellt schon war, empor, zwischen Himmel und Erde. Kurz, wie es mit mir ist, kann ich nicht sagen; ich will nichts mehr. Kein Plan, kein Bild; es schwankt und schwindet die Erde mit den Lebensgütern; der Lebensschatz ist alles! Sehen, lieben, verstehen, nichts wollen, unschuldig sich fügen. Das große Sein verehren, nicht hämmern, erfinden und bessern wollen: und lustig sein, und immer güter! So wie ich war und werde mögen meine Brüder mich sehen! Ich aber selbst will aus meinen Briefen alles suchen, und verwerfen; und nicht in vierzig, fünfzig Jahren, wie du der Guten schreibst, sondern viel früher; ich will noch leben, wenn man's liest."(I, 466f.) Not the recounting of especially concrete or even expressible actions produced the effect Varnhagen aimed to achieve in any autobiography she would publish. Rather the quality of a life and its honesty concerned her. That alone allowed readers their own expansiveness and encouraged the cultivation of their own inner freedom, the nerves and fibers of their souls.

From this perspective the openness of the epistolary form was ideal. A selective memory, a specific intent or even a single aesthetic principle could less easily reshape thoughts and desires which found only resistance and no resonance. If its potential for honesty were realized, letters would inevitably render conflicts more visible. Old desires would not be so easily removed or subordinated. But the perception of conflicts and their shapes depended on the readers' insights, it required active participation and was particularly demanding of readers. Foucault's call for "genealogy" was preceded by Rahel Varnhagen's.

This second plan of Varnhagen's to edit and publish her letters reveals a strikingly different intent from her earlier one. It was not necessarily only personal relationships that were to be the focus of such a work. On the contrary her statements indicate that she would have shown readers portions of her struggle with the social and historical situation into which she had been thrown. Nor would it have been shaped to show evolution toward a goal, harmonious or otherwise. Rather it would have focused on daily struggle and pain. She had not the social recognition or sphere of influence that someone like Goethe had, but she knew that her struggle and her life were no less important testimonies to history and human nature. Precisely because she held sacred inner desires, nerves and fibers of the soul, showing these would have meant sharing the history of her life.

We cannot know how she would have edited her letters: which she would have omitted, which *parts* she would have omitted, whether whe would have disguised certain correspondents. We know that when Karl August did edit them in 1834 he omitted much of her correspondence with men as well as women with whom she was intimate — to what degree is uncertain — and he disguised the names of certain correspondents. We know that he downplayed her sense of being an outsider and emphasized her mysticism. But many of the letters which he omitted or disguised (and to which Hannah Arendt had access) remain unpublished, and we still do not even really have as full a picture of Rahel Varnhagen's life as we might.

We do not even know why she changed her mind about editing her letters during her lifetime. If we may continue to speculate, we might suppose that the publication of the first volume of Goethe's autobiography *Dichtung und Wahrheit* (1811) had something to do with it. Varnhagen was one of Goethe's earliest and greatest admirers and it is not inconceivable that she allowed herself to feel overwhelmed by the brilliance of his autobiography. It is our loss, in more ways than one. For had she continued her plan, not only might we have a similarly brilliant, but very different autobiography from one of the most intelligent and insightful writers of the day; but nineteenth-century German women might have had more choice when contemplating appropriate models for their autobiographies.

As it turned out Varnhagen greatly influenced the lives if not the autobiographies of nineteenth-century Germany women. Her concept of the epistolary form allowed her passions to surface, and it was precisely the honesty of her struggle which provoked such a profound response in younger women like Fanny Lewald and Malwida von Meysenbug when the letters were published.[1] Varnhagen had not emphatically opposed women's oppression, although she felt it and articulated her frustration at the conventions which confined women. While thus abhorring all oppression, she felt the greatest antipathy for most women she knew, finding them far too slavish.[2] Her letters helped form her unwitting friendships with other women who needed recognition for desires denied them by their families. More than any of the autobiographies, Varnhagen's letters formed a link between women, and she and Bettina von Arnim begin a distinctly female tradition in German letters.[3]

Some writers have commented on the speed with which Karl August Varnhagen was able to edit and circulate three volumes of his wife's letters after her death in 1833. (The manuscript version of these selections was given to friends in 1834, the printed version appeared in 1835.) Naturally one wonders if some of the work might not have been done by Rahel herself before her death, but of this there is no clue. If the claim that Varnhagen never wrote an autobiography cannot be contested, her letters extend the historical and theoretical context in which we may consider the correspondence of Bettina von Arnim as a radical form of autobiography.

If she had written nothing at all, Bettina von Arnim (1785-1859) might have entered literary history merely as a personal link between several generations of German authors, as someone bridging diversities. Indeed she is most frequently mentioned as the granddaughter of Sophie von la Roche, the daughter of Maximiliane Brentano (whom Goethe had once admired), the sister of one romantic poet, Clemens Brentano, and the wife of another, Achim von Arnim. Even her writing combines elements of sentimentalism, classicism and romanticism. Any overly harmonious image of her, however, was doomed forever when, at the age of 46 and after her husband's death, she edited and published *Goethe's Briefwechsel mit einem Kinde* (1835), her correspondence with Goethe. Since that work she has been either glorified as a cobold, an electric spark, poetry personified, or criticized for lying and meddling.

Editions of her correspondence with other authors did not elicit the same concern vor her veracity: *Die Günderode* (1840) and *Clemens Brentanos Frühlingskranz* (1844), although the dedication of the former volume to the politicized students of the day occasioned some nervousness. A regular brouhaha stormed, however, over *Dies Buch gehört dem König* (1843). Dedicated and addressed to the King, she had the affrontery to offer him, in epistolary form, rather radical advice on political issues, accusing his bureaucracy with unresponsiveness and inner strife. Like Iphigenie this woman, too, sought to persuade the monarch of humane values, but the book fell on an unresponsive mind.

Another work, *Das Armenbuch*, was planned as a collection of biographies of the poor. It was withheld from publication because mere rumors of its content sufficed to elicit offical warnings of imprisonment. The Prussian government knew nothing of "freedom of the press". For this work and for the book dedicated to the King, in particular, Arnim acquired the epithets of atheist and communist in those pre-revolutionary days when the latter especially carried no specific meaning. Although the label "social monarchist" would best describe her political views, the term "radical" is not without some justification either in terms of her politics or her literary innovations.

These epithets need to be seen in terms of her "radical" view of the individual and of friendship. In this regard she shared Varnhagen's romantic philosophy. Mutual nourishment for the soul in friendship is practice for building generous spirits which encompass a whole nation or epoch. Clemens explains that for the world to come full circle, to return to its originality (*Ursprünglichkeit*) in full consciousness, what happens in the world must be seen in each individual. (I,90) Bettina wants to educate great personalities in the times and in history to a nobility of the will (*Wille*) ending caprice and the egoism of pretentious knowledge (*Klugheit*). "Und Freundschaft ist ein vorbereitender Egoismus jener Bildung. . ."(I, 154f) In her exalted vision, friendship practices that nobility of self which produces the egoism (seen positively) to encompass one's nation in its diversity, ones times and finally to redeem the world.

Ultimately it is this perspective on the individual's position in the world that produced the social and political stances that shocked her family and earned her the epithet of radical. Ardently insisting, as she did, on her individuality while recognizing her indebtedness to others, seeing that she was the product of history and the carrier of the future, meant bearing responsibility for herself and her neighbors. As an individual she insisted on her "self" as well as the dependence of that "self" on the evolution of other "selves". In the face of family pressure, therefore, she refused to recognize class or racial distinctions, befriending Jews and gardners.

Later Arnim would continue her democratic behavior in her political writings and deeds. She intervened privately and publicly with the King on behalf of the poor or of political prisoners, and in some individual cases she succeeded. She cared for those struck with cholera and acted in general as though she belonged to the whole and bore responsibility for it.[26] Although her utopian ideal imagined a society in which rules would be unnecessary, she never conceived of a political revolution to overthrow the monarch. Her idealism let her hope that proper advisors would aid the King to encompass his people as a great personality ought. He would then inspire and deserve their confidence. History, for Arnim, progressed toward a magnanimous goal that depended on the efforts of many, and she felt her generosity added to the general pool. There was a telos, perhaps, but a most uncertain one, for it depended on the assistance of human effort. The human spirit is like a seed which has remained dormant in various historical periods, "und erst indem sie sich zu wirklichem Leben entzündete, regte sich diese Saat selbstwirkender Eigenthümlichkeiten...jener elektrische Funke, der die Weltgeschicke durch große Charaktere heraus bildet und aufbaut".(I, 89) Great personalities, magnanimous souls (and to these she counted herself) incorporate the spirit of history and of the times and move it forward.

The three volumes of Arnim's edited correspondence with other authors could (and will) be considered to be autobiography: *Clemens Brentanos Frühlingskranz, Die Gündrode, Goethes Briefwechsel mit einem Kinde*. At first glance these works confront us with weighty doubts about their assignation to the genre of autobiography at all. Quite apart from the difficulty raised by their epistolary form, there is the question of her own description of them as "epistolary novels". Although the only interest they have held for traditional literary historians has been their biographical content, it is precisely that which is admittedly somewhat suspect; making her identification of them as "novels" seem appropriate![4] Even so they have been ignored in histories of the novel. However, since actual correspondence forms the basis of all these works, the question about the extent to which her portrait of herself is "true" must certainly be raised.

Although the issue of veracity and autobiographical intent will have to be raised again, it will help to clarify from the outset that the term "novel" was applied somewhat loosely at the turn of the eighteenth and nineteenth centuries, when the genre was in its infancy. In Germany, for instance, the terms novel and correspondence were sometimes confused. If she should ever write a novel, Friedrich Schlegel condescendingly advised his sister-in-law, Caroline Schlegel, she should have someone else draw up the plan and, in case it would not entirely be composed of letters, also write that part which is not![5] The veracity of both forms, in fact, was questioned equally by Sophie Mereau (1770-1806), a novelist and Bettina von Arnim's sister-in-law. She wrote her husband, Clemens Brentano, "Ein Brief ist mir immer wie ein Roman . . . (.) Das Papier ist ein so ungetreuer Bote, daß es den Blick, den Ton vergißt, und oft sogar einen falschen Sinn überbringt."[16]

Not only are these two forms confused, the term "novel" was frequently synonymous with a love story. Grimm's dictionary lists this as a third definition. Thus Rahel Varnhagen referred to her correspondence with her fiance, Karl von Finckenstein as a "novel". And Bettina von Arnim punned on the very ambivalence of the term. Her brother, Clemens, had chastized her for reading too many novels. He found they gave her the strangest thoughts. But Bettina responded that no novels could interest her except her own (meaning her own flirtations), and she found it annoying anyway to have them predigested for her.[17] Arnim's lost correspondence with a Major Wildermeth, which Karl August Varnhagen had characterized as "passionate" and compared to the correspondence with Goethe,[18] was referred to by a Swedish acquaintance, Malla Montgomery-Silferstolpe, as a "novel".[19] Insofar as each of the three volumes of correspondences with other authors tells the story of a passionate friendship each has earned the label, "novel".

From the point of view of autobiography there would appear to be several persuasive arguments against including them as representatives of this genre: the apparent lack of unifying perspective; the relative importance accorded the correspondent, rather than the author (in the titles and as characters); and the apparent lack of development, or plot. Nevertheless, when seen objectively none of these arguments withstands either Arnim's actual practice or the evidence we have of her intentional challenge to traditional concepts of the individual and of narration. These volumes can only be properly assessed when viewed as radical autobiography.

On opening any of these volumes a reader is confronted with what appears to be a collection of unedited letters between two friends. Since Waldemar Oehlke's careful and appreciative 1905 analysis, however, critics have known the extent to which these letters have in fact been reworked or actually invented.[20] He maintained that while all were based on original correspondence, they were essentially the products of her mature years. After comparing extant letters with the correspondences, he concluded that, unless there were proof otherwise, all letters in the published books had been tampered with.

Generally speaking, Arnim dismantled actual letters and dispersed their parts throughout a given correspondence. Material from different dates therefore appeared under one date; nothing hindered her, for instance, from reorganizing material under a season more appropriate to a particular mood. She preferred the Spring. She expanded material not only by adding passages or phrases as the composition demanded, but also by inventing and elaborating new themes and motifs. Letters from someone else were attributed to her current correspondent. She filled in time gaps in the real exchanges and called later knowledge and other sources to her aid. Her lack of regard for documentary material produced the chronological and factual errors which so horrified many of her first readers. Her most commonly observed error, for example, was the misdating of a letter from Goethe's mother — Frau Rath would have to have written Arnim from her grave. Facts in these volumes simply cannot be trusted without further verification. We can sympathize with the critic who called the Günderode volume a mixture of poetry and truth, "eine durch die Dichtung verklärte und aus ihrem Geist geborene Schilderung" and firmly maintained that it was neither biography (of the named correspondents) nor a novel in letters, that all three volumes were "true", but not "real".[21] However that critic failed to consider the works as autobiography. Since autobiography consists in any case largely of a "construction" of a story around certain unavoidable facts, hopefully expressing actual experience to some extent, the import of such a statement for a study of this genre is not greatly significant.

In rewriting her correspondences Arnim made every effort to imitate the style of her partner and to keep her own consistent. As Oehlke has also proved, however, her own letter-writing style is very different from that of these volumes. Arnim's son-in-law, Hermann Grimm, has recorded watching her write, reworking a text repeatedly and tossing earlier versions away: "Sie schrieb unaufhörlich wieder ab was ihr nicht gefiel, bis es die Leichtigkeit des Styls empfing als sei es flüchtig nur so hingeschrieben worden. Ihr Styl in den raschgeschriebenen Briefen ist von viel schwererm Gefüge als der in ihren Büchern."[22] So, thoroughly revised, these volumes really *are* the product of the years 1835 to 1844 and it is actually possible to claim for them the single life perspective preferred in an autobiography. After all, it was a shorter time than that in which Goethe wrote the four volumes of his autobiography.

The second major departure from traditional autobiographical form is intended and issues from profound differences in philosophical perspectives. All the works under discussion bear the name of the correspondent as title: *Goethes Briefwechsel, Die Günderode, Clemens Brentanos Frühlingskranz*. Arnim thus shifts attention away from the author, who by definition is the traditional focus of an autobiography. Indeed, except for Goethe, the correspondents seem to share authorship of the works to a large degree. Such an apparent breach of form, however, results from understanding character and personality in a manner radically different from the common concept of the self-identical individual and represents, in fact, a major challenge to the genre.

Like Varnhagen Arnim has taken the romantic concept of friendship seriously, but in these volumes she consciously fashions them to reflect portions of herself.[23] Her friends become her "mirrors" and her "echoes". To her brother she wrote, "[I]ch bin so stolz in Dir, weil Du oft mich anredest, als ob es die Stimme der Weisheit sei, auf die ich lange gehorcht habe in die Ferne, und jetzt ist sie mir so nah in Dir, daß ich sie von mir selber nicht unterscheide."(I,96) She tells Goethe, "Die Günderode war mein Spiegel; an ihr ließ ich jeden Ton widerhallen und bezeichnete sie mit meinen Empfindungen und Eindrücken. Offenbarungen wurden mir, indem ich mich übte, mich vor ihr auszusprechen."[24] She also had the audacity, which infuriated her critics, to refer to Goethe as her echo as well and wrote to him, "Ich liebe den eigenen Geist, Du bist die Pforte, durch die ich zu ihm eintrete."[25] Since all these voices echo hers, all these people mirror her, Arnim — in her multiple refractions — *is* actually the common focus of these volumes of correspondence.

This narcissism is not ego-centric in the common sense, and Arnim's tendency to absorb her correspondents into her own, all-encompassing personality can only be properly grasped if it is seen in its complexity and generosity. Indeed, as for Madame Guyon, love of self meant cherishing the ties perceived to connect her to other creatures. Her concept of love, like the romantic concept of friendship, meant growing and expanding through others. Thus she, too, became "ein fruchtbarer Acker" for the seeds of others. Clemens wrote: "Ich bin das Werk meiner Liebe zu Dir."(I, 188) She wrote Günderode, "Du sagtest, Du liebst Dich selbst in mir."(II,513) The author understands herself in a consistent fashion as both the reflection and the product of those whom she has chosen as friends. Thus, Arnim's concept of characterization is more externally non-identical than Elisabeth Stägemann's personification of part of her soul into an imaginary correspondent. But she also insists on her own "self". While writing of her "self", she also draws portraits of her friends as she knew them, and only she could.

Such an expansive view of friendship eliminates normal boundaries between individuals and tends to emphasize relationships instead. Distinctions between people merge and diverge, become blurred; personalities are more fluid and less dense. Distinctions between the foreground and the background, the individual and society are removed. The individual herself loses distinct contours (and society becomes the aggregate of individuals). And, the main character common to all three volumes, Bettina, is viewed in each from a different perspective.

Criticism of traditional biographical writing becomes explicit when Arnim has Günderode complain that such works never fully re-create a person. Biographers usually invent only one side of a person, while the complexity of human existence remains elusive and the image of the individual is not merely flattened, but falsified. All aspects of existence always shape an individual, and only such a presentation could make her/him understandable (II,4ll). Arnim's epistolary volumes answer that complaint. The correspondence with her brother is dated 1800 to 1803; that to Caroline von Günderode, 1802 to 1806; and to Goethe, 1807 to 1832, although only a few letters were exchanged after 1811. Not only do readers perceive a different side of Bettina von Arnim in each volume then, some events in the correspondence are repeated, giving the reader a multiple perspective on one event.

As a result, in part, of the variety of perspectives there appears to be very little plot or action in these volumes. Normally, autobiographies are expected to show the emotional, intellectual, or spiritual development of the author through clearly marked events. Certain moments become significant milestones in the development of the author: going off to school, finding work, wars. Even smaller events like reading a certain author, being unjustly punished, or being betrayed by a friend seem to have consequences, to produce certain behavior or attitudes. A life is often presented as a chain of events in a cause and effect relationship.

There are almost no outstanding events in Arnim's autobiography, certainly none that represent well-defined turning points or milestones. The three volumes seem to lead nowhere, seem to be without a telos. Arnim does not finally become a wife, or a mother, or an author, or acheive any particular social recognition. In her case this reflects a philosophical position. It is her character, rather than her social role which is of concern for her. Hence "events" are less important than interactions with other people and insignificant, daily occurences: a conversation with the gardner, conversations in general; a walk, walks in general; the contents of her music, math, and history lessons; her flights of fantasy; and her philosophical musings. Arnim's character reveals itself and shows its evolution, not in terms of her participation in events or reactions to them, but in terms of her behavior in various situations and with various people. What molds and builds her character are the relationships we witness in the correspondence.

Responding to a complaint about the unreadability of her Goethe volume, Arnim once wrote, "Lesen Sie mein Buch mehr wie einmal (. . .). Öff-
nen Sie es hier und da in jeder Stimmung, Sie werden gewiß einen Anklang
darin finden. . . (.)"[26] Recognizing the new form and the difficulty of finding the thread of the narration, she recommended a new way of reading as
well, one which removed the interest in plot. The sense of the present which
dominates these epistolary works contributes as well to the sense that they
do not constitute an autobiography. They seem, as some have said of Arnim herself, poetic. Yet, in what appears to be a contradiction, there is development. It is the gradual coming to itself of the soul, but the reader must
work with the author to see it.

In her emphasis on being and growth of the soul rather than doing, a spontaneous, epistolary form becomes integral to her intentions. Clemens, who
repeatedly urged his sister to write poetry, fiction, or autobiography used
her letters as examples of a talent she had which could be applied in other
forms.(II, 439) He even locked her in her room once until she could come
out with a poem. But his efforts to get her to write sequentially failed and
Arnim rebelled: "Dichten ist nicht nah genug, es besinnt sich zu sehr auf
sich selber."(II, 452) She would like "Poesie" to be intimate with nature so
that it might relinguish its sanctified laws for the sake of nature and burst
all conventional chains in order to throw itself into nature's embrace. She
knows form to be the empeccable body of "Poesie," "aber sollte es denn nicht
auch eine unmittelbare Offenbarung der Poesie geben, die vielleicht tiefer,
schauerlicher ins Mark eindringt, ohne feste Grenzen der Form? — Die da
schneller und natürlicher in den Geist eingreift, vielleicht auch bewußtloser
aber schaffend, erzeugend wieder eine Geistesnatur?"(II, 434) Even if she
rewrote these volumes repeatedly it was to give them the impression of that
uncontainable spontaneity, so that they might reach into the reader's mind,
because above all else she wanted to affect their souls, as nature itself affected hers.

When the reviews of her Goethe book appeared she claimed she could
not understand them; they only chastized her for providng erroneous information and false conclusions.[27] Clearly she had meant to convey more
than surface reality. She never completed the conventional narration of her
autobiography of the years she spent in the convent that Clemens had requested of her. The form itself unsettled her. Although it stretches our imaginations and causes us to rethink not only our understanding of the
autobiographical form and its history, but also the nature of the individual
and history itself, these epistolary novels are autobiography. Arnim sim-

ply refuses to relinquish the imaginative, intuitive, fantastic, and spontaneous side of her life. This series of relationships, of interactions, of ways of being in the world *was* the story of her life.

If we still want an "autobiographical pact", an admission on the part of the author, we will have to be satisfied by her actions. When she edited the first collection of her writings in 1853, she did not order her works according to their publication dates. Rather she grouped these three books of correspondence together, reversing their chronological order of publication, but placing them in the correct biographical order: *Clemens Brentanos Frühlingskranz* (1844) appeared first, with the correspondence from 1800-1803; *Die Günderode* (1840) appeared second, with correspondence from 1802-1806; and *Goethes Briefwechsel mit einem Kinde* (1835) appeared third, with correspondence from 1807-1832. *Dies Buch gehört dem König* which appeared in 1843, in the middle of these publications, was placed later. This is the only explicit clue to the autobiographical intent of these three volumes.

Arnim's great emphasis on "being" does not contradict her concept of the growth of a soul through relationships with others. "Being" is also a state of mind which is fluid and which must be achieved. Each of these volumes traces the growth and decline of a relationship on Bettina's way to understanding and asserting herself, and through and in herself "God". Inevitably, it is the *other* correspondent who initiates the end of the relationship: whether by striking poses and taking positions which limit her development so that she must distance herself — as in Clemens' case; or by directly or indirectly ending the communication — as in the cases of Günderode and Goethe. In some sense then there *is* a "plot" to each of these volumes, though it is the nature of this epistolary form that it is never immediately apparent. Precisely because these "plots" are never articulated in an expository fashion *and* because other of my conclusions about these works as autobiography will be based on my reading of them, it will be appropriate to summarize the progress of these relationships in somewhat more detail.

When Maximiliane Brentano died in 1793, her 8-year old daughter, Bettina, and two sisters were sent to the convent Kloster Fritzlar. There Bettina received that education typical for young women of the upper-middle classes: broad, but superficial and including instruction in music and painting. Flashbacks in the epistolary autobiography characteristically reveal few events of these years, but the young Bettina, lonely there, apparently learned then to appreciate nature. In 1797, after her father's death, she went to live with her maternal grandmother, Sophie von la Roche. According to the volume pertaining to their relationship, her re-acquaintance with her brother Clemens, seven years older, quickly evolved into the close friendship of which their correspondence was the fruit. Although the last of the three to be written it is the first in the chronology of her biography.

Clemens, so it would seem from *Frühlingskranz*, was the first to encourage Bettina's belief in herself and the divinity of her soul. Through these letters the young Bettina first became acquainted with general elements of romantic philosophy. He urged her to take herself seriously, to examine herself with insight into and consideration for her rights as an independent person. Together they held that it is everyone's task to find the truth in him/herself. (I, 23) This task was a secular version of Madame Guyon's — and any pietist's — search for God's voice in her inner nature. It was the search for and the faith in that inner voice, the "self", which gave women the courage to oppose oppressive structures. With her brother Clemens Bettina carries on an intimate conversation with a soul standing easily in the door, but so inclined toward the neighbor, so gently enticing that the neighbor expresses herself fully. (I,21)

If the condition for their mutual inclination is the desire to pursue the inner self and inner genius and to become unique, they also agree on any number of things: that insight, not knowledge of facts is true education (I,25); that thought is the most important activity (I,34); that a person is on earth to educate herself and then the world (I,34). They agree that pity with unfortunates is not a virtue, for it derives from scorn. One must be ashamed that such a misfortune could occur (I,46f.). They agree that it is not the practical, common-sensical citizen who represents the future, it is the person with an inner life who embodies the sentiments of her contemporaries (I, 145). They agree that one should act out of oneself and be inner directed and that religion means honoring that inner God (I, 163). Their concept of religion and God is highly secularized. They believe that it is this world, not the next, that should concern us (I,47) and, like Varnhagen and in contradistinction to mercantilist thought, that generosity is the source of all wealth (I, 388).

Eventually, and significantly, Bettina's introspection reveals and nourishes feelings and convictions with which Clemens cannot sympathize — as though the history of that belief in the "self" repeated itself in Bettina von Arnim herself. The assertion of that concept was more radical than many of its adherents cared to know — and this was true precisely for women. Though the differences between brother and sister are suggested from the beginning of the volume, only gradually do they form a gulf separating them.

98

The strength of character he sought to nurture emerges most clearly as Bettina insists on feelings contrary to those which social conventions prescribed for women. Not suspecting, apparently, that women harbored sensibilities which did not correspond to his notion of womanhood he innocently encouraged her independence. Issues of gender gradually emerge as the major point of difference between them and the one which ultimately ends their intimacy.

The "story" is not complicated. From the very beginning Bettina had complained that the world was very wide, while her circle was very small. Clemens comforted her by telling her that this was because she did not yet know her inner self. He warned her to appear dumb, rather than saucy (I, 257) and advised her to make herself loved on all sides so that her inner life could remain undisturbed; but she was outraged at the attempts to turn her into a pleasant, loveable girl and called convention "Polizei für Mädchen"(I, 182). She considered herself a caged bird and exclaimed, "O Sklavenzeit, in der ich geboren bin!"(I, 317). When Bettina befriended a young Jewish seamstress and even helped her sweep her stoop, her family admonished her—and Clemens joined them, advising her neither to befriend such people nor to demean herself in this manner. It outraged Bettina that the simplest deeds of kindness and friendship, of warmth and generosity were in conflict with correct behavior (I, 28). Isabella von Wallenrodt had exposed the same social hypocrisy, but Bettina—from a position asserting the validity of her inner convictions—rails loudly against that convention, insisting on the virtue of her actions and her right to have friends from whatever class of people.

Clemens asserts that the role of women is firmer and less mobile that that of man (I, 260) and looks forward to forming a foursome with her when they shall both have married. Not only does Bettina take offense at his assumption that her future lies in marriage, she finds marriage too prosaic an arrangement for her (I,218). She wants poetry and pleasure (I,218) and refuses all chains (I,206). Not unlike Elisabeth Stägemann's reaction to the genre painting of a family dinner, Bettina wants to be excluded from Clemens' holy portrait of the harmony of marriage, his idealized notions about men and women (I,288).

Just as Clemens had told her to separate her inner and social lives from the beginning, so at the end he still recommends separating being from becoming and fantasy from reality. In his opinion contemplating dreams at length is childish (I,198) and she should distance herself from her fantasies (I, 370). Bettina asserts that dreams are the most profound expression of the self (I, 282) and insists on retaining her fantasies. She will not separate those spheres of her life, she desires both to be and to become, both reality and fantasy (I, 162). Her emphasis on holding on to her desires parallels Varnhagen's efforts to bring them to the surface, as well as Recke's expression of her own need for integrity and Stägemann's expression of two sides to her "self". As Arnim finds herself gradually alienated by Clemens' reprimands and advice, she finds his letters strange, not familiar as they once were (I, 112,262,266). She finds his attitude as foreign as an inquisition (I,366). It would seem as though he reimposed a hierarchy, a harmony, when and where lack of one threatened him. Recognizing that the dish of morality he offers her comes from a brother's love, she claims no appetite for it but accepts it, opting to ignore his moralistic preaching because it would injure her love for him (I,281). Thus while the issue of Clemens' engagement to Sophie Moreau *appears* at the end of the volume to cause a weakening of the siblings' intimate ties, the rift, as Bettina von Arnim portrayed it, is actually one that has longer and more profound origins.

The late-romantic poet Josef Freiherr von Eichendorff (1788-1857), reading solely for his interest in Clemens, perceptively testifies to the likeness of Arnim's portrait of her brother and, inadvertently, also to her concept of friends as mirrors. "[Clemens Brentanos] Briefwechsel mit seiner Schwester Bettina...ist ein merkwürdiges Denkmal der in ihm arbeitenden Gegensätze. Er spielt hier den altklugen Hofmeister gegen seine jüngere Schwester (...). Überall aber ist die heimliche Angst vor sich selber fühlbar, vor dem eigenen Dämon, den er in der gleichbegabten Schwester wie ein erschreckendes Spiegelbild wiedererkannt und daher aus allen Kräften bekämpft (...)."[28] Eichendorff saw clearly both the mutual mirroring of the siblings, but also the rift, which he interpreted only from Clemens' point of view as "terrifying".

Bettina had loved her brother's "eingenmächtiger, selbstherrschender Wille" (I,85). And although he tries to tame hers, she identifies with it nevertheless, frequently referring to herself androgynously. She dreams of herself as a boy (I,156); imagines herself as Joan of Arc (I,290); outlines an opera in which her friend Günderode is the heroine and she the hero; repeats to Clemens that Günderode told her she knew no male company except hers (I,288). When others want to kill a chicken with mixed sexual parts (*Mannweib*), she rescues it, as it, too, is a product of nature.

Clemens, Günderode and Goethe are only the major mirrors for Bettina's development. Many others are also revealed throughout these correspondences. The issue of androgynous behavior and Bettina's attitude toward it is most thoroughly explored in her relationship to Madame de Gachet. Early in the correspondence Clemens announced that he had sent a remarkable Frenchwoman to Bettina with a letter of introduction; but even before she arrives his guilt begins to draw forth doubts about how appropriate this acquaintance is for his younger sister, and he tries to warn her. De Gachet had been forced to leave France and was a woman of revolutionary bent. She was also a physicist on a par with the most advanced in Germany. Clemens tries to soften what he gradually realizes could have a major impact on Bettina by noting that de Gachet had been seduced by her abilities and her delicate sensibilities had undoubtedly suffered because of it. He warns her to overlook "das männliche Wilde ihres Seins und Verstandes" and to remain innocent. When de Gachet first arrives Bettina, in fact, mistakes her for a man, since she arrives on horseback in masculine attire.

Clemens had not misjudged the impact on Bettina, but he had apparently misjudged her ability to remain true to herself. Bettina writes that de Gachet had spoken like a man about politics and the revolution, supporting the assemblee national. Her own heart had rejoiced when she heard her; she felt horizons open, saw new possibilities for existence, and began to trust herself and her own power (I,83). She was in fact nearly swept away. But, as if afraid of being overwhelmed, she discreetly withdraws, stating that she does not want to be Madame de Gachet (I,86). If Madame de Gachet represents an androgynous possibility, von Arnim ultimately rejects it for herself. The opposite of perversion (by which she means social convention) is truth, and to be somebody else is not to be true to oneself. "Dieser große Planet, de Gachet, erschüttert mich zu sehr, wenn er mir so nah rückt.— Sie redete von den Himmelskörpern, ihrem subtilen Ausströmen und von wechselseitiger Anziehung der Planeten in ihre Kreise, und vom innerlichen Sinn im Ozean der Gefühle, und ich war ganz betäubt. Wie komme ich ihr vor, da sie mir so was sagt! — Sie hielt mich fest in ihren Armen, ich hätte des Teufels werden mögen; ich schämte mich, da ich ihr zuhören mute, gefangen in ihren Armen, und nichts verstand." (I, 100) (The sexual overtones in this encounter are unmistakable and are repeated in her relationship to Caroline Günderode, but we will never be sure about the precise nature of these relationships.)

When de Gachet leaves suggesting that Bettina might accompany her to Spain, Bettina refuses — despite her longings to experience the world. She would rather stay at home, or so she tells the Frenchwoman (I, 114). But when she next sees her Bettina finds they speak the same language and agree on numerous subjects (I, 184). De Gachet has changed, too. She now purchases an estate and begins farming it. Bettina seems won over more by the useful, meaningful de Gachet than the one who told witty tales and made insightful comments about politics.

In the figure of this Frenchwoman Bettina recognizes her longings, but also the dangers of going to the extreme of becoming man-like. De Gachet has mirrored a possibility for her which she ultimately refuses because she could not be that and be herself. She must find her own way, and it is her experience with Günderode which helps her to define her strength in a less overtly masculine way. Indeed, in the latter part of *Frühlingskranz* Bettina mentions Caroline Günderode with increasing frequency and this new friend often sides with her against Clemens' inquisitional stance.

Die Günderode is the volume which perhaps best synthesizes Arnim's radical interests in changing society with an awareness of radical forms. When they met in Frankfurt am Main in 1804 Günderode was 24 and Bettina 19. Günderode had come there in 1797 when she acquired a position in the *Evangelische Damenstift*, a kind of self-endowed pension for unmarried women. Under the pseudonym "Tian," she would publish several uncelebrated works: *Gedichte und Phantasien* (1804), *Poetische Fragmente* (1806), and two dramas, *Udohla* and *Magie und Schicksal* (1806). Her friendship with the young Bettina Brentano ended when she distanced herself in 1806, apparently at the urging of Georg Friedrich Creuzer, the married man with whom she was in love. Her suicide in July of that year is most directly and most commonly associated with his rejection of her, but, as becomes clear in this correspondence, there were other causes for her unhappiness as well. She was a talented, melancholy person, and — like Baldinger, Engel, and Wallenrodt — sought esteem from a male intellectual establishment. She was not destined for happiness from that quarter, either.[29] Although her literary talent would seem to justify more attention than she received, her very desire for that elusive esteem would seem to resemble that of those autobiographers.

Even though the original correspondence is not extant there is reason to believe that one formed the basis of this epistolary work. The two friends were frequently separated when Caroline left Frankfurt on business or visited her grandmother or when Bettina stayed at her grandmother's in near-by Offenbach. Still, we have too much evidence of Arnim's cutting and pasting to believe that *this* is that original correspondence. And given what we do know of sources the precise resemblance of this to any original correspondence must be placed in doubt. For instance, we possess a letter of Arnim's to another friend, Claudine Piautaz, which was dismantled and included in various of her alleged letters to Günderode. Her description of her grandfather la Roche strongly resembles one in Goethe's *Dichtung und Wahrheit* (1811-33). Friedrich Hölderlin's comments on the translation of *Oedipus* appear here as statements made in conversation with Bettina von Arnim. As for Günderode's letters, they often appear to be reworkings of her published poems or prose placed to suggest that Bettina somehow provoked their authorship.[30] Perhaps it is best to consider all of these letters autobiographical constructions.

Compared to the somewhat unequal relationship between Bettina and her older brother, this one between these two young women appears to have been more of an equal exchange. Within limits Günderode indulged the flights of fantasy that so perturbed Clemens. For instance, unable to venture into the real world, they spent days imagining their travels to distant places and the details of their adventures. Bettina wondered why the mind had been given wings if they had not been meant to be used, and Günderode claimed that Bettina taught her to wear and use those wings. Günderode also supported Bettina in behavior which flaunted convention for the sake of higher principles, although the audacity of it sometimes unnerved her.

They shared a vision of a more noble and just world and together they determined to found a religion in which, laughing, they would turn the social order upside down. It was to be a "Schwebereligion" ("Hovering Religion") against injustice and for the purpose of sharing life and developing personal wisdom and "Poesie."[31] Among their principles were: "Der Mensch soll immer die größte Handlung tun und nie eine andere." (II,216); "Denken ist Beten" (II,217); one should be brave enough "das Große zu tun und die Vorurteile nicht zu achten" (II,224); "Echte Bildung geht hervor aus Übung der Kräfte, die in uns liegen" (II,243); "jeder soll neugierig sein auf sich selber und soll sich zutage fördern wie aus der Tiefe ein Stück Erz" (II,243); and God is "Poesie" and since humans are made in God's image, they are all born poets (II,213).

Both in the explication of the "Schwebereligion" and elsewhere in this volume, Bettina's political interests become more apparent. Although she disliked studying world history and could barely muster the patience to read a newspaper, she wanted to rule the world (II,300f.). When her grandmother suggests that she should respect the political opinions of intelligent men, since they understand the world and are called to govern it, Arnim responds, "Nein, liebe Gromama, mir scheint vielmehr, daß ich dazu berufen bin."(II,302) Since great deeds are the product of great character, she is convinced that she would rule greatly and with magnaminity (II, 307f.). Since all tyrants are "arglistige kleinliche Naturen" (II, 458) she feels well qualified, indeed, more qualified to rule. She could never degrade herself by permitting those injustices which pass for justice in the world, and she finds greater freedom in allying herself with the oppressed than the oppressors (II,456). But her definition of freedom differs from some: "[A]ber die Menschen verstehen nicht, was Freiheit ist, sie wollen sich ihrer bemächtigen, das ist schon sie ertöten. Der Freiheit kann man sich nicht bemächtigen, sie muß als göttliche Kraft in uns erscheinen, sie ist das Gesetz, aus dem sich der Geist von selbst aufbaut. Innere Gebundenheit und äußere Freiheit sind doppelt schwere Ketten, weil die Trunkenheit noch dazukommt, die die Sinne bindet und verwirret."(II,550).

She sought to cultivate that inner freedom which Lessing thought was the basis of a just society, and sought, as did Varnhagen, to avoid killing parts of herself in order to accommodate herself to the prevailing authorities. She sought the full exercise of her personality, not as later philosophers would, for the glory of the individual, but for the benefit of the human race. As far as she was concerned there was in each person a secret desire to be magnanimous (II, 210). That had to be unleashed. It was her Mathematics teacher, the Jew Ephraim, who, by his own deeds, taught her responsibility for others (II,542f.) and the exercise of that particular desire.

In matters of spontaneity and unconventionality the older friend, Günderode, seems to have learned from the younger. But if Günderode acknowledged she was Bettina's pupil in that untraditional sense, Bettina knew she was Günderode's in a more traditional one. She admired Günderode's clarity and grace, and in particular Günderode encouraged her to educate herself in new areas: in Latin and Mathematics for instance, but especially in History and Philosophy. In these areas she supplied Bettina with texts. Indeed, both she and Clemens shared a concern that Bettina's spirit was too chaotic, flighty, and undirected. They hoped reading would help her find a coherence and a firmer, more organized philosophy.

Although Bettina admits it will be difficult for her, she accepts Günderode's educational guidance. After reading ancient history, however, she writes her teacher a lengthy letter filled with the bloody deeds of ancient tyrants and teases her with the aridity and meaninglessness of such learning. Hearing that some ancient hero had disemboweled himself, she demands to know if he was young, beautiful, or in love (II,145ff). From her grandmother Bettina had learned: "[D]ie Vergangenheit [gehört] zum Tag des Lebens"(II, 406) and knows the value of understanding the past to understanding the present. But as with Varnhagen, it is a matter of how History is to be defined. Bettina is curious about her grandmother's tales, her *personal* narrations. Large-scale deeds do not interest her as much as the subjective, apparently irrelevant elements of history. She wants to record her grandmother's tales, but ancient History teaches her nothing except that tyrants are cruel.

Günderode also gives her various modern philosophers to read: Fichte, Schelling, Kant. If anything these readings are presented as even less helpful — although she has clearly absorbed something from them. Not only do they give her a headache and cause her to vomit, they send her to bed with a high fever. In her unconscious hallucinations she mutters the names of the philosophers Günderode had given her, especially Schelling. Since Arnim was fond of using images to represent her thought, it is very difficult to ascertain whether this portentous illness actually occured. She finds the logical abstractions of speculative thought senseless and imagines the frustration of a philosopher alone on an island. Nature there would be beautiful, it would be Spring with everything blossoming and the birds singing, but there would be nobody to whom the philosopher could preach, to whom he could explain his intricate leaps of logic. (II,129) Philosophers philosophize, she asserts, in order to teach others the most difficult and convoluted thoughts, not in order to be able to understand themselves and others better.

Bettina wants to teach Günderode to value "Alogik" (II, 178) and "Inkonsequenz" (II, 323). They are not so far removed from real concerns. When Günderode wants to escape to rainbows or be present in the dew, Bettina becomes alarmed. She fears Günderode will depart for regions that are not real, that are abstract and not of this earth. She wants, instead, to meet her on the garden steps or next to the stove (II,41). Not the poetry of abstract worlds concerns her, but the poetry of daily living, of concrete existence. Since Arnim wrote this correspondence long after Günderode's suicide, we will never know if she was really so prescient. She does seem, however, to attribute the danger of Günderode's "departure" to the abstraction and rarified atmosphere of the philosophy with which she was involved.

In effect, this is also a criticism of Günderode's poetic writings, which Arnim requests to see at the same moment she expresses her concern about Günderode's longing for rainbows (II, 50). Günderode had wanted to write in a "bleibende Form" (II,128), had longed for a certain type of "learning" and especially for reknown for her books. Bettina, however, is convinced that inconsequence, not consequence is the essence of the spirit (*Geist*) (II,323). She implies the need for a new aesthetic to accommodate inconsistency and these volumes of correspondence would seem to accord with such an aesthetic — indeed with many of Foucault's requirements of history and the formulation of the "self." Or it anticipates them.

Of all the volumes *Die Günderode* contains the most numerous reflections on aesthetics. Both Clemens and Günderode had urged Bettina to write. Clemens had found her letters so poetic he was convinced of her ability to draw scenes and events. He repeatedly urged her to record her experience in the convent (II, 310), to write poetry, or simply to write in order to concentrate her thoughts (II,310f.). Günderode also urged her to develop her thoughts in letters and to record her grandmother's stories (II,287). But Bettina repeatedly expresses her dissatisfaction with connected forms. Her thoughts are like butterflies lighting on different flowers, flitting about. Putting them on paper is like pinning the butterfly, killing it to preserve it.

She tells the story of how she learned the Tyrolean expression for butterfly. She had gone to see a certain Tyrolean because her sister wanted to buy gloves from him and because she wanted to see his face, which had been described to her as possessing great character. A butterfly landed on the flowers on his hat. Bettina called out that a "Schmetterling" had landed, but the Tirolean laughed and said it was a "Pfeilmuter." He then grabbed her and kissed her good naturedly. Neither she or her sister could be angry. Commenting that she had always wanted to write that story down, because she liked it, she adds, "aber zu einem Buch paßt sie nicht, denn sie ist ja gleich aus, und was soll dann weiter passieren?" (II,317).

The story is spontaneous and inconsequential, although she finds precisely such events quite simply beautiful. This makes it difficult for her to write long, cohesive works with a series of events related by cause and effect. She is pleased by the smallest daily realities of no apparent consequence. On a walk with Clemens she stops repeatedly to examine wildflowers and collect them for her study. Clemens comments: "Wenn du bei jedem Mauseöhrchen oder Vergißmeinnicht hocken bleibst, so werden wir nicht weit kommen."(II,313). She will never get very far by Clemens' criteria because she is drawn to what is simplest and nearest. Arnim knew this was the essence of poetry, but sought a form without firm lines (II, 434). And if she has Clemens suggest she would not get very far that way, i.e., become widely known (or consequential), she consistently argues against the need for fame or "learning" and in favor of insignificance.

Günderode admires her attitude, but cannot comfortably share it. Of herself Arnim has her write: "Ich fühl's, daß Du recht hast, und weiß, daß ich zu furchtsam bin, und kann nicht, was ich innerlich für recht halte, äußerlich gegen die aus der Lüge hergeholten Gründe verteidigen, ich verstumme und bin beschämt gerade, wo andere sich schämen müßten, und das geht so weit in mir, daß ich die Leute um Verzeihung bitte, die mir unrecht getan haben, aus Furcht, sie möchten's merken." (II,217f.) Günderode is timid and lacks Bettina's confidence to flaunt convention. She even disparages her own talents compared to those of her correspondent. Yet it is out of her relationship to Günderode that Arnim formulates her own particular aesthetic.

As Bettina senses Günderode lapsing into self-denigration she attempts to convince her of the importance of inconsistency and insignificance, but Günderode distanced herself consciously. Feeling the relationship cooling irrevocably Bettina blames herself for focusing too much on herself and for wandering paths too lonely in her letters (II,271). She knew their natures were too different. When the final break comes, Bettina is downcast. She writes Goethe's mother that she had inherited part of Günderode, that her friend had not totally gone: "Ach, sie hat vielleicht einen bessren Teil ihres geistigen Vermögens auf mich vererbt seit ihrem Tode."(III, 98f.). What she has learned from Günderode cannot depart; that part of her developed in and through her remains. As in the other volumes of correspondence, Arnim's character emerges with and in contrast to others; it defines itself and evolves because of their influence and in opposition to them.

Bettina Brentano had not known Goethe as well as she had Günderode or her brother, Clemens. She had gone to Goethe's mother to find a new friend when she noticed Günderode distancing herself. The relationship to Goethe's mother and the fact that she was the daughter of Maximilane von la Roche probably facilitated her access to his home. Goethe and Bettina first met in 1807 when she passed through Weimar with her sister and brother-in-law. She visited him only a few times thereafter. In 1811 however Bettina so outraged Goethe's wife Christiane (just how is not clear) that the latter tore Bettina's glasses from her nose and forbade her entrance to her home. This probably accorded with Goethe's own wishes as well, and he ceased writing her as well. Only after years of effusive apologies, an impulsive intrusion into his home, and Christiane Goethe's death was there a reconciliation of sorts. She twice visited him thereafter, but he continued not to answer her letters. Both the original correspondence as well as Arnim's reworked version reveal her to be the aggressive member of this friendship. She visited his mother frequently (perhaps as much at his request as for her own pleasure); continued to write even when he did not respond; sent presents to his entire family; and obliged his requests for music, information on the Jews in Frankfurt, and stories about his own childhood that she had heard from his mother. In short, she did everything to ingratiate herself.

Since we possess the entire original correspondence in this case, it is possible to compare Arnim's reworked version. As a first indication of her alterations it should be noted that the original correspondence comprises approximately 60 pages, while her version is more like 550 pages, to which she appended a diary of about 200 pages. Although she added some to Goethe's end of the correspondence, by far the larger portion of the additions were made in her own letters. Long discussions of music and poetic fantasies are included as well as descriptions of trips she made. The latter, especially, are narrated in such detail as to make it likely that she had recourse to diaries from that period. The most obvious manner in which she "misrepresented" the nature of the relationship has long been indignantly observed by critics. Whereas Goethe's real letters are friendly, but not enamored, Arnim implies that she was a veritable muse for him and elevates their friendship to a more passionate interlude. Thus in *Briefwechsel*, as opposed to the real correspondence, her letters are decidedly more passionate, describe suggestive romantic scenes with Goethe, and seem to elicit poetic responses, while Goethe expresses a more intense interest in her soulful explorations.

Those outraged by her alleged misrepresentations have been too narrowly focused on the portrait of Goethe and unconcerned with the other correspondent. While Goethe's real correspondence suggests nothing like the passionate involvement projected in Arnim's *Briefwechsel*, there is no reason for us to doubt the subjective truth of her portrait and her intimations that Goethe was her muse. In her dedication she foresaw accusations of inauthenticity and answered them by criticizing those who condemned her alterations of fact while they remained oblivious to "eine höhere Idealität" (III, 17). Perhaps for that reason, too, she preferred to label these correspondences "novels." Understood on that ideal level, however, this relationship was in fact one of the most intimate for Bettina von Arnim.

Arnim divided *Briefwechsel* into three parts. During the first part Goethe's mother mediates the relationship between Bettina and Goethe. The first half of this part contains her correspondence with his mother and the second half her correspondence with Goethe during his mother's lifetime. Part two consists solely of correspondence between Goethe and Bettina after his mothers death in 1808. Toward the end of this part however she relates stories of Goethe's childhood told her by his mother, as well as anecdotes about his mother. Frau Rat seems therefore to mediate and frame the entire correspondence. Part three is a diary, subtitled *Buch der Liebe*, and originally intended to be dedicated to Lord Byron. It is addressed to Goethe and in *Briefwechsel* she claims actually to have sent it to him in 1810 (III,419). It is a more explicit statement of ideas she works out in *Briefwechsel*, and here she attempts to illustrate how she has come to be so drawn to Goethe, to trace the evolution of her natural affinity with him. It is a spiritual confession remarkably close to those pietist ones narrating the author's path to God. In the process she relates stories about her childhood and her experience in the convent, stories which supply information about her biography until she began corresponding with her brother, Clemens. In this sense it provides and appropriate capstone for the three volumes, suggesting the connectedness of the beginning and the end.

The circular return to the beginning however also projects forward into Bettina's later life. It does so intricately through the rich associations of her concept of childhood. When Bettina Brentano began to write to Goethe, she was 23 years old and hardly a child in the literal sense of the world. Referring to herself as such in this correspondence has almost nothing to do with demeaning herself vis-à-vis Goethe. Rather this concept, like virtually all of hers, must also be understood in its "ideality." Moreover, the symbolic overtones to the concept do not exist in the original correspondence, a distinction *not* noted by privious critics, although it is undoubtedly central to her overall design for *Briefwechsel*.

Two lines from Goethe's poetry, quoted once toward the beginning of the first part and once toward the end of the second, provide a key for understanding Arnim's generally romantic notion of childhood which is the background for her concept, but only one of its allusions: "So laßt mich scheinen bis ich werde, zieht mir das weiße Kleid nicht aus." When it is cited the second time Arnim relates what she maintains is his mother's interpretation of these lines with which Bettina explicitly identified. Goethe's mother tells Bettina that he had described the only condition in which the soul might rediscover God (its divnity). It is a state of mind without prejudice or selfish deeds. Only pure longing initiates action. Virtues thought to win one a place in heaven are perceived as idiocies, mercy is different: "jedem Menschen sei diese Unschuld eingeboren und sei das Urprinzip aller Sehnsucht nach einem göttlichen Leben (. . .)." (III, 515) For Bettina God was in fact more of a pantheistic concept, related to nature, cosmic unity, and ulitmately Goethe as well.

When she had first quoted that passage in a letter to Goethe, she claimed that her magical attractions and abilities were her white dress, that innocent state, and she prayed she might keep it. Yet she knew that she too would have to take off that attire: "daß ich in den gewöhnlichen des alltäglichen, gemeinen Lebens einhergehen werde, und daß diese Welt, in der meine Sinne lebendig sind, versinken wird; das, was ich schützend decken sollte, das werde ich verraten...da, wo mir unbefangne kindliche Weisheit einen Wink gibt, da werd' ich Trotz biethen und es besser wissen wollen (...)."(III, 137) Although it would be a sin to leave behind the world of her senses and her childlike wisdom, she knew that she would betray that state of mind at some future time. Then, in 1807, she took Goethe as protector of her childlike innocence: "Du bist mein Schutzaltar, zu Dir werd' ich flüchten; diese Liebe, diese mächtige, die zwischen uns waltet, und die Erkenntnis, die mir durch sie wird, und die Offenbarungen, die werden meine Schutzmauern sein; sie werden mich frei machen von denen, die mich richten wollen." (III, 137f.) Her love for him would protect her ideal side against those who would wrench it from her. To be with him she cleanses herself of daily confusion like someone putting on festive attire (IV,32). His poems are seeds planted in her which liberate her from earthly weights (III, 153). Stägemann too had struggled against absorbtion into daily chores brought on by marriage. Arnim's relationship to Goethe would rescue her from this, but her autobiographical narration of this is far more indirect than Stägemann's.

The concept of Goethe as protector of Bettina's ideality yields another similarity with Stägemann's autobiography, for he serves her as a muse and as her other "self". When she writes Goethe she prays her guardian angel will speak to him for her, then she remains silent and lets her pen go: "Die ganze Natur zeigt mir im Spiegel was ich Dir sagen soll...alles sei von Gott so angeordnet, daß die Liebe einen Briefwechsel zwischen uns führe (...)."(III, 275). A letter early in *Briefwechsel* and not in the original, requests permission to write him unfiltered whatever springs into her head (III, 128). When she does she taps a "Herzensquelle, die nirgend wo ausströmen konnte...(.)" (III, 125) She tells him, "Du siehst mich an im Geist, und Dein Blick zieht Gedanken aus mir; da muß ich oft sagen, was ich nicht verstehe, was ich nur sehe." (III, 226) He allows her to rediscover part of herself. When he does not respond frequently in *Briefwechsel*, she asks permission to write as often as she likes. Writing what she can tell no one had become a necessity for her.

In fact writing Goethe is like writing herself or her twin (III,182). Goethe tells her he can give her nothing, she already has everything that could be given her. She writes to hold on to or to regain her unpragmatic, fanciful, and idealistic self, her own childhood, innocence, and harmony. Goethe is a catalyst for her discovery of herself. While her outpourings to him unite them, there is an implied paradox when she suggests he divides her: "Du bist inmitten meines Innern, es ist nicht mehr eins, es ist zu zwei in mir geworden." (IV, 13) In *Briefwechsel* then she corresponds with the ideal part of herself in "Goethe," much as Meta had with Elisabeth in Stägemann's autobiography. Only here the correspondent has been modeled on a real person. Also oppressed by the restrictive role society urges on her, Bettina works to realize that ideality in herself. Arnim values that side more highly and abstracts it. She writes to reawaken the child in herself, to let it supercede her pragmatic side, not to establish a harmony between the two. In this sense the child in her is not merely a retrospective image, but also a prospective one.

The romantic concept of childhood, of innocence and harmony, and the longing to regain it form only one aspect of Arnim's allusions to childhood. Although it was to be understood spiritually, her suggestions of Goethe's paternity have also offended some critics. In the Spring of 1806 Bettina Brentano had read letters to her grandmother which Goethe had written in 1772-1775.[32] Since they revealed the nature of his attachment to her mother, Bettina alludes in the *Briefwechsel* to her spiritual attachment to him as an inheritance from her mother and to herself as his child. In the diary she explains the childhood loneliness caused by not having a mother to help her define her character, to reflect her, and support her true personality. In the convent, where she was sent after her mother's death, she found no one who did this for her. There was, in her language, no mirror there. She learned to be with nature, to find resonance in it. Only when she went to live with her grandmother and found herself surrounded by her siblings did she see herself in a mirror for the first time (IV, 61). Throughout the three volumes she refers to her various correspondents as mirrors or echoes of herself. She needs them to reflect and build particular parts of her "self." In the diary her relationship to Goethe, her reflection in him, seems anticipated, even destined because of his former relationship to her mother.

If in some sense Arnim associates herself with Goethe's mother (through Frau Rath's mediation of their relationship as well as her transmission of stories of Goethe's childhood through Bettina back to Goethe) then Arnim also finds metaphors for herself as Goethe's lover as well as his child. That she learns of herself through Goethe implies for her this kind of romantic love, exalted friendship: "die Aufgabe der Liebe zwischen Freunden, [ist] das Rätsel [der Natur] aufzulösen; so daß ein jeder seine tiefere Natur durch und in dem Freund kennenlerne."(III, 244) She believes that people become one in conversation: "wenn ich Dir die Wahrheit sage, so muß Deine Seele in meine überfließen, — daß glaub' ich."(III, 246) She says repeatedly that she embraces his soul, or that she nourishes his poetic seed. The intimacy of such a relationship suggests a passion to Arnim: "Dein Geist wohnt in mir und entzündet mich."(II, 238) To comprehend beauty, for Bettina, is to love Goethe. Her own spirit ripens on her love for him. Thus, in a purely ideal sense, Goethe *was* Bettina's lover.

It is in the diary that she most frequently takes note of the fact that Goethe does not reciprocate her feelings. There is a sense of onesidedness which she attempts to correct in *Briefwechsel*. On at least one occasion she attempts to imagine that Goethe must love her, because he loves nature and she is part of nature (IV, 16f.). But such a compliment to his great soul does not prevent her later from bemoaning his lack of attentions. In *Briefwechsel* she draws some consolation no doubt from a tale Goethe's mother had related about herself. When she was seventeen Charles VII had visited Frankfurt. She had instantly fallen in love with his blue eyes. Nor was this attraction a passing infatuation. She felt this love, so chimerical from the beginning, to be much more than a fleeting intuition of affinity. At the end of her life, when she tells Bettina the tale, she is still moved by the memory of him. Bettina has her say: "Soll man da nicht wunderliche Glossen machen, wenn man erleben muß, daß eine Leidenschaft, die gleich im Entstehen war, alles Wirkliche überdauert und sich in einem Herzen behauptet, dem längst solche Ansprüche als Narrheit verpönt sind?" (III,519f.) However Bettina does not ridicule the idea. In *Briefwechsel* Goethe's mother goes on to admonish her to continue loving her son, since she understands him. Their spiritual bond appears to have the blessing of his departed mother.

If Bettina is, in a sense, a child of Goethe, like any child she does not merely replicate her parentage. She brings something of her own. In part, her contribution is a love for music, and she takes credit for bringing Goethe and Beethoven together. In part, it is also her belief in political action. This emerges most clearly when Bettina urges Goethe to take a stand for Tiroleans fighting for their independence. When Goethe does not, Arnim suggests that he has retreated into the realm of his novels (at that time he was writing *Wahlverwandtschaften*) in order to escape reality. Ultimately generous in her interpretation of Goethe, however, she finds Goethe resigned to what seems inevitable and attempting to give the times what they lack, a sense of their ideality (incidently the kind of ideality she, too, would like to give the times). Gently, she chastizes Goethe, but she also permits her own difference to emerge in a favorable light. Anecdotes in the diary bear repeated witness to her own active concern for the poor, endangered, or handicapped.

She saves the life of a French (enemy) soldier, admires the personal strength of a blind man, and details the lives of people living in the ruins of medieval castles. Her ability to recognize shared human qualities in enemies, handicapped, and poor manifests itself in her later political activities. She worked on behalf of those imprisoned for political reasons, those impoverished through no fault of their own, and those struck down with cholera. As in the other volumes the evolution of her character and the defining of it thus occurs with and against her correspondent. For all her admiration of Goethe she does not dissolve her personality in his.

Bettina von Arnim turns the poetry of concepts over in her mind, latching on to multiple associations, considering them from different perspectives, and allowing their tones to resonate. Thus the notion of her childhood in Goethe is enriched by the one of her creating him. The reciprocity of friendship is developed a little differently here. The concept of her elective affinity with Goethe is not merely passive: "indem wir die sinnliche Schönheit gewahr werden, erzeugt sich in uns ein geistig Ebenbild, eine himmlische Verklärung dessen was wir sinnlich lieben (...)." (IV, 63) Insofar as she loves him, then, she creates his spiritual image in her soul and constructs him in her—as she also describes in *Die Günderode*. When she dreams him she imagines him: "O, lerne schöne Träume durch mein Geschwätz, die Dich beflügeln und mit Dir den kühlen Äther durchschiffen. Wie herrlich schreitest Du auf diesen Traumteppichen! Wie wühlst Du Dich durch die tausendfältigen Schleier der Phantasie und wirst immer klarer und deutlicher, Du selber (...)." (IV, 86). Writing *Briefwechsel* means creating his image on paper. Insofar as she presents here her image of Goethe she gives birth to him through her imagination.

She gives birth to him in yet another sense as well. She both sketched plans for a standing monument to Goethe (described in her last letters to him) and created a literary one in *Briefwechsel*. Hence the subtitle, "Seinem Monument." In each case she has drawn Goethe. But she also created a living monument to Goethe in herself. Goethe may have nourished her ideal self, but insofar as she nourished his image in her (and she actively pursued it) his eternal spirit continued to live in her. Indeed the inscription on her sketch for a real monument was: "Dieses Fleisch ist Geist geworden." She had written Goethe's mother that she was Günderode's heir after she died and she claimed Goethe had told her Schiller continued to live in him. In the same sense she was a living monument to his spirit. Without her, and others like her, he would die.

The three volumes of correspondence do not illustrate the workings of cause and effect in Bettina von Arnim's life. The only events in these works are interactions with people and, as has been noted, the gradual definition of self which resulted from struggling with these personalities and others portrayed in each of them. If it is possible to imagine any overriding conception at all, perhaps it is best done in light of an essay she wrote and included in the *Günderode* volume. There she wrote: "Es sind aber drei Dinge, aus diesen entspringt der Mensch, nicht nur ein Teil oder eine Erscheinung von ihm, sondern er selber mit allen Erscheinungen in ihm, und sein Same und Keim liegt in diesen drei Dingen, die aber sind die Elemente aus welchen die ganze erschaffne Natur sich in den Menschen wieder bildet."(II, 46f.) Dimly one might discern the influence of her three correspondents in shaping these elements of her person. The first of these is faith, which she describes as the appearance of God in time, certainty and eternity. If divinity in time is understood in a pantheistic sense to mean the divinity residing in the soul of every human being then Clemens, as she herself admitted, was the first to encourage her faith in the divinity, integrity of her "self." "Der Glaube aber ist Befestigung, und ohne diesen schwebt alles und gewinnt keine Gestalt und verliegt in tausend Auswegen." (II, 46f.) Only with faith in the truth of one's own judgement can perceptions or thoughts, scripts or discourses, acquire any shape. With such a faith one rejects anything one had not first worked through for oneself and from oneself. This is why it firms the self. One begins to take responsibility.

The second element in her trinity is thought. Bettina wrote Goethe's mother that Caroline von Günderode was the one who taught her to read with understanding (III,88). Certainly it was through her that she received and read many books about history and philosophy, studies not included in her training at the convent or usual for girls at all. With thought though one must take care: "der Gedanke geht in sich selbst zugrund', weil er ein Kleid der Zeitlichkeit ist, nicht aber eine sichtbare Erscheinung des ewigen Geistes" (II,48). Evil is when the temporal and mundane consume the eternally divine. Her abstractions become somewhat more pointed when she writes, "Böse also der Selbstmord, denn der Willen der Vernichtung ist zeitlich." (II,48) Arnim had tried to wean Günderode away from her philosophers' manipulations of logic and the aridity of historical fact; she had encouraged her to let her soul soar on its wings, to fly and hover.

Goethe did not require such encouragement and one might associate him with the third element of personality, spirit (*Geist*): "das Gute aber ist wenn das ewige Himmlische das Irdische in sich umwandelt und alles zu Gott in ihm macht." (II,48) Good is also when the divinity in oneself takes the mundane and transforms it into the divine. Arnim does not reject reason, she would only put it in its place: "Die Vernunft aber ist eine Säule, festgepflanzt in dem Menschen, sie ist aber ewig und also eine Stütze des Himmels...und in ihrer Wurzel liegt die Zeit, aber wie sich aus dem Stoff der Geist entwickelt, so entwickelt sich die Ewigkeit, und der Mensch wird durch die Vernunft aus einem Irdischen ein Himmlisches." (II,48) It is the infusion of reality with the divine which she learns, in part no doubt, from Goethe. Her poetic language invests reality and nature with its ideality.

Although the interactions with these sides of her character were in fact sequential in her biography, such a portrait of the definiton of self is not innately linear. Viewing these works as autobiography requires viewing them as a secular form of spiritual autobiography, the autobiography of the soul. In this sense they have a great deal in common with early pietist confession which restricted themselves to the life of the soul to the exclusion of worldly affairs, or at least in opposition to mundanity. Somewhat surprisingly, the "Briefromane" of this radical "atheist" bear witness to the persistence of the pietist tradition. They are perhaps not as traditionally religious as Elise von der Recke's autobiography, but they are more intrinsically spiritual. Arnim's style contains baroque elements of pietist mysticism: paradoxes, contrasts, the juxtaposition of worldly and spiritual lives. Certainly metaphors in *Briefwechsel* associate Goethe with Christ or God and her passion for him mystically unites her with him in spirit.

Ultimately it becomes necessary to place these unusual volumes in the context of Bettina von Arnim's life, to read them backwards, as it were, in the order in which they were written. One might suppose, for instance, that Arnim would not have been inclined to expose Goethe's determined distance in response to her so passionate courtship, for despite her repeated (real) efforts to renew their correspondence Goethe remained totally silent. While she gained access to his home on visits to Weimar in 1824 and 1826, after 1811 her letters to him, full of adoration, remained unanswered. Rather than ending the correspondence in 1811, however, when it actually ended, she included her own later letters (reworked) and invented some warm ones from Goethe. Just these efforts however may have been important to her own biography. Although it was a coincidence that her falling out with Christiane Goethe occured in the same year as her marriage (in fact during the first trip she made with her new husband, the poet Achim von Arnim), it may well have remained a symbolic incident for her.

Bettina seems genuinely to have loved Achim, but it was not an untroubled marriage. Rather than single-mindedly pursuing his literary career, as

Bettina urged him to do, he chose to live on and to work his rural estate only barely managing to remain solvent. They were not wealthy, and although he had originally refused to use any of the money she brought into the marriage, when subsidies for the War of Liberation from the French made their financial situation truly precarious, she insisted he accept her funds. In addition to bearing seven children Bettina immersed herself in the necessities of managing an estate — although it was surely as foreign to her as it had been to Elise von der Recke. This child of fantasy learned to cook and weave. She raised the children (nursing them herself), cared for all the sick on the estate, managed servants and craftspeople. By 1817 she wrote, in a real letter, that she felt she had been destined only to endure burdens.[33] That summer she attempted to reestablish contact with Goethe. Her letter remained unanswered. Gradually the Arnims began living in Berlin during the winters and gradually Bettina remained ther over the summer as well. From their estate in 1823 she wrote her sister, "Das Schreiben vergeht einem hier, wo den ganzen Tag, das ganze Jahr, das ganze liebe lange Leben nichts vorfällt, weswegen man ein Bein oder einen Arm aufheben möchte. Ich kenne kein Geschäft, was den Kopf mehr angreift als gar nichts tun und nichts erfahren. . . Ach, wie sind meine Ansprüche an das Leben gesunken, und je weniger ich fordere, je mehr dingt es mir ab, und es wird mir nichts gewähren, als daß ich mich zum Schelm oder Lump mache."[34] Her poetic flights of fantasy, when they transcended the mundanity of her existence, all fell to earth again. The following year she again attempted to renew the correspondence with Goethe and finally visited him with her sketches for his standing monument. However all her attempts to renew their correspondence failed. Judging by comments to Malla Montgomery-Silfverstolpe, she may have begun working on *Briefwechsel* as early as the winter of 1825/26.[35] It seems likely that she began with the diary as an actual diary addressed to Goethe, but left it unsent as a consequence of his continued silence. Ranke seems to believe that he heard these ideas from her in 1826/27.[36] However, if it began as a diary, she also reworked it for publication, for she apparently included the content from some letters she had written to Prince Pückler-Muskau from 1832/34.[37]

The constellation of these events permits the interpretation that the period of her marriage represented an intellectual and spiritual wasteland for her, that she lost contact with her fantasy, her poetic self, her childlike self during this period and found herself becoming absorbed totally by daily chores. Attempts to be heard by Goethe were likely attempts to reestablish contact with that lost part of herself and truly had less to do with Goethe than with her own situation. She seems to have written herself out of it by using Goethe as muse.

Although Bettina von Arnim had compiled and reworked her letters to three poets, she never did that for her correspondence with the poet closest to her, her husband. As autobiography, therefore, these three volumes omit precisely that period in her life which was the focus of the epistolary autobiographies of Isabella von Wallenrodt, Elisa von der Recke, and Elisabeth Stägemann: her marriage. Despite the difference, however, Arnim's reconstruction of her early life informs us just as clearly that a certain side of her character was repressed by her marriage, just as Recke and Stägemann reveal that their marriages radically interrupted the development of their personalities. Bettina von Arnim skirts the issue, but it is there by implication and obvious in its omission. Her concentration on her ideality in all three works would not have allowed her to treat the daily and real struggles with her husband. She could not refashion it as a poetic life. After all, she and Günderode had made it a principle of their "Schwebereligion" that no matter what befell them they would accept it, and the world would not know they were unhappy.

If they are read in the order in which they were written, these volumes reveal a different kind of development of her character. With each volume she emerges more clearly as a personality. Not only is her mystical union with Goethe not repeated in the succeeding volumes, she becomes more and more distinct, and her writing acquires more precision and clarity. After reading *Clemens Brentanos Frühlingskranz* in 1844, Adolf Stahr, the later husband of Fanny Lewald, wrote Karl August Varnhagen von Ense that he found it "das reinste, einfach-schönste und lieblichste von allem was sie geschaffen hat."[38] Certainly her sense of her political self is the most concrete of all volumes. She stands her ground on the issues of befriending and helping Jews, gardners, on refusing traditional restrictions for women and on not desiring to become like a man (like Madame de Gachet). Indeed she articulates "feminist" thought most clearly in this volume. One critic finds that this volume represents a turning point in her career.[39] When it appeared *Frühlingskranz*, although a rather innocent work, was confiscated by the police. It had two strikes against it, neither related to the work itself. One was that it followed immediately on the heels of *Dies Buch gehört dem König*, an assault on the lack of justice under the reign of the King. Dedicated to that King, appealing to his justice, and warning him of the subterfuge of his advisors, it had not been possible to confiscate that work. In some measure, the action taken against *Frühlingskranz* was revenge for *Dies Buch* gehört dem König. The other strike against it was that Bettina von Arnim had had it published by a radical publisher, Egbert Bauer, brother of the better known radical Bruno Bauer. Eventually the King himself intervened to have the book cleared for sale, but the experience no doubt confirmed the political direction in which Arnim was already headed. In the turbulent forties, before the Revolution of 1848 would shake the foundations of government, Arnim was beginning to agitate for the release of political prisoners and to collect material for her *Armenbuch*. However, if she realizes concrete political concerns in the forties, that side of her character had in fact found expression as early as 1835 in *Briefwechsel* when she distinguished herself from Goethe on political grounds.

It is as though she strove to become more fully that which she had claimed to be in her earlier epistolary works, to realize her ideal image of herself. What Bettina von Arnim really was, how she really experienced events in her life is, on the basis of material currently available to us, virtually impossible to reconstruct. She appears to have wanted to realize the ideal image she understood to be her true self and to build herself/nurture herself on descriptions of that ideal. In so doing, she did more consciously what others did unconsciously. Most of the autobiographies under discussion have suggested the elaboration of an ideal self in both their structure and content. They were ideal constructions which did not necessarily accord with reality, although some of the authors attempted to live those ideals. Bettina von Arnim recognized the role of the ideal and of the fantasy, of that which escapes the grasp of positivists, as an essential part of her "self."

In the tradition of romantic philosophy, which validated subjective experience as real experience, both Rahel Varnhagen and Bettina von Arnim proposed that the epistolary form was better suited than connected narrative to convey that more profound level of existence, the non-rational realm of fears and desires. Both incorporated dreams, desires, and fantasies into the letters they acutally sent — or some of them. In reworking her correspondence, however, Bettina von Arnim elaborated even more fully that subjective side of herself. Both would have claimed that that non-rational experience, which allegedly surfaced in unguarded moments, was more authentic than ordered concrete reality. At the same time, Bettina von Arnim already worked very hard and very consciously to lend the editions of her correspondence an appearance of naturalness and spontaneity her real letters did not possess. Even the authentic letters of Rahel Varnhagen bear evidence of polishing. The air of spontaneity in the letters of both women was quite as deliberate as the image they projected of themselves. Sophie Mereau had asserted that letters and novels offered the same degree of imagined reality. Around 1800 however both genres also pretended to be closer to reality than more traditional, Aristotelian forms. The two perspectives are not contradictory. From the latter the proximity of women's autobiography both to novels and to letters seems absolutely consistent. From the former, *all* representations of reality are recognized as fictions.

Both the concept of a de-centered self and its structural manifestations pose profound challenges to "classical" autobiography, in which one, harmoniously organized individual ideally emerges. Rather than the model of an individual relinquishing or subordinating facets of the self to a dominant image or position, the de-centered self presents the model of a multifaceted self in which doing or achieving in one area is less important than becoming in general. Despite Arnim's graphic representation of Fichte's philosophy making her ill, she was clearly influenced not only by him, but by Friedrich Schleiermacher as well. As such, this concept cannot be claimed as innately or naturally female. Neither Rahel Varnhagen nor Bettina von Anim would have accepted this model for women only. Each encouraged her male friends to recognize and nurture all sides of their personalities as well. Nevertheless women (and others on the margins of society) surely had a greater stake than successful males in proposing this model for recognizing and validating aspects of their personalities not recognized or validated in the dominant culture.

Understood historically, the epistolary form *is* peculiarly female. Had Baldinger, Engel, or Wallenrodt elected that form, its implied validation of subjective and personal experience might have permitted them to portray their lives with less pretense. For they were in fact more personal and private. The absence of public events or public importance in any of the epistolary autobiographies was an accurate representation of most women's lives. Recke, Stägemann, and Arnim also chose models, "fictions," for their lives, but the discrepancy between the model and real experience diminished. Baldinger, Engel, and Wallenrodt attempted to accomodate their life stories to formal models based on male lives and/or dominant morality. The contradictions which emerged as a result were inevitably antagonistic. Baldinger doubted her intellect, although she aimed to trace its development. Engels actual "amazonian" experiences were minimal and the historical adventures on which she focused belonged to her husband, not herself. Wallenrodt mouthed social platitudes, although she had lived and felt their opposites. None of these women achieved the recognition in male culture which she coveted.

Recke, describing her socially marginal behavior, turned mainly to women for her personal and formal models. The character of "Sophie Sternheim" and the person of Madame Guyon appear to be models with which she could live and which explained her aspirations and/or experience to some extent. She may have identified with the situation described in Goethe's *Werther*, but neither "Werther" nor "Lotte" was a behavioral model for her. Similarly, Stägemann's literary and even formal emulation of *Werther* did not imply a personal one. Her less violent conclusion insists on the integration of qualities associated with women and her ideal appears modeled after real situations and figures of contemporary intellectual salons. Stägemann, affirming the validity of subjective (here also, aesthetic) experience, does not feel the need to kill that person to which that impractical side corresponds. Arnim's personal models may be more elusive or complexly organized, deriving from her brother, from Günderode, from Goethe in the main, but also from others like Goethe's mother, Madame de Gachet, her grandmother la Roche, or the Jew Ephraim. Both her models and her difference from them are consciously formed. As exemplified in the interchange with Madame de Gachet, she refused to accept wholly a masculine model, but she clearly incorporates aspects of Goethe and her brother as well as other male philosophers. Regardless of gender she takes individuals as models for aspects of her own nature. Out of this she attempts to create her own, personal model. Ultimately, the distinction between model and author becomes shadowy at best. Women's struggle for an appropriate autobiographical form is complicated by their struggle for an appropriate biographical model. Clearly none of these women is totally free of male tradition, but some are better able to modify that tradition for their own needs that others.

The autobiographies of Elise von der Recke and Elisabeth Stägemann did not appear until after Bettina von Arnim had published at least two of her volumes of correspondence. And Rahel Varnhagen's letters, written in part at the same time as Recke's and Stägemann's autobiographies and Arnim's original correspondence, appeared before any of these works. There is therefore no possibility of actual influence of one work on any of the others. The context in which the epistolary variation of autobiographical form arose is unique. Stägemann, Varnhagen, and Arnim all lived in Berlin and held salons there. All surely knew each other, although even in the case of Varnhagen and Arnim the relationships were not the friendliest. Certainly it is possible that the Berliners at least may have discussed the form of epistolary autobiography, but of that there is no evidence. It is far more likely that the concurrence of dominant intellectual movements—

romanticism, the unrest and increasing literary awareness of women, and the persistent association of women's lives with letters — produced this form. If the period in which these concepts were formulated was not conducive to the publication of such works, women's voicing of their differences with dominant culture became possible in the period after 1835 and around 1848, when they no longer hesitated to use the pen in their own defense and when they began to open the doors of their homes and walk out into the realm of public history.[40] They may not have ventured far, but even those few steps created a new situation for them as autobiographers.

4

THE CASES OF ASTON AND MEYSENBUG

When Louise Aston and Malwida von Meysenbug wrote their autobiographies the correspondences of Rahel Varnhagen and Bettina von Arnim had been published, but neither was read as autobiography. Elisabeth Stägemann's autobiography appeared in the same year as Louise Aston's, but was not especially well known. Epistolary novels had long since ceased to hold sway in the literary market; and the dominance of the objective narrator in fiction, clearly signaled by Blanckenburg as early as 1774, remained unchallenged in autobiography. Epistolary narration was anachronistic by the time these two activists joined the generally progressive movement for liberal democratic rights in Germany and worked for women's political and personal freedom. Although the radical students in Berlin, to whom Bettina von Arnim had dedicated *Die Günderode*, honored her with a torchlight parade, her epistolary campaigns against the King of Prussia inaugurated no tradition.

Rahel Varnhagen and Bettina von Arnim had believed that connected narrative prevented presentation of their desires and fantasies. They took advantage of the flexibility and openness the epistolary form afforded to formulate and demonstrate their visions of more humane social structures. In the 1830s and 1840s younger women sought to realize the dreams these romantic women had helped them acknowledge. Louise Aston, Malwida von Meysenbug, Fanny Lewald, and Marie von Ebner-Eschenbach belonged to a generation which witnessed and participated in the growing activity and respectability of women in public and literary fields. They were outspoken, liberal authors, who in some ways turned their backs on that radical female literary tradition and took up what must have seemed to be more efficacious forms of political and/or literary protest.

As women engaged in public discourse they were in a position to write a different kind of autobiography. Their personal, philosophical, and formal models included famous men, but also the powerful women they had read as girls. Although they witnessed the frequently condescending recognition accorded writers like Varnhagen and Arnim, as well as de Staël and Sand, these women admired their forebears. They began to take themselves

121

seriously as authors and no longer presented themselves as idle dilletantes. They admitted writing because they so desired and because there were issues they longed to discuss.

In their youth these four women had been excited by Germany's progressive intellectual movement, but they aged quickly during the sharp repression following the failure of the Revolution of 1848. Thus, like those women who had placed their trust in friendship, these younger ones would also see their dearest hopes dashed. Varnhagen and Arnim had persisted in voicing unacknowledged desires and painting unconventional fantasies. But women like Aston and Meysenbug, who had pitched their whole lives into the fray, would speak from still different experience.

When Louise Aston published her autobiographical fragment in 1847 it was in the heated spirit of the times, the spirit of political *and* aesthetic rebellion; and the public figure against whom she most decidedly took a stand was none other than Goethe. In part it was a necessary position. After *Dichtung und Wahrheit* it became more difficult to write autobiography in Germany. Appearing in 1811, 1812, 1814, and 1833, its four volumes quickly began to dominate and rigidify thinking about autobiographical forms. The authority it embodied became a disideratum for autobiographers, a model to which few could aspire. Still, while autobiographers in the latter part of the century could not easily avoid its influence, the nature of that influence depended greatly on the particular interpretation of *Dichtung und Wahrheit*.

In many ways Bettina von Arnim had already manifested the overwhelming influence of Goethe. Certainly she had borrowed specific anecdotes from that work for her own. But more importantly she likely owed Goethe her emphasis on becoming; her image of human growth and its parallels with plant life; her awareness of her indebtedness to others and to the times; and her reluctance to impose human logic or abstract rules on nature — inner or outer, social or organic. Or at least she owed him the seeds for these thoughts, which, as she had phrased it, she then cultivated in her own way. In the real correspondence Goethe himself had acknowledged vague outlines of his thinking in her letters.

Ultimately Arnim's monument to Goethe, which was to have been the testimony to his living spirit, failed to prevail. Whether a true one or a false one, it was not the generous and passionate image Arnim had painted for posterity that was to become the dominant image of Goethe. His refusal to involve himself directly in political movements had caused Bettina von Arnim some disappointment. In this she was not alone. But while she finally came to terms with the fact that he would not be what she wanted him to be, other radicals bitterly lambasted that socially aloof stance in Germany's leading intellect. They perceived him retreating into the abstract realms of aesthetics, looking down from Olympus while real people became injured in real circumstances.

Louise Aston (1814-1871) belonged to this camp. When she introduced her autobiography, she asserted: "Das Leben ist fragmentarisch; die Kunst soll ein Ganzes schaffen!"[1] She meant to reject Goethe's aestheticized autobiography and its harmonious form in favor of a fragmentary one more appropriate to modern life — "our life". Unlike Goethe's her text would not display the cool and distanced beauty of a classically and harmoniously created work of art, its noble simplicity and quiet grandeur, but would evince the full turmoil of modern life, indeed, would participate in it. The value she placed on her own work was its proximity to and involvement in life. She rejected those unnamed "others" who sought to make themselves immortal along with their aesthetically pleasing works of art. Her self-portrait would belong to this earth.

The full title of Goethe's autobiography had been *Aus meinem Leben. Dichtung und Wahrheit*. Aston pointedly entitled hers *Aus dem Leben einer Frau*. With that she not only suggested the difference between the life Goethe had been able to live and that of a woman, she also indicated her intention to portray herself as typical. This contrasted radically with classicists like Goethe, who sought to represent the uniqueness of their individual lives. Throughout her short preface, Aston refers to "us" and "we", clearly identifying herself with a larger movement and not as an isolated rebel or a representative giant. If she was representative it was because she felt herself to be typical, not the more profound expression of the age. She intended to present a case history.

To a limited degree Aston's claims to speak for a movement were justified. She was not merely a literary rebel. She was one of the more colorful and notorious participants in the Revolution of 1848. Born the daughter of Johann Gottfried Hoche, advisor to the church consistory and senior minister in Gröningen bei Halberstadt, she twice married (1835, 1841) and twice divorced (1838, 1844) the English manufacturer Samuel Aston, who resided in Magdeburg. She first drew the attention of the Berlin public in the mid-1840s when she arrived in the capital desirous of beginning a literary career. Convinced by her own experience of the necessity for women's emancipation and inspired by the model of George Sand, Aston shocked middle-class Berlin (probably even more susceptible to scandal than mid-nineteenth-century Paris) by wearing trousers, smoking cigars, and apparently living up to her belief in free love. More specifically she provoked the suspicions of the Prussian authorities by forming a club for emancipated women and by associating with progressive intellectuals like Rudolf von Gottschall (1823-1909), Bruno and Edgar Bauer (1809-1882 and 1820-1886), and Max Stirner (1806-1856).[2] She was also close to the radical circle around Gottfried Kinkel (1815-1882) in Bonn. In 1846, on grounds of subversive and immoral behavior, the Prussian authorities refused to renew her residency permit.[3] In 1848 she was also forced to leave Hamburg.

During the Revolution of 1848 Aston accompanied the volunteers (*Freischärler*) as nurse on their campaign in support of the rebellion in Schleswig-Holstein and edited the short-lived radical newspaper, *Der Freischärler für Kunst und soziales Leben*. The initial successes of the Revolution made it possible for her to return briefly to Berlin. However after its failure reactionary forces once again expelled her, and she moved to the free city of Bremen. When Bremen too came under the sway of the reaction in 1850 she married Dr. Eduard Meier, who was then relieved of his hospital post as a result of this liaison.[4] Thereafter she followed him on assignments in Russia, the Ukraine, Hungary, and Germany, but she wrote nothing further. She died in Allgäu in 1871. In addition to *Aus dem Leben einer Frau* (1847), Aston published two volumes of poetry, two novels, and an account of her difficulties with the Berlin authorities — all between 1846 and 1850. Thus, her literary activity was confined to the years between her second marriage to Aston and her marriage to Eduard Meier.

Aus dem Leben einer Frau opens *in media res* on a scene in a country parsonage during a lively discussion in which the daughter, Johanna, refuses to marry the wealthy, unattractive Oburn, because she has given her love and her promise to another man. Although the father stresses the importance of money in building a good marriage, Johanna still refuses to marry Oburn. In a fit of rage the father curses his daughter and suffers an attack which leaves him speechless. Driven to remorse Johanna quickly consents to marry Oburn that very evening. After the unhappy wedding the bride swears that, if she is to enter grand society, she will live strictly according to its rules.

Four years later Johanna visits the health resort of Carlsbad without her husband. Although all the aristocrats are enchanted with the lovely, fresh, and mysterious Madame Oburn, and although she has discovered true love in her feelings for the doctor of Prince C., she renounces all liaisons. She so despises the hypocrisy and superficiality of grand society that she will have no secrets which could put her at its mercy and jeopardize her pure and virtuous reputation. However Prince C. himself tries everything to compromise her and she is just barely able to maintain her virtue. Fortunately she has also found an admirer and protector in the politically liberal Baron Stein, and when the Prince breaks into Madame Oburn's room, Baron Stein appears on the spot to save her. Forcing the Prince out the window, he takes some of her jewels to make the attack look like common robbery. As Madame Oburn leaves Carlsbad the following morning, she learns that Baron Stein has been killed in a duel with the Prince. No one suspects the cause.

Several months later her husband's factory is on the verge of collapse. Johanna sells her jewels, dismisses a few servants, and begins to do the housework herself — thinking to aid the wageless workers. The outraged Oburn can do little to stop her, and the narrator discourses on the need for thoroughgoing reform and redistribution of wealth. Coincidently, the Prince is visiting the area on the very morning Oburn discovers his bank has collapsed. Unable to obtain credit quickly elsewhere, he turns to the Prince who agrees to loan him money in return for a night with Madame Oburn. Oburn's attempt to persuade Johanna arouses her indignation. She packs and leaves immediately for the capital, preserving the honor of the institution of marriage as well as her own. The narrator again denounces the venality of women and the idea that they are the chattel of men.

Despite the highly romantic and novelistic aspects of the work there is enough material to justify Aston's allusions to Goethe's autobiography and her references to her own work as a "confession". The phonetic similarity of names strongly suggests the intended identification: Aston/Oburn and Louise/Johanna. "Johanna" is also the female version of Aston's real father's first name, "Johann". Details of the fathers' lives correspond, as do the facts of her marriage. Aston had married her husband twice and the narrator concludes the autobiography, "Das war der erste Abschnitt ihrer Ehe."(154) The character of the protagonist is much as Rudolf Gottschall described it: "kokett, aber prüde dabei".[5] Indeed Gottschall also believed the Karlsbad events in *Aus dem Leben aus einer Frau* (among the most unbelievable in the text) to be at least partially true. Both Prince Metternich and a Prussian Prince appear to have been attracted to Louise Aston. Moreover the text was originally to have been titled *Louise, eine Ehestandsgeschichte.*[6] The final title retained Aston's assertions for the representative character of the text, but thinly disguised the autobiographical nature of it. The reasons may well have been those traditional to women revealing scandal in their own lives.

Like Recke's and Stägemann's autobiographies (and unlike *Dichtung und Wahrheit*) *Aus dem Leben einer Frau* is fragmentary. It only renders that period in her life and those issues which concerned her marriage to Aston. Like Recke's autobiography there is less a sense of growth than one of the defense of her integrity, the story about her protection of her "self". The fragmentary narration contributes to the sense readers have of following stations in her ordeal, rather than the evolution of a position. *Aus dem Leben einer Frau* begins *in media res*. We enter in the middle of the critical discussion about her marriage. Just as readers never learn about her childhood, they never learn what happens after Madame Oburn leaves for Berlin. Indeed the work itself consists of nothing but fragmentary scenes: the country parsonage; Carlsbad four years later; Oburn's estate months later. No attempt is made to supply information about the gaps or suggest biographical sources for her defense.

Unlike Recke's narration of her marital difficulties this is a polemical autobiography. Aston does not recoil from publicly exposing her husband's callous treatment of her. She uses her experience to provide a model, to make a more general statement about marriage, to assert the rights of women to dignity and respect, and their right to take their fates into their own hands. Speaking not only out of indignation for herself, but for others as well may have provided impetus to the courage to break the convention of not publicly criticizing her husband — though of course she disguised the names. Through her pointed polemic Aston intends to influence life, to improve conditions for others. She aims to participate in life rather than observe it from Olympian heights.

The assertion of her rights belongs precisely to her assault on German classicism. The rejection of classicism is an unexplained process of emancipation for Aston. Before she leaves her father's house Johanna vows, "Geld war mein Verhängniß — es soll mein Verhängniß bleiben, dem ich willig folge; gegen das ich länger nicht thöricht kämpfe!"(27) Like Schiller's "Maria Stuart", who willingly accepted an unjust death penalty to atone for a crime for which she was not tried, Johanna steps across the threshold of the parsonage with a changed stature that reflects the nobility of her voluntary resignation to the demands of social forces beyond her control. Her altered countenance and farewell recall "Maria Stuart's" dignified acceptance of her fate. In contrast to this scene of classical freedom through submission, the scene in which she parts from Oburn finds her telling him, "Oburn. . . Du willst mich verkaufen, wie eine Sache, wie Dein Eigenthum verhandeln!. . . Du hast kein Recht, über meine Liebe und meine Ehre zu bestim-

men. Ich werde die heiligsten Rechte meines Herzens und Lebens wahren —
dies ist die Stelle, die uns auf ewig trennen muß."(150f.) Johanna no longer
submits to her monetary fate with a mercantilist husband.

As she rides off in her carriage at the end of *Aus dem Leben einer Frau*,
her situation contrasts with the conclusion of *Dichtung und Wahrheit* which
has Goethe riding off in a carriage to a court position in Weimar. In a self-
quote from his play *Egmont* Goethe had claimed only to be holding the
reigns of a chariot running wild, almost beyond his control. Aston however had decided to leave for Berlin entirely on her own accord, breaking
with society. She rides in a carriage fully on her own responsibility with a
destination of her own choosing. To whatever limited degree she struggles
to take fate in her own hands and revolts against society and classicism.

Aston's rejection of classicism had been part of the progressive literary
movement prior to the Revolution of 1848. Young authors of the 1830s and
1840s criticized Goethe's aesthetic aloofness and sought to redefine literature as part of life, developing new journalistic and poetic forms. Authors
of these movements were familiar with the letters of Varnhagen and Arnim, begrudgingly admired the strength, poetry, and spontaneity of their
epistolary styles, and may have schooled their own sharp witted style on
theirs. However Aston's autobiography shows no traces of having been affected by either of these German women, despite what one could take as
a stated similarity of views. Aston had wanted to portray life in its inhar-
monious reality and desired that art not be separated from life; like Varnhagen and Arnim Aston had believed that passion should conquer social
norms; and she conceived of herself as part of a larger whole, albeit an elu-
sively defined "we".

Aston had wanted to describe life and not to paint fantasies or idylls. She
rejected certain literary and social scripts in favor of the reality of her experience. She alludes to eighteenth-century pastoral idylls in which the poet's
imagination populates the landscape with ideal characters, "welche in dem
Comfort eines stillen, in sich befriedigten Lebens das letzte Ziel und den
ganzen Werth der Existenz zu erschöpfen wähnen."(1f.) Such poets have
translated the broad prose of life into longwinded verse. These works are
"Utopien einer spiessbürgerlichen Phantasie"(2). Like the family dining scene
on Meta's wall in Stägemann's autobiography *and* Bettina von Arnim's rejection of Clemens' portrait of her eventual marriage, this genre painting
is one of which Aston wants no part. Such paintings have lost their audience,
Aston maintains, because life invades even the most removed parsonage.
She knows all too well, perhaps even from Goethe's own criticism of his

Sesenheim experience, of the dangers of projecting one's fantasies of life onto real experience. In this view she unconsciously repeats Varnhagen's and Arnim's desire not to impose such prescribed images onto anything living. But she does not have at her command the means to carry this through.

Indeed despite her criticism of the confusion of poetry with reality, Aston herself has clearly succumbed to the temptation and accepted an already modeled existence for herself. When the narrator reveals that Johanna's reading material in Carlsbad was George Sand's *Indiana* it becomes difficult not to view her own characterizations as modeled on those of Sand's novel. Readers of the autobiography can discern Sand's heroine in a loveless marriage to an inconsiderate, brutish man; her passionate love for another man; the platonic friendship with an honorable man who deeply respects her and tries to aid her; the adventure of narrow escapes and barely kept virtue; the contrast between the natural settings and "grand society". Through it all Johanna's character is every bit that of the "femme incomprise", a type originating with *Indiana*. Instead of rejecting literary models altogether, Aston seems to have replaced one with another, and her imitation of George Sand in Berlin indicates that she even imagined herself living a life already modeled by someone else. This is hardly unusual. Elise von der Recke so admired "Sophie von Sternheim" and Madame Guyon that they influenced the actual living of her life. The scripts Aston chose are merely more obvious, and at least she chose one fashioned by a vigorous woman and not one of idyllic domestic bliss. While one must admit that, like her perception of her adversary Goethe, she too had imposed fiction on reality, it is important to stress that she consciously chose the model and at some discomfort to herself.

The particular model she (and Sand) appropriated, however, merits some comment. Noteworthy is the way in which she appropriates male accoutrements: pants, cigars, sexual freedom at the same time that she adopts a less complex and rich idea of her own identity. Bettina von Arnim had rejected not only the image of women found in bourgeois genre paintings as a model for her future, but also the image projected by the strongly male-identified Madame de Gachet. Absent are Rahel Varnhagen's and Bettina von Arnim's radically non-gendered images of themselves and powerful alternative visions of the nature of the individual in general, of a different way of Being. The model Aston chose challenged stereotypical views about women, but not the very concept of gender itself or the dominant view about human beings as they exist in the world.

As for allowing passion to reign: Aston's narrator concludes the work:

"Sie rettete ihr besseres Selbst vor der brutalen Gewalt, die sich in hundert Gestalten gegen sie verschwor! *Sie rettete die Heiligkeit der Ehe, indem sie dieselbe zerriß*! Doch noch hatte sie eine Gewalt nicht besiegt, die mächtiger war, als Rang und Geld und Freiheit; die im Hintergrund zurückgedrängt, bald siegsgewiß auftrat, ein Gestirn, das ihr Leben beherrschte von jetzt ab, eine Kraft, welche in ureigener, angestammter Heiligkeit die Formen zerbrach, die das Gesetz und die Sitte der Menschen geheiligt — *die Liebe.*"(154f.) Passion, for Aston as for Arnim or Varnhagen, can and will conquer conventional social forms. Yet in her autobiography Aston defines passion more narrowly than had those romantic authors. For her it is restricted to love between men and women and is no longer a passion for all of nature's creation.

Similarly the "we" which Aston announces is clearly not the sense of unity emerging from the epistolary forms of Varnhagen and Arnim. It is a very partisan, exclusionary "we", where in the letters one aimed not to exclude any possibility, attempted to open any dialogue. Generosity and magnanimity coincided with individual struggle. Varnhagen and Arnim insisted on their great, unrepeatable characters, but knew the extent to which they relied on others. They grew through others and found themselves mirrored in others, but they never identified fully with any other or collapsed their selves into others. They held firm a powerful and dynamic balance between awareness of their uniqueness and difference from any other and awareness of their merging with others and Being in the whole.

Although a brave and spirited activist, Aston lacks the radical content — and form — of her stated desires. It is as if by entering the public sphere in a fashion which would receive recognition (viz male), she were required to relinquish the beauty and richness of a truly alternative vision. For she clearly was recognized as a threat in a harder, more tangible way than Arnim. Is that the only way to be heard?

The Reaction eventually silenced Aston. And it ultimately rid Germany of the presence of another outspoken radical, Malwida von Meysenbug (1816-1903). She was descended from the lower aristocracy. Her father held the position of personal advisor and court marshall to the Hessian Elector, Wilhelm I, and later of Private Cabinet Advisor and Minister of State for Wilhelm II of Hessen. Due to the political disturbances of 1830 and the voluntary exile of the Elector, her family led a somewhat nomadic life when she was a child. As a young woman she rejected one proposal of marraige and experienced an unhappy love affair.

When she met Theodor Althaus her life changed; but she would never marry. He was six years her junior and an idealistic young theologian, freshly inspired by the democratic circles around Gottfried Kinkel in Bonn and by Bettina von Arnim and the Young Hegelians in Berlin. His ideals opened her eyes to social injustice and they maintained a close friendship based on common ideals. After he became interested in another woman and after the defeat of the Revolution, Meysenbug could endure the narrow confines of her family no longer and left them for a women's school (*Frauenhochschule*) in Hamburg. That school had been founded by Johanna and Karl Fröbel and Emilie Wüstenfeld as an extension of Johann Ronge's *Freie Gemeinde*, in turn modeled to some extent on the early pietist communities. There she felt, finally, that she was doing useful work and that she was valued for it.

Reactionary forces soon closed the school however, and due to Meysenbug's correspondence with revolutionaries she was threatened with imprisonment if she did not leave the country. She departed for England the very night following her interogation. In London she met the Russian revolutionary, Alexander Herzen (1812-1870). Growing steadily fonder of his daughters, she soon volunteered to move in and order the motherless household for no salary, but on the condition that either was free to break the arrangement if any dissatisfaction arose. When differences of opinion on pedagogical matters eventually dissolved this agreement, Meysenbug began supporting herself by translations and journalistic work for the Italian revolutionary, Giusseppe Mazzini (1805-1872).

After his departure for Italy, she moved to Paris where she was introduced to Richard Wagner (1813-1883) and became both a friend of the family's and one of his earliest admirers. Although residing in Paris, she was soon asked by Herzen to accept full charge of his daughter Olga's education. Meysenbug would spend the rest of her life devoted to this girl and cultivating her friendships. Her European connections continued to expand, and she remained now in Italy. These would include friendships with Friedrich Nietzsche (1844-1900) and Romain Rolland (1866-1944). Her autobiography was well known and admired throughout Europe and, unless one wishes to count her relationships with famous men, it remains her single claim to fame.

The three-volume *Memoiren einer Idealistin* was not planned as a whole. The first volume, covering her life from her birth until her exile in 1852, was originally published in Switzerland in 1869 as *Memoires d'une idealiste*. She translated this work and added two more volumes for the first German edition, published anonymously, in 1876. The second volume treats her life in England from 1852 to 1856, when she left Alexander Herzen's household, and the third her wanderings in England and France from 1856 until 1861, when she formally took charge of the education of Olga Herzen. The publication history and its own structure make it necessary to discuss this autobiography as two separate works: one published in 1869 and a second in 1876, the first volume and the second two.

In the first volume her exile from Germany appears as the logical consequence of the "holy restlessness" which she claims to have cultivated since childhood. In numerous confrontations, especially with her family, her strength of character triumphed over social convention. It was that insistence on her right to an individuality which led her family to ostracize her. And when she left them for the school where she could exercise her beliefs, the German state similarly ostracized her. The pursuit of her own needs and interests had driven this woman into political exile — unmarried and alone.

By devoting scant attention to the first fourteen years of her life, Meysenbug suggests that her real life began at fourteen with her incipient individualization and her awakening faculty of reason. In 1830 she sided with her father against the demonstrators outside their house. For Meysenbug this marked the end of her childhood, since this was the first time she was called upon to take sides in a real conflict. Her gaze began to encompass "wider horizons" as she gradually left her dolls for the newspapers. But she had already experienced her "zweite Taufe. . .durch die Hand der Revolution".[7] From the beginning then Meysenbug establishes a political context for her life.

As she progresses through various phases she emphasizes her passion for truth, her continual questioning, and her continual dissatisfaction with conventional answers. First she seeks them in religion, but when questions of dualism lead her to doubt the dogma, she is ready immediately to pass on to another possible solution. One of her friends is not. The contrast serves to characterize the young Meysenbug as a restless, striving soul, and it hardly seems unreasonable that the author of *Faust* rescues her from the agonies of dualism. In Eckermann's conversations with Goethe she finds the sentence: "Jedes tüchtige Streben wendet sich von innen heraus auf die Welt."(I,78) This points her in the right direction. Soon she gives up going to church at all and writes instead her own thoughts on Sunday mornings. Thus she gradually evolves her own "philosophical system". Not unlike Recke's diaries, Stägemann's imagined dialogues with herself, and Varnhagen's and Arnim's letters, these notebooks provide a vehicle by which Meysenbug comes to know and define herself.

After her experiment with religion she seeks answers in "grand society". When her aspirations to nobility of soul cannot be supported midst the petty vanities of grand society, she seeks her ideal in art (I,109f). As she describes it, her perpetual restlessness and unrelenting search for the truth mark her for a lonely existence. On a journey through the Alps, surrounded by high, isolated peaks covered with snow and ice, Meysenbug pledges herself to that lonely pursuit of the ideal. Those who dedicate themselves to it commit themselves to "ein Kampf ohne Aufhören, ein Weg, der durch einsame, unfruchtbare Wüste führt."(I,155) She asks herself, "Willst du die Aufgabe annehmen und nicht zurückschrecken vor den Opfern, die sie dir auferlegt? Willst du bereit sein, dein Herz, das den ewig brennenden Durst nach Schönheit hat, unaufhörlich kreuzigen zu sehen?" (I,155) And she answers with a resounding, yes.

Only a little later she explains that it is not enough to feel and to love, above all one must think and act. Every effort that is lost for the great task of life becomes a sin against the law of progress (I,159). As her belief in the process of history becomes more concrete so too do her actions. She turns her energies to caring for the sick and poor. Her association with Theodor Althaus, democratic publicist, as well as her own democratic views cause her alienation from the society in which she was formerly welcomed. Asking why her former friends should avoid her, she realizes that she has transgressed against social convention. "Es fiel. . .ein Schleier von meinen Augen. Ich sah ein, daß ich nicht mehr das sanfte, nachgiebige Geschöpf war, das, um Niemand zu verletzen sich Allem unterwarf, und den Weg, den Allen gingen, mit ihnen ging aus Gehorsam und Gefälligkeit. Ich fühlte, daß ich eine Individualität wurde, mit Überzeugungen und mit der Energie, sie zu bekennen. Ich begriff nun, daß dies mein Verbrechen sei."(I,183f.) The more she allows her own interests and talents to evolve, the more she alienates herself from society. When she supports the democrats in the Revolution, even her family ostracizes her. The teleological process of her individualization leads away from acceptable social norms, not toward social integration.

Hamburg brings her into closer contact with the working classes, and she begins to admire their moral strength. Growing respect for them accompanies a new understanding of their situation. Her strong sense of morality gives way to sympathy for prostitutes when she realizes that the state makes a profit on their degradation by taxing them (I,319f.). Although her immediate reaction is to work for reform by urging education for women, she soon reasons that this will not get at the base of the problem and that more radical political and economic reforms are necessary. At the very end of the first volume she comes to the materialist view of history that the ideal is only to be achieved through economic revolution. When the state threatens to imprison her then, her self-imposed exile is but the physical consequence of her own internal alienation and refusal to submit to irrational authority.

In her eyes she had experienced bitter battles "durch welche [sie] hindurch gegangen war, weil [sie] [ihr] Leben [ihren] Überzeugungen gemäß hatte gestalten wollen".(I,364) These were part of the rigorous process of building her individuality: "Das grosse Recht der Individualität an Alles, was ihr nötig ist, um Alles zu werden, was sie werden kann, stellte ich mir in bitterer Klarheit dar. Daß es erlaubt sei, jede Autorität zu brechen, um dieses Recht zu erobern, war mir keinem Zweifel mehr unterworfen."(I, 234)

In her letters Rahel Varnhagen had also presented herself as a determined, restless, and lonely individual. As a girl, Meysenbug notes she felt a strong sense of identification with Varnhagen's struggles. In that feeling of affinity, she seems also to have incorporated aspects of Varnhagen's self-image into her own. The restlessness and the struggle to uphold her individuality in the face of social demands brought with it for each woman — and it was unusual for women — the image of herself as an exceptional individual. Varnhagen had written that she was as unique as the greatest phenomenon of this earth. Like her Meysenbug felt her significance because she had struggled honestly with history and social convention. Both emphasized their independent intellect and unrelenting effort to confront reality and the truth. They boldly announced their disdain for dissimulation, circumspection, and compliance. For Varnhagen as for Meysenbug, this had led to isolation and conflict. Each had taken the difficult step of moving out of her family's house, and Meysenbug denounced "die dreifache Tyrannei des Dogmas, der Convention und der Familie"(I,268f)

In all likelihood it was the tyranny of the family which had convinced both of the importance of freely chosen relationships. As Rahel had insisted that Karl August love her without constraint or coercion on her part, so Meysenbug (also the older woman) attempted not to place chains on Althaus. Disappointment in love became for each "das errungene Gut des durchschmerzten Herzens".[8] Each woman ostensibly avoided placing demands on the free choice of the man she loved. Ultimately Meysenbug's theme of the loss of Althaus would rival that of her own restlessness in the structuring of her autobiography.

Despite the obvious power of Varnhagen's personality on Meysenbug's self image, some profound differences emerge. Unlike her romantic fore bear and more like her contemporary Louise Aston, Meysenbug asserts a "self" which evolves in isolation from all other people. Both Varnhagen and Arnim had known and stressed their dependence on others if they were to evolve as individuals at all. While cultivating their unique qualities, they simultaneously announced they shared parts of themselves, owed parts of their souls to others. They balanced their individualism and their sense of loneliness with the religion of friendship and the ideology of community. Meysenbug's radically individualistic stance requires *she* illustrate her evolution as absolutely self-generated. In part at least Nietzsche's admiration for this autobiography was surely inspired by the image of Meysenbug defining and shaping her life on the basis of exclusively personal drives and in a condition of social exile.[9]

Perhaps it is precisely because she insists so vehemently on her independence that one becomes sceptical finally. Meysenbug rarely discusses the evolution of any of her preoccupations — not her interest in religion, in grand society, in art, or in politics. Reading the autobiography closely one finds suspicious gaps in the narration at those moments when a relationship we know is important for Meysenbug is rather obviously not credited with encouraging a certain direction in her thinking.

The case of Theodor Althaus is the most striking. Another critic, observing Meysenbug's tendency to attribute the origins of all her ideas to herself alone, studied the recollections of Elisabeth Althaus, Theodor's sister, and concluded that he was very much the origin of Meysenbug's interest in social and political matters.[10] In fact there is almost no indication of political concerns on her part until after she hears Althaus preach. Then, having recorded her enthusiasm in vague terms, she dryly comments that he returned immediately to the university. Suddenly Meysenbug feels her life has been too comtemplative and that she must act. Painting seems egotistic compared to acts of true Christianity, so she founds a local society for charity. She also plans a corresponding society for women, since they are generally isolated within the domestic realm. There can be little doubt that Althaus was the vehicle through which Meysenbug was placed in touch with democratic circles in Berlin and Bonn, but a reader of these pages would not know it. Dora Wegele has asserted that Meysenbug influenced Althaus as well, and while she may well have and might have made something of this in her memoirs, both debts are camoflaged.

If her intellectual debt to Althaus is obscured by her desire to secure a particular self-image, her stance ultimately also produces a rather ungenerous attitude toward women. When Varnhagen wrote her letters at the turn of the eighteenth and nineteenth centuries there had been much discussion but nothing strongly resembling a movement for women in Germany. This was not the case in the 1840s when women like Aston specifically demanded women's rights. Novelists like Fanny Lewald took up the pen for the cause. Louise Otto-Peters (1819-1895) and Franziska Anneke (1817-1884) also made known their opinions on women's issues in radical newspapers they themselves edited, in Otto-Peter's case a newspaper aimed particularly at women![1] They raised issues about marriage and education which Meysenbug illustrates with examples from her own life, but she does not relate her ideas to any movement.

And yet Meysenbug counts herself among the pioneers of this movement. In the introduction she specifically looks forward to the day when women's emancipation shall have been completed, when women shall have "dasselbe Recht zur Entfaltung aller Fähigkeiten"(v.f.) as men and shall be equal with them before the law. In just such a spirit she conceived the idea of recording her life as "ein bescheidenes Gemälde einer jener Existenzen unbekannter Pfadfinder, welche den Weg noch im Schatten der Nacht suchen, wenn eine neue Idee sich Bahn brechen will in der Geschichte, und die, wenn sie nicht als Narren oder Verbrecher behandelt werden, für Idealisten gelten, welche Unmögliches verlangen".(v.f.) As someone in advance of the world historical idea, in Hegel's terms she becomes its instrument. It is an audacious and powerful self-image.

Memoiren einer Idealistin fails to mention the burgeoning movement for women's rights as an having any influence on Meysenbug. References to reading Rahel Varnhagen, Bettina von Arnim, and George Sand never indicate just how important these women almost surely were for her own self-image. More immediately even, there was her own mother whom she described as an "unabhängige Natur".(I,11) Nowhere does the mature Meysenbug suggest that she may in some way have been a model, and yet it was she who introduced her to the ideas of Arnim and Varnhagen; who, like Varnhagen, opened her house to artists when they were still considered socially unacceptable; and who maintained an independent and highly moral position on issues of court intrigues — on occasion in oppostion to her husband and his interests (I,23). Indeed from this scant evidence alone one might deduce that Meysenbug strongly resembled her independently minded mother. But she is intent on portraying her independence as self-generated.

The authenticity of Meysenbug's reports of her "holy restlessness" are not in question; nor is the pain imposed by a process of "engendered" socialization. What is of interest here is the degree to which she felt it necessary to assert that radical individuality. When she wrote her autobiography she occupied no socially recognized position, was engaged in no socially recognized profession, and was living in exile, a single woman. Althaus was dead, the movements of which she had been a part dissolved, and their participants dispersed on at least two continents. Like Rahel Varnhagen she claimed that it was her personal struggle with history which entitled her to a place in it. Was the radical assertion of her great individuality compensation for her loss and legitimation for her autobiography? We cannot know with certainty.

What we can observe with more certainty is a conflict of themes in her autobiography with ramifications for its structure. The extreme assertion of her lonely restlessness would have produced — and for a time did produce — a structure of spiraling progress. When Meysenbug records the earlier phases through which she passed (religion, society, art, politics) something of this structure becomes clear. But, writing in 1852 from exile, she had another script in her head as well; and it is one which counteracts that progressive motion, suggesting that no life is ever that independent.

The countervailing theme of course is her attachment to Althaus. In accordance with her model of development, she might have portrayed this relationship as one of the many stages through which she passed as her individuality struggled to find itself, however her relation to Althaus is represented as "die höchste Blüte des Lebens" and "die schönste und edelste Blüte meines Wesens".(I, 168, 181) When he finds another woman suicidal thoughts convey the importance she had placed on this one relationship and she refers to the end of the Spring of her life (I,200).

The issue is more difficult than personal attachment. Althaus is virtually identified with her political aspirations: "Liebe und Freiheit (waren)...eins in mir geworden".(I,199) When, through her association with Althaus, she becomes ostracized from society, she realizes that her social sin was to have become "eine Individualität...mit Überzeugungen und mit der Energie, sie zu verteidigen".(I, 184) Althaus and the ideas to which he surely introduced her are not merely another stage in her progression. They are a turning point for her. Through the ideas of freedom and political action which he transmits to her she begins to recognize herself as empowered. Structurally, however, the dramatic quality of their relationship is not emphasized in order to allow for her concept of continual progress, rather than climactic moments. The dramatic story of suddenly seeing things in perspective is a different plot.

Although the causal relationship remains unexplored, the theme of becoming an individual is intimately and dramatically bound to her association with Althaus. Although separated during most of 1848, she feels especially close to him through the events which would realize their common ideals. Toward the end of 1848, as the Revolution falters, so too does her relationship with Althaus. In her account, the end of 1848 saw her mourning both the end of the Revolution and the loss of Althaus (I, 272). Both of these events occupy a central position in the autobiography and represent a distinct turning point. Hereafter her fate and her aspirations no longer seem to rest in her own hands.

At the school in Hamburg the esteem her peers accord her allows her to feel she is "eine Individualität...die eine gewisse Macht ausübte"(I, 313) and she tells herself she is happy again. But when Althaus arrives looking for a job after his incarceration, her fragile happiness is shattered. She notices then her unhealed wounds and, when he leaves, the hole in her life that cannot be filled (I, 328f.). Meysenbug still oriented her life around Althaus and has difficulty maintaining her image of independence. The coincidence of his death (as a result of prison illnesses) and the closing of the school once again compounds her sense of loss and creates further parallels for her narration: "In Theodors Grab, in das der Hochschule, begrub auch ich die Jugend, die Hoffnung, den freudigen Mut, der noch an eine Erfüllung in der Zukunft glaubt."(I, 367) Meysenbug's hope was so bound up with Althaus and the school that the focus on her self-generating individuality was overpowered by their loss. All that remains for her to relate in this volume is the process by which she was exiled.

If Meysenbug's primary image of herself is as an independent woman, then the undercutting theme of her dependence on Althaus represents a conflict between a self image she wanted to uphold and genuine sentiment. Like Varnhagen she suffers personally because her struggle with history is decided against her. Unlike Varnhagen however she sought a structure for her life story that would not easily permit the full range and complexity of her personal and historical situation to be told without appearing somewhat contradictory. In a sense the form she chose belied a portion of her experience, dependence on others—not just Althaus.

Unwittingly Meysenbug reveals what must have been the fate of many in that generation. The awareness of sharing an unjust fate and the rewards of working with others for common goals had, some might say paradoxically, given individuals a firmer sense of themselves as individuals and produced a dynamic literature. As the political reaction imprisoned, killed, exiled, or silenced its opponents it broke the channels of communication between them. Louise Aston had ceased writing. Franziska Anneke had exiled herself to the United States, where she became active in the American women's movement. Louise Otto-Peters' newspaper was closed by the authorities. The isolation which followed produced that sense of suffering alone, which Fanny Lewald would acknowledge to be the one feeling which had most oppressed her in her youth, before reading Rahel Varnhagen's letters. With the channels of communication and the identification with others, the Reaction undoubtedly also broke the strong sense of selfhood cultivated by many individuals during the struggles of the 1830s and 1840s. The resulting isolation was ultimately far more real and far more terrifying than Meysenbug's determined lonely quest for an ideal.

Meysenbug's own development after leaving Germany only amplifies some of these issues. In the preface to her memoirs she states that the idea for her autobiography had been conceived while sitting on the white cliffs of England (I,v). In the second volume, she mentions writing something during her summer vacation in Broadstairs near the white cliffs in 1852 (II, 164). If she began the first volume of her memoirs during that second summer in England, they were almost surely not finished immediately. They were not published until 1869 and in 1865 she wrote a friend that she was writing something she had long carried around with her, something "das einen wichtigen Grundgedanken hat . . . [der] ganz selbständig in meiner Seele erwuchs, schon ehe ich Schopenhauer kannte"![12] Already in the first volume of the memoirs, Schopenhauer's pessimistic tone and desire for cosmic identity become antidotes for her continual disappointments. This accounts for what are major discontinuities in that text. Indeed ranking the first volume of Meysenbug's memoirs with Rousseau's *Confessions*, the novelist Bertold Auerbach (1812-1882) had also noted that much appeared to have been written later![13] Resignation and pessimistic idealism characterize the end of the first volume.

After learning of Althaus' attraction to the other woman, Meysenbug writes, "Sterben wollen, um nicht mehr zu leiden, ist Schwäche. Lebe für das Ideal, um das Gute in dir und um dich her zu vollbringen!"(I,245) By negating one's own pain, that devotion to an ideal can become not self-sacrifice, but a means to self-preservation, so she believes. The ideal can become "der Schild der eigenen persönlichen Würde, die unversehrt aus jedem Kampf hervorgeht und über alle Enttäuschungen siegt".(I, 245) In that letter of 1865 Meysenbug applauds "[den Menschen], der das Leben hingibt für eine Idee, den Willen zu Leben ertötet, um des Objektiven, des Erkannten willen".[14] In the memoirs the tendency toward self-abnegation, if not masochism, in love surfaces when Meysenbug remains faithful to Althaus even after he has deserted her. Since she feels she could never love that way again and that to marry without that love would be a desecration of the institution, she relinquishes any thought of marriage for herself (I, 293).

One wonders how the same person who wrote about the necessity of economic freedom for women could have written the following passage: "wie könnte der Mann je in vollem Umfang seine Pflicht im öffentlichen Leben tun, wenn ihm daheim am häuslichen Herd nicht ein großes Frauenherz zu Seite stünde, das Teil nimmt an seinen grossen Interessen und bereit ist, ihnen, wenn es sein muß, sogar das persönliche Glück zu opfern?"(I, 246) Meysenbug, staunch individualist and spokeswoman for women's rights, extols the virtues of martyrdom. By 1869 she had willingly dispossessed herself of the individualism for which she had struggled before 1852.

In striking juxtaposition to her Alpine pledge to hold her inner restlessness sacred and to wander lonely paths, Meysenbug places a scene at a mountain monastery on a moonlit night: "Nach und nach versanken die flüchtigen Erscheinungen der Welt, die Phantasmagorien der Einbildungskraft, die ungestümen Wünsche, wie in einem fernen Traum...Lange, lange schaute ich hinaus und hatte das Gefühl meiner Individualität verloren."(I, 158) She would negate the individuality she proudly observed emerging in her association with Theodor Althaus. For Schopenhauer the sense of losing individuality, accompanied by a heightened awareness of cosmic identity, allowed one to acknowledge one's limitations and gave peace of mind. Meysenbug studies astronomy, "und indem mir das Universum erschloß, kam es mir zuweilen vor, als seien die ephemeren Leiden dieser Erden nicht der vielen Tränen wert, die um sie fliessen."(I,276f.) Could the horrible pain of that disappointment of 1852 only be shed by negating her earlier ideals and denying pain altogether? Malwida von Meysenbug quashes her individuality, virtually anaesthetizes herself by dissolving herself in the universe.

She is a woman of extremes. Where before she powerfully asserted her self-generating individuality, later she dissolves herself into the cosmos. Varnhagen and Arnim had held the two poles of the dialectic together. Malwida von Meysenbug withdraws from the world of political action into the world of art and pessimism after bitter public and personal defeats. Varnhagen and Arnim had held politics and aesthetics to be inseparable. Aston had too. For Meysenbug art becomes a refuge from politics, even though in the person of Richard Wagner it becomes politically charged again.

The radical change in Meysenbug's philosophy which occured during as many as the 17 years in which she may have been writing the first volume produced a more consistently pessimistic perspective in the second and third volumes of her autobiography, written between 1873 and 1875. The foreword to the first complete German edition of 1876 suggests the clear shift of emphasis. She is no longer the self-acclaimed world historical person, the pioneer of historical movements. Her life, she reports, has lost contact with public events in these years, but the personalities with whom she had become involved merited "Kränze der Erinnerung"(II, viiif.) While she does not totally subsume her own fate and development to the description of refugees from the continental revolutions of 1848 (Herzen, Mazzini, the Kinkels, Louis Blanc, and others) she devotes at least as much energy to them and to travelogue-like descriptions of life in England as to her own life.

The structure of these two volumes underscores the movement toward Schopenhauer's pessimism. The household arrangement with Herzen, her social experiment with a "Familie der freien Wahl"(II, 246) had given her full happiness again. Leaving it at the end of volume two represents a second painful nadir for Meysenbug and parallels the end of the first volume as a kind of exile. The third volume opens, as the second had, to find her isolated and uprooted and gives her cause to emphasize the repetitions of isolation in her life, the perpetual return. Toward the end of the third volume she observed: "Treue war ein Grundzug meines Wesens, und doch trieb der seltsame Widerspruch, in dem sich das Geschick zuweilen zu gefallen scheint, gerade mich immer von Neuem hinaus, von dem sicheren Boden, den ich mir erworben, in das Schwankende, Ungewisse neuer Verhältnisse, riß mein Herz mit Schmerzen los von dem, was es in fester Liebe umfaßt hatte, gönnte dem Geiste nicht in fester Conzentration an einem Werke seine Kraft zu üben und die Freude des Erfolgs zu erleben."(III,223) The terms of her self image have changed. She has selected a different model for her life story. Her innate "holy restlessness" has been replaced by an innate desire to stand constant on one ground. It is no longer internal forces which drive her, but external ones.

Repeatedly her efforts to satisfy her needs and exercize her talents are frustrated by circumstance. No sense of a meaningful teleological development is possible for her in that political and personal situation. Not only does she now emphasize, with Schopenhauer's conviction, the constancy of her character and the perpetual repetitions in her life, she is glad to transcend this vale of tears. According to Meysenbug, those who realize the inevitable hopelessness of their situation are drawn to the ultimate ideal, Nirvana: "die selige Einheit des Grundes der Dinge, in der alle Unruhe der Erscheinung aufgehört hat, und die Vollendung, die wir im dunklen Drang gesucht...(.)"(III, 223f.) She is glad now to transcend her "holy restlessness" and would withdraw from the struggles of the world, which she considers pointless, to rejoin the unity of all things. The final volume closes in an apotheosis of philosophical resignation and self-negation. She glories in becoming a mother by choice when she accepts Olga Herzen as her ward; she becomes friends with Wagner during the premier of *Tannhäuser*; and she reads Schopenhauer. These events "gab [ihrem] Leben den Abschluß".(III,274)

This new stance is necessarily reflected in her political views. On her arrival in England she had still been a materialist. She saw a lack of schools and commented that those who consider public education impractical should recall that the public had formerly supported extravagant courts (II, 62). She observed that the lavishly beautiful country estates were maintained at the expense of the workers (II,41). The misery of a proletarian quarter disgusted and repelled her, but she excused the curses of its inhabitants, the miserable creatures, since she had not come to rescue them (II, 133f). Herzen's descriptions of Russian villages convinced her that property should be held in common and that those who work should reap the benefits (II, 194).

After leaving Herzen's household, she became disillusioned with this class. As she organized for Mazzini among the working class, she beccame ever more cynical, surprised to find normal human traits of envy, jealousy, egoism, personal ambition. (British industrialism had also produced a class very different from the craftspeople she had met in Hamburg.) Gradually her opinion of the working class reversed itself: "Zu *einem* Schluß führten mich jedoch diese Gedanken, nämlich daß wir, die wir alle Idole und falschen Götter zertrümmert zu haben meinten, uns freiwillig einen neuen Götzen geschaffen hatten: das Volk nämlich"(III, 75)

Naturally her views on women are similarly affected. Although she still harbored a belief in the right of women to the full development of their natural capabilities, she now presumed to define "[den] wesentliche[n] Bestandteil der weiblichen Natur".(II, 276) That was motherhood, biological or chosen. Instead of arguing that each woman should enjoy the right to define and evolve her nature for herself, Meysenbug was now persuaded of "die heilige Aufgabe der Mutter im höchsten ethischen Sinn"(III, 270). Love she defined as a dependency relationship in which the soul became a slave

(III, 264) and on this account she had expressed some reservation in accepting Olga Herzen as ward. However she finally accepted, for: "[das] Mütterliche in mir wallte hoch auf (. . .)."(III, 264) And she decided to dedicate the last powers of her life to this task accomplishing it according to the highest principle of "des mütterlichen Berufs" (III, 271). Meysenbug became a mother without husband or giving birth. Motherhood (in which the soul also becomes a slave) was a profession, she now maintained, in which she fulfilled her life's plan: "Daß die Frau um ihrer heiligsten Überzeugung willen einen ebensotreuen Kampf kämpfen und um ihretwillen die Schranken der Verhältnisse durchbrechen könne, so gut wie der Mann — diese meine Ansicht war nicht Theorie geblieben, ich hatte sie verwirklicht. Daß ferner die Frau auf sich selbst ruhen und sich eine ehrenhafte Stellung durch Arbeit und achtunggebietendes Leben erwerben könne — auch hierin war ich meinen ausgesprochenen Grundsätzen treu geblieben."(III, 271) As far as it goes this statement cannot be disputed. And yet the specific meaning of these principles had changed considerably.

In the final volume of her autobiography Meysenbug rejected her earlier materialism, identifying it with positivism and describing it as a transitional phase (III, 158). She also connected this philosophy with illusions of personal happiness and the possibility of realizing her ideals for humanity. Several passages in *Memoiren*, however, make the origin of her philosophical turn more concrete. In discussing her former hopes for happiness as having been sought "im Lande der Täuschung, im Bereiche des Wahns"(III, 164). In a statement of extreme pessimism Meysenbug asserts: "Das Herz, an das wir uns gebettet, erkaltet und die Lippen, die uns Worte der Liebe geflüstert oder erhabene Weisheit verkündet, verstummen; die Menschheit, der wir wohltun wollten, zuckt die Achseln und kreuzigt oder verspottet uns."(III, 164) Meysenbug's interaction with public history caused her to lose hope in political movements as catalysts of her ideal. Rejecting concrete political action she fled, again like Schopenhauer, to the ethereal comfort of music (especially Wagner's): "Mir ging die Überzeugung auf, daß, wie sich einst in Italien nach dem Scheitern des lombardischen Städtebunds und mit ihm des Scheiterns eines geträumten, vollendeten Zustands politischer Freiheit die ideale Sehnsucht in das Reich der Kunst flüchtete und dort eine verklärte Menschheit, ein ideales Vaterland schuf, so auch jedes, selbst das größte Erreichen auf politischem Gebiet nur mangelhaft bleiben würde, wie Alles, was der Beschränkung des Irdischen anheimfällt."(III,296) Unlike Arnim, Meysenbug includes political action in her category of mundanities. The only realm which cannot betray her ideals, which cannot betray *her*, is art. The ideality for which Arnim had also striven becomes, for Meysenbug in the wake of personal and political defeat, the absolutely abstract realm. Even motherhood has become relatively abstract. Unlike Arnim who waxed enthusiastic about the particularities of nature, Meysenbug would dissolve reality and the atomization she perceived as part of it: "Der gebundene Gott in uns muß sich befreien aus den Schranken der Individuation, in die ihn der ungestüme Drang zum Leben gebannt hat. Das lange, qualvolle Ringen des Daseins hat keinen andern Sinn, als den der Auferstehung nach dem Kreuzestod, an dem das Ich, das Persönliche stirbt, um als Universelles fortzuleben."(III,284)

If she had seriously wanted to dissolve herself into the universal she would have ended her autobiography. Yet, to justify having written it at all, she concludes that a person who struggles continuously always has moments in life where the general yearning and searching of humanity expresses itself in individual form. Such an experience is of more general interest and should be preserved. She has ceased however to view her life historically, as representing a new idea taking hold in the world. Now far more abstract, she claims her life until 1860 represents the general vision and search of humanity, not the history of women. Her own individuality is subsumed in Olga Herzen, Richard Wagner, and Aruhur Schopenhauer: "unsere persönliche Geschichte hört dann auf".(III,297) By negating her own needs and aspirations, by acquiescing to the disappointment and pain, Meysenbug has by her own standards relinquished her individuality and eliminated the justification for her autobiography.

That she published yet another continuation of her life—*Lebensabend einer Idealistin* (1898)—indicates that she did not totally dissolve her sense of identity. And yet, the form this sequel takes is one which all but obscures its author. She arranged diary-like entries chronologically without reworking them. They are essentially unconnected and without a coherent perspective. Most contain her philosophical musings since the late 1870s, although she also includes a story she wrote. Narrated episodes from her life relate in a removed way anecdotes focused on other people—Nietzsche or Rolland, for instance. There is no indication of evolution or change. Her life remains a "verification". Despite what might be called an open form, these entries bear no resemblance to Bettina von Arnim's passionately engaged epistles in which she wrestled herself in relationships to people and ideas, or in which her caring and sense of responsibility for others led her to extend herself. Meysenbug has resigned from the world, seeking nothing more since she finds nothing more to hope.

144

Viewed together the autobiographies of Aston and Meysenbug reveal a truth about women's lives in this period. It is a partial truth which will be balanced by other autobiographers (like Fanny Lewald), but one which is not therefore invalidated. Both Aston's *Aus dem Leben einer Frau* and the first volume of Meysenbug's *Memoiren* had ended in a voluntary exile of the author. But it was voluntary only insofar as the alternative was none. For Aston the alternative would have been loss of honor and integrity through her husband; but later she would also be banished from two cities by public authorities who considered her a danger to the civil population and cease writing. For Meysenbug it would have been loss of physical freedom through the state; but she had also earlier left her family for a sphere where she would be able to exercise her talents and energies. To preserve their "selves" they were forced to remove themselves, not unlike Recke's experience on a personal plane. Women who claimed a right to integrity and the evolution of personal talents were obliged to leave.

The personal costs of their rebellions were great. Aston had begun her radical autobiography by renouncing the rarified realm of aesthetics in favor of politics and life. Meysenbug ended hers by retreating from the pain of political *and* personal engagement into a realm that could not betray her, aesthetics. Calm descended over Germany. Women like Anneke and Meysenbug were in exile. The *Frauenhochschule* in Hamburg and Louise Otto-Peter's newspaper were closed. Women like Aston ceased writing. Women like Meysenbug resigned themselves to the unity of the cosmos, to individual negation and submersion in the whole. Silence.

Less obvious from a political and biographical point of view, but more significant for the discusssion of women's autobiography is the fact that even before these women had been defeated in the revolution they had been defeated in their heads. Their ability to imagine other ways of thinking and being in the world was restricted to that of the male revolutionary movement. The richness and dynamic balance of vision articulated by Varnhagen and Arnim were gone. This becomes all the more apparent in a woman like Meysenbug, who we know was familiar with their letters. Indeed on some very abstract level one might suppose that the remnants of that desire, emptied of the fullness that might have given some solace, placed them in all the more vulnerable position when the reaction triumphed.

It is inevitable that an autobiographer avail herself, at least to some extent, of some fiction to narrate her life. But there are more open and more closed ways to accomplish this. Even, perhaps especially, Bettina von Arnim created a fiction through which to narrate her life. But Arnim opens form with her efforts to portray — in action and through epistolary styles — her various correspondents. Her correspondents also acquire depth through Arnim's mirroring of them. Through them she gives life to the different facets of herself, instead of killing them. Aston claimed she would not impose fictions on the story of her life; but she clearly modeled her experience after novels of George Sand. Her imposition of the boundaries of fictional characters on those people she knew reduces them to one-sided personalities without adding dimensions to her own self-portrait.

In her title and introduction Aston emphasized what she had in common with others, the experience she shared with women and the goals she shared with the movement of the *Vormärz*. But the *we* she asserts is never brought to life in terms of drawing characters with whom she might demonstrate a *we*. To be sure, Sand's implied influence on her through novels like *Indiana* represents a clear expression of connection and debt to another. But rather than exploring the relationship, the action Aston finally took was to move to Berlin and imitate George Sand's rebellion. Assuming a false and foreign identity, in her autobiography as well as in her action, she collapsed and simplified herself unnecessarily. There is no suggestion of a multifaceted person in such a style, and the creation of that partisan and exclusionary *we* actually inflicts damage on the fullness of its creator.

Meysenbug too suffered from a too limited sense of her identity. Her assertion of and desire for absolute independence was impossible to maintain. Her autobiography shows the strain. Her reaction to it is to lose herself in others, to become their slave. The language recalls that Wallenrodt used to describe herself in her marriage, but the concept is very different. Meysenbug defines love as the slavery of the self. There could scarcely be a greater difference between her view and that of Varnhagen and Arnim, for whom love meant encouraging all facets of an individual to expand and evolve.

Meysenbug's mystic sense of union with the whole, as she articulates it, is the subversion and negation, not the empowering of the self. In her view the self withdraws from active engagement. Arnim and Varnhagen believed the awareness of one's connection to the totality implied expansion of the self into the world and responsibility toward others as the ultimate responsibility toward one's own self. For them there was no necessary polarity between strong, assertive individualism and caring for the growth of all possibilities in others.

Varnhagen's and Arnim's powerful vision of the diffusion of the self while developing that self was one which was lost for these strong, talented, and committed women. Had they possessed it history may not have been changed; but without it they suffered greatly and parts of themselves died. Their autobiographies reveal a radical longing without a radical vision. Even before the revolution failed the reaction had won.

THE CASES OF LEWALD AND EBNER-ESCHENBACH

The Reaction did not silence Fanny Lewald (1811-1889). But this was not because she sympathized with it. Indeed, like Aston's Lewald's first novels, published in the early 1840s, contributed to the radical literary movements preceding the Revolution of 1848. Thereafter she continued her career, without relinquishing a certain liberal tendency, despite the decline of those movements and the defeat of the Revolution. Unlike Aston and Meysenbug she had not had to leave her family in order to uphold her integrity or find an outlet for her talents. She had not assaulted public morality as had Aston. Nor had she the strong ties to political radicals which led to Meysenbug's expatriation. She lacked their fire and intensity, and perhaps also their longing. Her struggle to find legitimation for women professionals led her to invoke, rather than reject, the name of the patriarch of German literature — Goethe.

Fanny Lewald merits a place in German literary history as one of the first women writers to be taken seriously. She was clearly no dilettante wiling away empty hours, for she supported herself as a respected professional long before she married at the age of 43. While the phenomenon of the writing woman had become less and less unusual, Lewald's own high standards and self respect for her work contributed greatly to the acceptance of such women. In full consciousness of her historical role as pioneer for women in a male profession, she wrote her autobiography in her early 50s. That work reveals in content and form the struggles she endured and those she never resolved.

Born to a jewish merchant family in Königsberg the young Lewald (then Markus) attended private school which encouraged her discipline and individuality. By the age of 11 she knew and recited poems and plays of Goethe and Schiller, but she was never permitted to read novels or allowed to go to the theater. School ended for her when she was 14 and Lewald devoted the next 7 years of her life to housework, which she found both demanding and boring. When an adolescent boyfriend died, her parents sought to divert her grief by permitting her to convert and allowing her to accompany her father on a business trip. During her visit with relatives in Breslau she fell in love with her cousin Heinrich Simon. She waited seven years for specific rather than vague encouragement from him, before he finally wrote that he had fallen in love with another woman. Proudly but painfully, she rejected her father's pleas to accept an arranged marriage. Unlike Aston she stood her ground early enough not to be shackled in a marriage of convenience.

Confused about what to do with her life she began to listen to suggestions from her cousin, August Lewald, that she write. Finally asking permission from her father, she told him at the same time that if she were to do it at all she must be allowed to write truthfully about her family and friends. At first unwilling, he finally consented on the condition that she write anonymously. Her first two novels, *Clementine* (1842) (influenced in all likelihood by George Sand) and *Jenny* (1843) reflect that radical literary movement of the 1840s. They speak passionately against social injustice and anti-semitism. Income from these novels permitted her to move to Berlin where renting her own apartment gave her a new sense of freedom. And when she learned that her novel *Jenny* had in fact affected people's thinking on anti-semitism, she began to regard her profession as a kind of mission.

After a trip to Italy in 1845-6, which the sale of her books afforded her, Lewald's style gradually changed. Since her childhood she had known and admired the works of Goethe, but in Italy she had frequented the circles of Ottilie von Goethe (the widow of Goethe's son, August) and Adele Schopenhauer (daughter of Johanna Schopenhauer, who had also known Goethe). There she also met the publicist and classical scholar, Adolf Stahr (1805-1876), with whom she fell in love. Stahr was unhappily married and, although he and Lewald attempted to end their relationship, he ultimately divorced his wife to marry her in 1854. In Italy, in 1845, Stahr read Lewald's novels and expressed his admiration, recommending at the same time that she study Goethe!

Returning to Berlin, Lewald attracted the attention of an even larger reading public in 1847 when her novel *Diogena von Gräfin Iduna H.* appeared. It was a biting satire on the excesses and sentimentalities of the popular salon novels of the Countess Ida von Hahn-Hahn (1805-1880). Like Lewald herself, Hahn-Hahn has been labeled the German George Sand,[2] and Lewald's criticism of her may have been associated with her new interest in classical aesthetics. Clearly Lewald's novel *Wandlungen* (1853) was a conscious attempt to create a classically harmonious work of art.[3] For the rest of her life Lewald's novels elicited modest but respectable praise. Many of them were serialized in bourgeois family journals as was frequently the case with female authors in the nineteenth century. She wrote often for the *Kölnische Zeitung*, and her books were circulated in at least 800 lending libraries throughout Germany.

With an established reputation and after her marriage to Stahr, Lewald published her autobiography, *Meine Lebensgeschichte* (1861/2). A cursory comparison of this work with Aston's and Meysenbug's immediately reveals the gulf separating them in temperament and style. Although all recognize the oppressive situation of women and are generally concerned with their own liberation as well as that of women as a whole, the differences between these autobiographies could scarcely be greater.

In the main that difference may be summarized in terms of historical breadth and biographical length. Aston of course had totally omitted both historical background and childhood experience in her fragmentary work. Meysenbug quickly passed through her childhood, commencing the detailed narration of her life when she was fourteen. She could hardly omit historical phenomena which so affected her life, but those events are not portrayed as necessarily influencing her growth. However Lewald both details her childhood experiences and carefully situates her own life against a very broad description of her times.

Of the autobiographies surveyed so far only Regula Engel's adventuristic travels with Napoleon convey a historical perspective approaching Lewald's. And perhaps only Recke painted such a concrete and detailed portrait of her childhood and youth. It is really the first time that a woman has attempted an autobiography of this scope, one including both private affairs and their public connections. It is a continuous narrative covering childhood as well as young adulthood, with repeated reference to European, but specifically German history. Both of these distinctions may be attributed to the influence of Goethe's *Dichtung und Wahrheit*.

In a diary entry from 1855 Lewald had compared Sand's *Histoire de ma vie* (1854/5) and Goethe's *Dichtung und Wahrheit*. Although her own first novels had been strongly influenced if not by Sand's style, then by her passion and commitment, here she finds the French author's work vastly inferior and formless. Indeed she characterizes it as "capricious".[4] *Dichtung und Wahrheit* however epitomizes the ideally structured and focused autobiography. Like Aston, Lewald wanted to convey the realities of women's lives. Where the former consciously rejected classical aesthetics as inappropriate for this task, however, the latter explicitly adopted Goethe as a model.

In the introduction to *Meine Lebensgeschichte* Lewald invokes Goethe's patronage as a traveler would carry letters of recommendation from esteemed persons on a journey to strange parts.[5] In particular, she cites Goethe's concept of the individual as a product of his time and its spirit. Indeed Goethe becomes the model for the integration of history into her autobiography. The diary entry of 1855 makes this explicit when Lewald explains the ideal manner of integrating historical material: "In [Autobiographien] hat nur das Wichtigkeit, was das Leben des Erzählers gerade zu diesem Leben machte, und Personen und Ereignisse haben für uns keine weitere Bedeutung als durch ihren Einflu auf dies *eine* Leben. — Goethe fühlte dies . . . (.)"[6] Thus while the broadest possible historical perspective is desirable, this should always appear only as it is relevant to the one life under discussion. This is the kind of hierarchical and teleological narration of history which suppresses "extraneous" elements which do not happen to accord with the focus of narration. Goethe's masterful manipulation of this style of narration has led many literary historians to interpret history around 1800 from his perspective and label it "The Age of Goethe". In Lewald's case of course, the startling fact — and challenge — is that a woman attempted to appropriate it for her own life story.

Not inconsequential in this regard is the fact that while Lewald emphasizes Goethe's sensitivity to the role of history in shaping the individual, she neglects the other side of his formula: that the autobiography show the influence of the individual on history.[7] Goethe must have assumed that only those who had would write autobiographies. While Lewald thus intended to stress the uniqueness of the autobiographer rather than her typicality, she does not reiterate Goethe's preference for those autobiographers who have influenced history.

When Lewald commences her autobiography, she begins with the geographical importance and recent history of her home town, Königsberg. Since she had not been permitted to wander about the streets as a young girl however the kind of first-hand exploratory impressions of the city, which Goethe had included of his native Frankfurt, are missing. The fact of her restriction to the family circle — a historical phenomenon which remains unexplored — prevented her from intensely experiencing the more public history to which Goethe referred. From the very beginning then Lewald appears more disconnected from historical events, and her attempt to handle them as Goethe had is undermined by her own real relation to history.

In part stylistic differences ought to be acknowledged. Like many of her contemporaries Lewald's style was more realistic and less symbolic than

Goethe's. The significance of this for the integration of historical phenomena in autobiography can best be illustrated on an example. European history intruded on Königsberg with the occupation of the town by Napoleonic troops in 1812. Lewald remembers a popular French song and a wounded soldier quartered in the house. In order to explain the more complicated issue of her father's support for the Prussians, she expands on general attitudes towards the French and the complicated position of Jews in that war.

But, as if intentionally invoking Goethe's tale of his father's fight with a French officer quartered in his home during the Seven-Years War, Lewald describes a similar occurance in her own home — although at age 2 or 3 she could scarcely have been aware of the particulars. Lewald's description remains an anecdote while Goethe, through his symbolic manner of characterization, portrayed the clash of two ways of life. That clash made visible Goethe's sense of distance from his father, something that would have consequences for his later actions. In Lewald's case the fight remains personal and wanting in larger implications or later consequences. It is realistic when Goethe's had been symbolic. In this way she inevitably shared more with contemporary autobiographers — like George Sand — than with Goethe.

However, Lewald actually fails to establish herself in relation to what is usually assumed to be "the spirit of the times". On one occasion, for instance, she presents several contemporary actresses, describing their acting styles in great detail. She explains that she had included these descriptions to preserve for a later generation what had given her own so much pleasure and edification. (2/2, 65f.) This rather positivistic collection of material is not seen from any particular historical perspective, nor are the acting styles related in any way to her own development. Goethe's descriptions of his youthful attraction to the theater had, of course, carried implications for his later literary and personal development.

Even the description of that literary movement which most influenced her own early novels appears disassociated from her in some measure. Of her experience reading these authors, before she thought of becoming one herself, she wrote: "Wir alle [begrüßten] jene [Werke]...in Pausch und Bogen mit Überraschung und mit großer Zustimmung...(.)"(2/1, 116) Lewald remains undistinguished in that generation of readers and similarly fails to distinguish particular ideas or authors which may have influenced her in particular directions. She also remains a passive recipient of that literature, not suggesting in what areas her own later contribution lay. In similar cases Goethe had detailed the significance of various literary movements for him as well as where he would differ from what had preceded him. Thus, even where she might have alluded to her active role in history and her integration into public history, she appears removed from it.

This does not mean that Lewald does not sense her role in history. It merely implies that history was differently composed for Lewald than it was for Goethe. It was both more immediate and personal and also more closely identified with the role of women. Without her being fully aware of the distinction, her history was not abstracted from the thoughts and deeds of men. Thus the passage displaying her positivistic interest in acting styles concludes one chapter, but the consideration of her real interest in these women opens the next. "Für mich hatte die Begegnung mit den weiblichen Bühnenkünstlerinnen noch eine ganz besondere Bedeutung, weil sie mir das Bild einer Unabhängigkeit und einer persönlichen Bedeutung vorführte, nach denen meine ganze Seele trachtete."(2/2, 67) Implicitly and instinctively Lewald recognized the difference in public and private history. It was not any particular evolution of acting styles which riveted her attention on these women so much as the very existence of independent women. Nor does the theater acquire the philosophical position in her life that it did for Goethe when he also became interested in acting. It is neither a historical nor a philosophical experience. Rather it is a highly charged and particularized vision of what she might become as a person. Because becoming anything at all was so unusual for a woman, that single fact overrode other questions of history. In her autobiography however she subordinates her particular interests to those of a more general history.

That scarcely means that Lewald was not explicitly aware of other women as role models. The earliest women she knew provided only negative examples. An aunt, who was pressured into marrying a man far less educated than herself, represented something Lewald would not do. Her own mother, who had never had the chance to become educated, could not be a model for her. Lewald's Aunt Minna was the first example of an intelligent, independently-minded woman she knew. Even more important was another woman. In the midst of her depression over Heinrich Simon she had had an enlightening experience: "Es kamen mir damals, nach christlichen Begriffen, ein Trost und eine Quelle der Hoffnung recht eigentlich vom Himmel; denn sie wurden mir durch eine Todte, durch Rahel Varnhagen zu Ense zu Theil... (.) [Die Briefe] waren eine Offenbarung und eine Erlösung, die sich für mich durch die hinterlassenen Briefe dieser Frau vollzogen. Was den Menschen am Tiefsten niederwirft, das ist die Vorstellung: ein Besonderes zu erleiden... (.) Was mir auch begegnet war, was ich Unbequemes, Peinliches, Schmerzliches zu ertragen und zu erleiden gehabt hatte, Rahel

Levin hatte das Alles gekannt, hatte das Alles durchgemacht, hatte über Alles mit der innewohnenden Kraft den Sieg davon getragen, und sich endlich an den Platz hinzustellen gewußt, an dem sie gefunden, was sie ersehnt: die Möglichkeit zu genießen und zu leisten nach dem eingebornen Bedürfnis ihrer Natur."(2/2,20f.) In Varnhagen Lewald acknowledges her first public model. Indeed when she moves to Berlin, she seeks out those women with ties to that generation of women which included Henriette Herz, Sara Levy, Bettina von Arnim, Henrietta von Paalzow, and Therese von Bacherach. Although most of these women were dead, Lewald was well aware of their tradition. The history that is finally important to Lewald's development is after all a particular one, it is women's history.

Recognizing her common experience with women meant recognizing that that experience was fundamentally different from that of men. It was impossible that she portray herself as the spirit and embodiment of her entire age, as Goethe had sought to portray himself.[8] No woman could. Her integration of and in history must be perceived as more particular than Goethe claimed his had been, and that imposed particularity lends her work a conscious tendentiousness Goethe had sought to avoid. She writes: "Von meinem ersten kleinen Roman an, bis hin zu diesen gegenwärtigen Geständnissen über mich selbst, habe ich es als meine höchste Aufgabe betrachtet, in meinen Arbeiten dichtend den Zwecken und Tendenzen zu dienen, welche mir Ideal und Religion sind, seit ich zu denken gelernt habe."(3/2, 46) Drawing on her own experience she allows herself to plead for various reforms for women in her autobiography. She hated her piano lessons and argues that this senseless traditon be abandoned. She articulates respect for the intricacies and demands of housework and the difficulty of performing it in earlier days. She notes the transferral of many tasks outside the home and suggests that communal kitchens be established to further free women from household tedium. She had not been permitted to continue in school or train for a profession and pleads repeatedly for educational reform. On the basis of unhappy marriages she has observed, she urges that women not be forced to marry. That institution would only regain its dignity when it was founded on love, not money. Lewald's autobiography evinces a strong awareness of her particular place in history although she is not able to assert that she embodied her history and represented it entirely. Although she exposes the distinctions, she is not conscious of the difference this would mean in the manner of her integration into history as opposed to Goethe's.

Unlike Goethe, for whom autobiographies could not provide examples to others and particularly not his, Lewald wants to provide other women with hope and with a model. She rightly considers herself a path-breaker for other women and with Rahel Varnhagen she believed "in der für sich selbst errungenen Freiheit und Anerkennung auch für Andere ein Stück Freiheit zu gewinnen. Denn das ist das Schöne und das Ermuthigende an der Freiheit, daß Niemand sie für sich allein erkämpft."(3/2, 230) Of autobiographies in general she had written in her introduction: "Der Hinblick auf das arbeitsvolle Ringen Anderer hat mich im Arbeiten und Beharren bestärkt. Bevorzugte, glückliche Lebensläufe haben mir Hoffnung auf Erfolg und Streben nach ähnlicher Befriedigung gegeben; und wenn ich Menschen, die ich über mich zu stellen hatte, mit Migeschicken kämpfen oder gar den sie umgebenden Verhältnissen unterliegen sah, so hat mich das vor thörichten Anforderungen an ein sogenanntes unbedingtes und müheloses Glück behütet, sowohl das Gute, das mir durch meine angeborenen Verhältnissen geworden, als dasjenige, welches mir durch eigene Kraft zu erringen gelungen ist, in jedem Augenblicke doppelt bewußt zu genießen, doppelt dankbar anzuerkennen."(1/1, 5) Despite her intent and in contrast to her explicit model, Lewald does not portray herself as the product of her times or its spirit. Her experience is too specific to enable her to do that in any larger sense. She does succeed in positioning herself in the particular history of women.

However if Lewald intended her autobiography to encourage others to follow her example, she failed. And it is the very structure of *Meine Lebensgeschichte*, once again modeled on her understanding of Goethe, that undermines her tendentious aspirations concerning group identity with women. Lewald had been inspired not only by the historical breadth of *Dichtung und Wahrheit*, but also by the pattern of biographical development which structures that work as well. Like Goethe Lewald began her autobiogaphy with her birth and childhood and concluded just as she was on the verge of a journey which would solidify her career and prove significant to her future development. Goethe's talents had been recognized in the highest circles, and he had just broken his engagement to Lili Schönemann. Lewald had already published two successful novels and overcome her dependence on Heinrich Simon. For both, the end of their autobiographies marked the beginning of more classical influences on their work. As the anticipation of his journey to Weimar for Goethe, so the pause before entering Italy signaled a professional arrival and the joyful acceptance of it. Lewald's youthful depression and awkward domestic situation lay behind her. She was recognized by society and felt free of spirit (3/2, 294). It is an unlikely coincidence that both should conclude their autobiogaphies at such similar points in their lives. Lewald might have chosen the moment when, in the flush of excitement and great release, she sat down to write her first novel. Or when she married Stahr, or when she wrote her autobiography, or any number of points in time. The choice of conclusion was deliberate and clearly modeled on *Dichtung und Wahrheit*.

The biographical pattern which Lewald perceives in and adopts from *Dichtung und Wahrheit* is teleological. In the introduction she stated: "Und was uns im Affekte des Erlebens einst rätselhaft, was uns getrennt und zusammenhanglos, was uns zufällig, unwesentlich oder auch gewaltsam ungerecht erschien, das gestaltet sich vor dem überschauenden Blicke zu einem übersichtlichen Ganzen, in welchem unser Denken und Streben, unser Mißlingen und unsere Erfolge uns nur noch als eben so viele Ursachen und Wirkungen entgegentreten. Jedes Menschenleben trägt eben seinen vernünftigen Zusammenhang in sich."(1/1, 4) From Lewald's all-encompassing perspective on her life at the age of 50, achievements at the end of the autobiography appear as a telos, the innate goal toward which her personality was naturally evolving. This "objective" narration is not so dissimilar to the perspective on their fates attributed by Recke and Guyon to God. Lewald's life appears neither fragmentary nor accidental, but rather as a meaningful whole, necessary and inevitable, the result of a series of causes and effects. Most importantly for her self-portrait then, she opined that she had contained the germs of the logical evolution of her character within her own being from childhood. The end of her autobiogaphy was not only the perspective from which she surveyed her life, but also the innate destiny toward which it was meaningfully progressing. Hence, early in the text Lewald asserts that environment tends less to produce anything new in us than to develop and firm that which was already present in childhood (1/2, 55). Youthful character traits thus convey for her the essence of her life and future development.

It is hard to imagine a theory of autobiography differing more strikingly from that of Varnhagen and Arnim. They sought precisely *not* to obscure what was unjust, inconsequential, illogical, or even mysterious. The power of the objective narrator to select and order according to the principle of cause and effect was one they explicitly rejected. In the age of positivism however it was a principle that Lewald accepted. It is the one that corresponds to Foucault's understanding of "History" rather than "Geneology". But it was one ultimately inappropriate to her life, as contradictions within the autobiography make abundantly clear. Indeed the concept of a consequential order was every bit as distorting as Aston's appropriation of George Sand characters to narrate her life.

Since she had become a writer, the teleological perspective required that she, like Goethe, give early indications of her inclination to write as well as of her strength and independence. Any information pertinent to her writing is included. She records her reading in detail: Goethe, Schiller, Walter Scott, Heinrich Heine, Ludwig Börne, Rahel Varnhagen, George Sand, Ida von Hahn-Hahn, Bertold Auerbach, Spinoza, and Rousseau. Although Lewald confronts us with her diverse literary interests, readers never perceive any particular development in taste. Her interests are presented as cumulative and eclectic.

Omens of her literary talent include her childhood propensity for fantasy (which Lewald interpets as plasticity of imagination), as well as her early cleverness. She remembered a French song from her second year and had an unusual ability to recall sensations and to memorize poetry. She loved reading and reciting and she possessed a natural curiosity about her environment. Numerous early attempts to write are mentioned. Her teacher praised her imaginative essay when she was twelve. At twenty she composed a poem for a party and noted: "Ich erndtete einen großen Beifall, fand lebhafte Bewunderung für meine Verse, und von dem Tage ab stand es unter meinen jungen weiblichen Bekannten eigentlich felsenfest, daß ich eine Dichterin sei."(1/2, 226) When her sister's eye operation forced her to remain in a dark room, Lewald told her stories. Her audience responded enthusiastically, and she had to repeat them. She left a novel unfinished. Her cousin published excerpts from her letters in his journal, *Europa*. Sparse and sporadic though they are each of these episodes would seem to provide evidence of her early interest in writing.

Some autobiographical information is included only as it pertained to her literary career. For instance, she does not characterize any of her siblings, with the exceptions of the younger sister to whom she told stories and the brother whose fate in Russia provided material for her second novel, *Jenny*, and whose indecisiveness formed the basic character trait for a figure in her novel, *Wandlungen*. Clearly, the treatment of material is fairly selective and self-conscious. Like Goethe in his introduction, Lewald noted specifically that she felt obliged to relate the origins of her works for readers who had enjoyed them and "ich habe hauptsächlich den Zusammenhang zwischen meinem Leben und meinem Dichten zu erklären."(3/2, 147)

The teleology of her career parallels the development of her selfhood. Just before entering Italy she writes of herself: "Ich war meiner Freiheit, meiner Verhältnisse, meiner selbst Herr geworden, und damit erst recht fähig,

sie zu benutzen und zu genießen."(3/2, 302) One is not surprised to find
earlier statements about her youthful propensity for independence and her
need for freedom. She describes the two as fundamental to her character:
"Ich weiß nicht, ob in allen Menschen und namentlich in andern Frauen
das Bedürfnis nach Unabhängigkeit und nach persönlicher Freiheit ein so
unabweisliches ist, als in mir. . . (.)"(3/2, 78) She claims her first sense of
this need in adolescence: "das Verlangen nach einer gesonderten Selbststän-
digkeit (hörte) nie wieder auf."(1/2, 119) Her development as an integrated
personality and discreet individual appears as the natural course of events.

But Lewald's development was far more problematic than she asserts and
the structure of *Meine Lebensgeschichte* ultimately resists, even belies, a
teleological interpretation of her life. The structure is actually quite different from Goethe's despite her clear intentions to convey the gradual unfolding of talents and character she perceived in Goethe's life. The three volumes
of this thoughtfully composed autobiography outline three phases in her
development. Volume I "Im Vaterhaus" relates Lewald's childhood while
she still partakes of the family's comforts. Volume II "Leidensjahre" follows Lewald as she ventures beyond this narrow circle and encounters a wider
world. Returning home, she rejects an arranged marriage and feels isolated,
useless, and misunderstood. She experiences unrequited love, becomes
alienated from her family, and gives up on herself. Volume III "Befreiung
und Wanderleben" shows her regaining her balance by finding a place and
occupation where she feels useful. She becomes self-sufficient. The organization of the volumes alone immediately reveals a development more
problematic than Goethe's gradual, harmonious unfolding. In addition to
success it suggests obstacles, pain, and struggle. The tri-partite arrangement
even implies a redemptive pattern of happiness-suffering-better happiness.

Despite the incidents which she herself presents as evidence to the contrary, Lewald's development into a writer was far from a natural and inevitable unfolding of her interests and abilities. Ultimately it is her keen attention
to psychological detail and her passion for truth which contradict her intentions. Lewald realized very early the dangers of accepting ready-made
and especially romanticized images of women for a description of her life.
Shortly after leaving school and in a melancholy state, she had decided to
keep a diary. A popular novel, *Rosaliens Nachlaß*, by an obscure author
Friedrich Jacobs, gave her the idea. The young men and women in the book
had pleased her too well. The gentle mixture of noble sentiment and blue
and white ribbons, of balls and religiosity, of love, fainting spells and pious intimations of death had strongly appealed to her. Since she was phys-

ically ill at the moment, it was all the easier to imagine a multitude of pains and to fantasize suffering with Rosalie. (1/2, 70f.) With considerable self-irony she portrays herself trapped in romantic images of her life. Aston's model for her persona had also been a romantic literary figure, "Indiana". But where Aston had chosen one of some integrity and fortitude Lewald had not, at least not as a young girl.

Fortunately she was not satisfied with Jacob's particular model and rejects it in ridicule. Curious to see what posterity would learn of her after she died, she was inspired one day to read what she had written. Tearfully she began to read — and she read and read and the wool fell from her eyes. Not one word of what she had written in the last three months was true! She had spoken of suffering she had not known, of longings she had never experienced. She found herself repulsive and ridiculous at the same time. Only burning every last page of her "lyer's chronicle" would bring her peace (1/2, 76f).

Rather than using the diary form to explore her psyche, Lewald had succumbed to novelistic fantasies. The unfortunate result of this painful experience was that she never kept a diary again. Her adamant refusal to accept ready-made stereotypical postures or literary models however is generally consistent with her autobiography. Despite her stated intentions and pretentions of following Goethe's model, her interest in her inner development joined with her detailed descriptions of her personal life become remarkable revelations of the social pressures on bourgeois women in mid-nineteenth-century Germany. And herein lies a real strength of her autobiography. The particular irony in it all is that her very realism ultimately undermines her attempt at reading a teleology into her life. For her own precise observations and psychological perceptivity confront us with patterns of development radically different from that model. Her experience contradicts the "dictionary" of accessible concepts in terms of which she would have been able to conventionally view her life.

Unlike Goethe whose urge to write appears natural and unrestrained, the young Lewald is virtually pushed into each of her efforts by a teacher, girl-friends, a sister, her uncle. Even more than the accurate record of external promptings, the descriptions of her reactions to her own work or to suggestions that she write prove the impossibility of a harmoniously developed character or talent. When Heinrich Simon asked if she had ever written, she had responded that the suggestion was ridiculous. At that moment, she comments, nothing had been further from her mind. (2/2,160) The novel she had begun she considered ridiculous. She was familiar with the best literature, disdained mediocre writing, and did not trust herself to accomplish more. She had always ridiculed bad women authors, who (she accepted the common myth) wrote out of boredom and empty lives. She would not condescend to amuse simple women and sleepy servants with her deepest emotions and most secret thoughts. She thought too highly of writing, too little of readers, nothing of her own talent, and all the more of herself as her father's daughter and a woman of character. So she crossed out the pages and wrote no more (2/2, 151f.).

Only by accident was she dragged into the profession. The only thread on which her entire metamorphosis hung — as Lewald actually reveals it — appeared in the form of a cousin who encouraged her. August Lewald had requested a description of the King's oath of allegiance taken in Königsberg in 1840. Lewald's description, modeled in detail on Goethe's description of the coronation of Joseph II in Frankfurt, so pleased her cousin that he requested permission to print it. He then wrote her father testifying to her literary talent, amazed that she had not considered writing herself. This time Lewald responded with excitement. "Mir stieg, als ich diese Worte las, das Blut vom Herzen schnell und warm zu Kopfe; ich sah meinen Vater an, er mochte mir die Freude von den Augen ablesen. Ja! das war es! das könnte mir helfen! Es war mir ein Blick aus der Wüste in das gelobte Land, es war eine Aussicht auf Befreiung, es war die Verwirklichung eines Gedankens, die Erfüllung eines Wunsches, die ich mir einzugestehen nicht getraut hatte."(2/2, 254) She had not dared to admit such unconventional desires until someone else suggested the possibility. That Lewald escaped the narrow confines of her parents' house seems more like a miracle than the destined fulfillment of inner drives. In such a context it is not possible to talk meaningfully of teleology.

Similarly on a personal level Lewald's adolescent goals belie her stated need for independence. Even late in the autobiography she reflects: "Meine Aussichten für das Leben waren in meiner ersten Jugend so beschränkt gewesen, nun weiteten sie sich mit jedem Tage mehr, und ich hatte beinahe Mühe mich daran zu gewöhnen. Es war ja Alles ganz anders geworden als ich es erwartet, als ich es gewünscht hatte. So weit menschliche Einsicht es in meinem sechzehnten Jahre voraus berechnen konnte, war es mir bestimmt gewesen, als eine christliche Pastorsfrau in einem stillen Dorfe des Harzes zu leben. Ich hatte mir dies als das größte Glück gewähren können, was es mir einst gewesen sein würde."(3/2, 29f.) In other words her prospects and with them her "telos" had actually changed radically, and the change had been occasioned more by chance than her own action. Due to his own

160

initiative, Goethe was a published and controversial author when he received the invitation from Weimar that would determine his fate as an author and court advisor, rather than a lawyer. For reasons of convention Lewald had taken no such initiatives.

As an adolescent and young adult, she had been at best only vaguely aware of her unhappiness and never dreamed that she might become independent. For eight long years she had lived in a state of depression and stagnation, waiting for Heinrich Simon. Her character is portrayed as not developing at all during this period. In the second volume therefore, rather than her own life, she describes her family's life or events in Königsberg and Berlin. For a time she lived vicariously through the travel diaries of Heinrich Simon. Only on a sojourn to Berlin does Lewald learn anything new — "good social form" — and notes that this makes her feel more comfortable in good society. Despite her desolation she makes no move to break out. Her depression is severe and perceptively rendered. After Simon writes that he loves another woman, Lewald records her loss of hope and the sense that her life has ended by noting that she began consciously to dress in more somber tones. After rebelliously rejecting the suitor her father had chosen for her, she feels she is an economic burden to her family and keeps a notebook in which she affixes prices to the handiwork she does at home, thus determining her contribution to the household economy.

The very concreteness of these details conveys dramatically Lewald's utter desperation as well as her sense of worthlessness. She seems unable to effect any change in her situation. It becomes impossible to believe Lewald when, at the end of her autobiography, she claims: "So lange ich mich zu erinnern vermag, habe ich immer ziemlich bestimmt gewußt, was ich wollte, und das Ziel nicht leicht aus dem Auge verloren, dem ich zustrebte. Ich hatte unabhängig sein wollen, nun war ich es."(3/2, 225f.) This extremely positive assertion falsely characterizes Lewald as a goal-oriented person. She claims this virtue of modern bourgeois society for herself at the same time she provides the evidence which contradicts it. The harder, less easily acknowledged psychological oppression of women surfaces in this very contradiction.

As her salvation in the desert, writing acquired a significance for Lewald it could not possibly have had for Goethe. Of writing she recalled: "Dieser Freude an den Gestalten gesellte sich nun noch die Wonne hinzu, durch ihre Vermittlung einmal Alles sagen zu können, was mir seit so vielen Jahren auf dem Herzen gelegen hatte, und es sagen zu können, ohne daß man mich zurecht wies, ohne daß man mir widersprach, ohne daß ich mich zu mäßigen und Rücksicht zu nehmen und ohne daß ich es zu meiner Vertheidigung zu sagen brauchte."(3/1, 18) Writing becomes the battleground on which she fights for her freedom and the process by which she achieves her independence. As though addicted, the minute she finishes her first novel she begins the next: "Ich kann es nicht oft genug wiederholen, welch' ein Glück das Arbeiten mir war, welch' einen Genuß das Schaffen mir gewährte. Wie mit einem Zauberschlage entrückte der Moment in welchem ich mich an den Schreibtisch setzte und meine Hefte zur Hand nahm... Ich war froh, frei, mächtig und unverzagt, ich hatte fortwährend ein Gefühl meiner Kraft und auch ein gewisses Gefühl des Gelingens."(3/1, 60f.) Only in writing does she first sense her own strength, realize herself.

Of particular interest for us is the apparent fact that she gave voice to long suppressed views only in her novels. Lewald had required of her father that she be allowed to write the truth as she saw it. (He required it be disguised, behind a pseudonym.) In her novels a side of her comes to life that would not have otherwise, and insofar as it does it reminds us of the fictional epistles which Recke and Stägemann had used to give vent to opinions normally unacceptable. Rather than letters, Lewald now puts them in the mouths of her heroines — disguising them in her own right to some extent. It may indeed well be that women's novels had obliquely exposed much truth about their own lives and thoughts.

Lewald's new role as someone who earns money forces her to change her self image. Again concrete details perceptively trace her gradually changing consciousness. The initial discomfort at accepting money from August Lewald for her story moved her to assuage her guilt by buying a present for her mother. Increasingly she is proud and happy to be able to pay for certain luxuries for herself — like a trip through Bohemia. Similarly, the self-pity at finding herself alone one evening on the streets of Berlin becomes both the loneliness and the joy of having her own apartment. Whether as a model for describing one's relationship to history or one's personal development, Lewald's perception of *Dichtung und Wahrheit* was absolutely inappropriate for a woman's life. Her departures from it were conditioned by her experience as a member of the female sex.

Despite her awareness of what her sex meant for her development and her acknowledged identity with her sex, Lewald's choice of a teleological model obliged her to create a harmonious resolution. (Or she chose that model because she believed she had found one in real life.) Just such a resolution, however, suggests that those who so desire will find similar good fortune. She failed to consider adequately that her own emancipation was first of all a matter of good fortune rather than the inevitable realization of her own particular teleology. Despite her acute awareness that women are relegated to an inferior position in society, she suggests that her success was the result of her natural development and implies that if other women are less successful, it is because they lack her drive for independence and her urge to write. Neither of these qualities, we recall, could be ascribed to Lewald during the "Leidensjahre". Her own experience does not prevent her from asserting that the individual contains within him/herself the ability to derive happiness from life: "Man hat es so sehr in seiner Gewalt, sich die Gläser zu schleifen, durch welche man die Welt betrachten, und die Farbe zu wählen, in welcher man sein Schicksal ansehen will. Wer die Welt und seine Obliegenheiten in derselben im trüben Lichte zu schauen geneigt ist, dem fehlt es in der Regel an Einsicht und an Selbsterkenntniß, und vor allen Dingen an der rechten Liebe."(3/2, 34) Never mind real injustice. As long as nature is beautiful and there is art one can never be totally unhappy (3/2, 35). By focusing the dissatisfaction of women or other oppressed groups away from society and on their own supposed lack of insight and self-knowledge, the societal problem becomes internalized. The issue becomes privatized and women alone responsible for their own inferior status. Ultimately, for all her liberal views, Lewald's autobiography assumes a quietistic and legitimist stance.

The tripartite construction of her work thus differs radically from Aston's innocence-compliance-emancipation scheme. Lewald's childhood growth-stagnation-emancipation emphasizes integration, not the need to break with social convention. The years between Aston's 1847 publication of her autobiography and Lewald's in 1861/2 had witnessed the radical quashing of the revolution of 1848 and with it many hopes of liberals in Germany. Those revolutionaries who had not been captured were in exile, or, if they stayed, experienced either the concrete pressures of censorship or the more ethereal ones to conform. Among those ideas repudiated by the bourgeoisie in the wake of 1848 was the concept of the emancipation of women. The 1840s had nourished the emancipatory ideals of the young Aston, the young Meysenbug, and the young Lewald, but the strength of the intellectual reaction strongly affected women as well. In this climate Goethe's autobiography, conservatively interpreted, became a natural model for legitimatory autobiographies in general and for Lewald's in particular.

This does not mean that Lewald became a conservative and relinquished all desire for change. The conscious tendentiousness of her autobigoraphy, in contrast to Goethe's, was intended to motivate changes for women. She also explicitly sympathizes throughout with the poor and expresses her hope for liberal reform. None of this however really overcomes the weight of the autobigraphy in the direction of legitimation.

She concludes the narration of her life a good two years after her initial flush of freedom – a point at which she might more easily have inspired other women to take initiatives – and states that that sense of freedom can never replace love, over time between a man and a woman (3/2, 267f.). And, although she had not even met Stahr at that point, she anticipates their union which she calls "die höchste Liebe, die Erfüllung aller meiner Wünsche."(3/2, 305) From the latter part of the second volume on in fact Lewald had periodically mentioned her future husband – the first time just before she received Simon's devastating letter. It is as if she expected the knowledge and reassurance of her future marriage both to soften the blow of her immediate desperation and to moderate eventual joy at independence in the final volume, when she herself does not know what lies before her, but relishes the risk. A reader thus assured would not be driven to unmanageable extremes of emotion – either depression or liberation. Moderation and sanguinity are crucial for Lewald. This explains, perhaps, why – despite general critical acceptance[9] – it did not find the same resonance among women as Rahel Varnhagen's letters or Malwida von Meysenbug's *Memoiren einer Idealistin.*

Lewald's inappropriate appropriation of a male form of autobiography is a very different phenomenon from that of say Baldinger or Engel. For one thing she is quite explicit and detailed about the personal difficulties she has had to face as a woman. For another she is an established professional who can speak from the vantage point of some real success about obstacles to the development of her already proven abilities. For yet another she speaks in a clearly tendentious way using her experience not to bemoan her fate, but to argue for reforms in the education of women. She writes sensibly and sensitively to perpetuate improvement in the lives of women.

Acknowledging that, it is also crucial to recognize that the potentially disruptive, despairing, and profoundly unsettling moments of her experience are strongly ameliorated by her appropriation of Goethe's teleological model. Not only does *she* gain from this strategy – her talent has proven itself and she has associated her development with the authority of the master – the establishment is also legitimized. If her talents had finally evolved and found recognition by virtue of her own inner drive toward independence and activity then the situation for women is not all that bad. Careful readers will perceive the role that mere chance played in her success, but even so will not be greatly unsettled.

If Aston and Meysenbug had shown us the longing without the vision, Lewald has left us without the longing. Despite the impact which Rahel Varnhagen had made on her, very little of that openess which permitted her struggle to become so visible is apparent in this autobiography. There is no longer a desire for a different way of being in the world, for a different order. In this Lewald is hardly alone of course. Her contemporaries are engaged in a positivistic pursuit of knowledge and understanding. It is a tendency she tried to counteract with Goethe's more totalistic understanding of history and human evolution, but it is a tendency she could not ultimately escape.

Naturally one wonders whether she would have been able to counteract it more effectively with Varnhagen's epistolary style. But Lewald had already rejected much in Varnhagen by 1849. In that year she wrote a novel *Prinz Louis Ferdinand* in which Varnhagen and her salon play a central role. Lewald placed Varnhagen squarely against a background of jewish intellectual women and in a society which legalized prejudices. In the salon of Varnhagen the right of various types of people to freer, more appropriate development was recognized.[10] Lewald's political consciousness was high. Varnhagen knows she cannot be happy because she still cannot believe in "diese innere Nothwendigkeit der Weltordnung, der man sich ergeben unterwirft."(256) But she later resigns herself to her unhappiness because she knows "daß der Boden gesund sein muß, auf dem Glück aufgehen soll."(III,105) By giving up her hope for happiness, Varnhagen gives up what Lewald had identified in the beginning as her last shred of egoism, her refusal to submit to the status quo. It is this "refusal to submit to the status quo" that Lewald defines as "egoism" which she has relinquished in her autobiography as well. (In fact Varnhagen's letters suggest that she never relinquished that refusal.) Lewald has in fact submitted to it and considers it a virtue – as indeed had Meysenbug when she virtuously shed her individualism. And since the corollaries to Varnhagen's, and Arnim's, individualism – namely, the awareness of the necessity of the development of others to one's own development – were no longer perceived, that egoism could only be identified with unmitigated self-interest and capitalist greed.

Perhaps it is not surprising that shortly after the appearance of the novel Lewald commented that she had retreated somewhat from her unqualified admiration of Varnhagen: "daß das Springende in ihren Einfällen und in ihrer Ausdrucksweise etwas Unheimliches, Unschönes und Unruhiges für mich bekommen hatte."[11] Regardless of the historical situation, one can only express sadness that the appreciation for the generous openess of Varnhagen's epistolary style had been lost.

The pessimism of Schopenhauer consistently informs the autobiography of Marie von Ebner-Eschenbach. With the aid of that philosophy she relinguishes any claims to historical connections or even personal evolution. Appearing in 1905, *Meine Kinderjahre* thus seems to continue the historical progression of pessimistic thought in some members of this first generation of women to participate in the public sphere in sizeable numbers. And yet, well concealed but still visible and not so irrevocably repressed as she would seem to wish lie the remnants of her earlier hopes, muffled sounds of another voice.

Marie von Ebner-Eschenbach (1830-1916) was born to the second wife of the Austrian Baron, Franz Dubsky. Her own mother had died two weeks after her birth, so the young Marie was raised and educated by two stepmothers and a series of governesses. Her childhood was spent alternately in Vienna and on the family's summer estate, Zdißlawitz, in Moravia. Although the family as a whole objected to a young girl writing, in 1847 a receptive step-mother sent samples of her work to the Austrian poet Franz Grillparzer (1791-1872) for his professional opinion. His response was moderately encouraging, as was that of the poet Betty Paoli (1815-1894), whom Marie adored and to whom she had also sent her work. Aged 18 in 1848 Marie Dubsky was old enough to sympathize with some of the goals of the Revolution (although not its tactics), but not really old enough (or in a position) to have her life interrupted by those events. Indeed she was probably preoccupied with her marriage in that year to a cousin who had been supportive of her writing. For a decade they lived in the provinces where she read voraciously. In the early 1860s they moved to Vienna, where the liberal-minded Marie von Ebner-Eschenbach attended the salons of Iduna Laube and met prominent intellectuals.

By that time Ebner-Eschenbach was already a published author. In 1858 the anonymous appearance of her satiric travelogue, *Aus Franzensbad. Sechs Episteln* had afforded her the opportunity to criticize the society assembled at the Bohemian spa![12] The work displayed the author's familiarity with the novels of Madame de Staël and her contemporary, Sophie Gay![13] Its form and tone recalled those of George Sand's *Lettres d'un voyageur* (1834-1836). Between 1860 and 1874 she worked on thirteen plays, two of which were never completed. Although she received encouragement from such prominent theater people as Eduard Devrient (1801-1877), Friedrich Halm (1806-1871), and Heinrich Laube (1806-1884), none of her dramatic efforts was a commercial success. Several plays in the grand historical style of Friedrich Schiller, portray heroic, sharply profiled women.[14] Two of these — *Maria Stuart in Schottland* and *Madame Roland* — attempt to rescue the reputations of these women misunderstood by history. The heroine of *Die Schauspielerin* is an actress who refuses to marry a man unable to respect her profession. Several of these plays of social criticism had difficulty finding a stage because they were too unsettling. In 1863 Heinrich Laube rejected two of her plays — *Die Schauspielerin* and *Das Geständnis* — because the endings were too bitter.[15] Eduard Devrient rejected *Madame Roland* in 1867 explaining, "Die Gifthauchatmosphäre der Revolution is zu treu darin geschildert."[16] Nonetheless, beginning in 1860 with Devrient's Karlsruhe production of *Maria Stuart in Schottland*, various of her plays did reach the stage.[17] Once performed however they met with extremely harsh criticism and little success. The reviews of *Das Geständnis* were so acid and personal that Moritz von Ebner-Eschenbach, concerned about his good name, was on the verge of forbidding his wife to write. Like Fanny Lewald's father therefore Moritz von Ebner-Eschenbach considered a writing woman in the family a social liability. In Marie von Ebner-Eschenabch's case friends had to intervene.[18]

Some critics consider these dramas dilettantish,[19] and some agree with Ebner-Eschenbach's own later assessment that these historical plays were out of joint with the times, which expected realism.[20] Not all of these plays were historical however and the histories of at least two suggest peculiar prejudices against the author for writing at all. When *Dr. Ritter* opened anonymously the public received the play "enthusiastically", according to Ebner-Eschenbach herself.[21] When the play's authorship was revealed, the criticism became quite bitter, suggesting that the author had done well to hide her name.[22] This unexplained rancor has been attributed to bourgeois critics' resentment of nobility participating in *belles lettres*, certainly a possibility in late nineteenth-century Vienna.[23] However bias against women dramatists was probably just as strong if not a stronger motivation. One of the harshest reviews of *Das Waldfräulein* asked: "Machen diese kleinlichen Hauskrakehle nicht auf uns in der Art, wie sie hier nach echter Frauenart detaillirt und von Akt zu Akt neu vorgenommen werden, den kleinlichen Eindruck eines Familienklatsches, der zu dramatischer Publizität gebracht wird?"[24] Although the action of the play revolves around preparations for a ball and an engagement, the focus of it is the pretentiousness, uselessness, and imbecility of the aristocracy. The character through which the satire emerges is a young woman, and the absurdity of aristocratic society is seen from her perspective. Criticisms like the one above reveal that sexual bias almost surely colored reviewers opinions of her plays.

Continued harsh treatment of her works in the press was undoubtedly one reason for Ebner-Eschenbach's turn to the less exposed form of prose fiction in the 1870s. But this shift in genre was accompanied by a profound shift in subject matter as well. After reading Turgenev in the 1860s, she gradually ceased portraying heroic figures and world historical events and began to turn to the lower middle class and the peasantry for her characters and to everyday occurrences for her plots. Characteristic of this change is the motto she chose for *Das Gemeindekind* (1886), taken from George Sand's *Histoire de ma vie*: "Tout est l'histoire". Her prose efforts of the 1870s, with their more generous interpretation of history, resulted in wide-spread success in 1880 with the serialization of *Lotti, die Uhrmacherin* in the prestigious journal *Deutsche Rundschau*. It is the story of a principled, generous, and unerring female watchmaker. With the author Paul Heyse's (1830-1914) selection of "Die Freiherrn von Gemperlein" for his anthology *Deutscher Novellenschatz* in 1883 her literary success was firmly established.

Only in her fifties then did Ebner-Eschenbach begin to write the type of prose fiction on which her reputation is exclusively based. None of her early plays has appeared in any edition of her collected works, and only *Das Waldfräulein* has been published in any but manuscript form.[25] In later years Ebner-Eschenbach herself did nothing to call attention to these works and disowned *Aus Franzensbad* as an "uneheliches Kind"[26] Judging from her later ambivalence, she wanted to expunge the memory both of these works and of the influence of the French women on her.

Ebner-Eschenbach's views on women undoubtedly underwent a change during her lifetime. One critic characterizes the transition by juxtaposing *Die Schauspielerin* (1861) and "Ihr Beruf" (1901).[27] In the former a woman artist foregoes marriage in order to pursue a career. In the latter a woman sacrifices her persoanl goals in order to be a good mother. Although there was obviously a shift, it was probably not as uncomplicated or as drastic as this contrast implies. There is no reason to assume that the early Ebner-Eschenbach was as outspoken on the issue of women's emancipation as were various Frenchwomen in pre-1848 France (or Germany). And even her later works are remarkable for their unusually strong and intelligent female characters. In part the richness of these portraits is surely the reward of a sensitivity trained on the female characters of de Staël and Sand.

In addition Ebner-Eschenbach's own bitter experience of the difficulties facing women artists was articulated in various ways, even in the latter part of her life. She has expressed part of this awareness in "Die Visite" (1901), where she satirized the demeaning and contradictory treatment women authors received at the hands of male critics. A diary entry expressed her delight when a woman won a prize for drama.[28] She intervened with her publisher on behalf of the publication of the letters of Anette von Droste-Hülshoff (1797-1848) and of another work co-authored by three women.[29] The Ebner-Preis was awarded to ten women authors between 1900 and 1910.[30] Her own close personal association with women, especially the popular German novelist Louise von François (1817-1893) and with Ida Fleischl and Betty Paoli, suggests that she sought and received support mainly from women. The letters of Hermine Villinger testify to the personal and professional support she gave other women authors.[31] Her real belief in women and support of them as artists while not covert, is nevertheless as implicit and subdued as it is in her autobiography.

That Ebner-Eschenbach chose the title of Theodor Fontane's (1819-1898) autobiography *Meine Kinderjahre* (1894), for her own (1905) does not seem coincidental. Both authors achieved literary reputations only in their fifties (Fontane after two other careers), and yet both encompass only the first thirteen years of their lives in their autobiographies. In each case however the narrow focus on childhood reflects less a nostalgic longing for lost innocence or joy than the belief that the story of one's entire life is already manifest in childhood. For Ebner-Eschenbach at least this concept will not represent the Goethean striving to evolve traits present *in nuce* since childhood, but rather a more Schopenhauer-like eternal return. Fontane had suggested more of a personal evolution by projecting his own adult characteristics onto his father, thereby subtly disclosing the course of his entire life through the father's portrait.[32] The Austrian author also projects forward, though in a different way.

Ebner-Eschenbach believed that events in her childhood prefigured and set the tone for events throughout her entire life. In the process of sorting out her correspondence, diaries, and other papers at Zdißlawitz in 1903, she began to write her autobiography. On April 26, 1904 she wrote her publisher Julius Rodenberg explaining why she would not continue that work beyond her fourteenth year: "Die ganze Zukunft, mein ganzes an äußeren Ereignissen arme Leben ist da schon vorgezeichnet gewesen. Es war bei mir ausgemacht, daß ich die Frau meines lieben Vetters und Schriftstellerin werden würde."[33] The basic pattern of her later life: her interest in literature and fairy tales; her desire to write and be read; fundamental attitudes on justice, courage, kindness, religion, sympathy, even public reactions to her work are therefore prefigured.

Unquestionably the two experiences she portrays as pivotal both in her childhood and later life are her fascination for literature and writing and the silent rejection with which her literary efforts were met. Above all Ebner-Eschenbach's autobiography is a literary one, but she is more persuasive than Lewald about her early desire to become an author. Her later career appears foreshadowed in her childhood. Not just genres or specific works, but the very tone of her later works are evoked without overt reference to them. Play acting the role of dragon slayer or various of Schiller's heroes, she anticipates her own heroic historical plays. The fairy tales she later wrote had precursors in the fantastic adventures she experienced sitting in her grandmother's chair. Characters in her later fiction are described in their original forms. The doctor in "Kreisphysikus" (1884) bears an uncommon resemblance to the Jewish doctor in *Meine Kinderjahre*. Fantasies about a picture in her father's antechamber suggest the story "Krambambuli" (1883). She narrates the original episode on which she based "Die erste Beichte" (1874). This specifically literary quality brings the narration of her childhood close to that aspect of Goethe's and of Lewald's autobiographies.

Of importance for her claim to the anticipation of later life in her childhood are the references to her efforts at writing and her family's rejection of them. From the very beginning Ebner-Eschenbach couples her writing with rejection. A very young Marie wrote admiring letters to the actress Louise Neumann (1818-1905). She discovered by chance however that the person to whom she had entrusted them to be mailed had never done so. As she scatters them to the wind; not knowing if they will be found she wonders how anything can come into the world for nothing: "In späteren Jahren habe ich das kleine Erlebnis in anderem Maßstab und in anderer Form sich an mir und um mich zahllose Male wiederholen gesehen."[34] Her allusions remain vague, but we might assume she meant her plays.

Repeatedly whatever she writes meets with family resistance. Her sister's frequent response to her writing was a mere "curious!", and Marie instinctively senses something "disgraceful" in such a comment (799). This too she takes explicitly as a prefiguration of later rejections, perhaps even her husband's efforts to keep her from writing: "Alles wiederholt sich im Leben. Der Grundton, auf den das Schicksal des Größten wie des Kleinsten gestimmt ist, kommt immer wieder hervor. Die stumme Ablehnung, die mein erstes poetisches Gestammel durch eine Getreueste und Geliebteste erfuhr, wurde meiner Schriftstellerei bis ins reifste Alter durch andere Vielgetreue und Vielgeliebte zuteil."(808f.) It is not the evolution of talents on which she focuses, but rather the repetition of entire patterns of fate.

Even more painful than the inexplicable disregard for her writing is the sense she received that she had sinned. While praying for the strength to resist the temptation of writing she vows not to reveal her transgressions to her family. But she cannot help herself. Corneille's poem "Meditation sur la mort" takes hold of her imagination one day and she cannot keep herself from reciting it to her grandmother. Receiving praise for having learned the poem she blurts out, in confused phrases, her desire to write like Corneille: "Großmama unterbrach [die Schilderung] mit einer Strenge, die ich noch nie von ihr erfahren hatte und die mir bis zum heutigen Tage unerklärlich geblieben ist."(813) She could only conclude that writing was something "ungerechtes und sündhaftes"(813) and prays again for God to redeem her. Her sister advises her not to speak of it, perhaps it will just go away. Still she is left burdened with "das peinvoll demütigende Gefühl eines angeborenen geheimen Makels".(814)

The mature Ebner-Eschenbach does not believe her persistence in writing to have been either sinful or rebellious, but rather the result of an irresistible natural urge or divine destiny. Having vowed to keep silent about her writing, she comments, "Ebensogut hätte ich aber eine Brut Singvögel mit mir herumtragen und sie bewegen können, stumm zu sein."(811) One is strongly reminded of Madame Guyon's description of her own inner voice as "songbirds". Even the prayers in which she begs for strength to resist writing were nothing more than "ein armes, kindisches Versgestammel"(811). This drive, like Schopenhauer's "will", is perceived as fundamental to her character, and as such it is impossible to change through rational efforts to conquer it.

Even more than Schopenhauer whom we know Ebner-Eschenbach read and reread, this concept is reminiscent of the irrepressible and divine voice heard by Madame Guyon. Although there is no clear evidence that she was familiar with that seventeenth-century mystic, we know of Schopenhauer's admiration for her. Just before unburdening her heart to her grandmother, the young Marie knew only "da alles gesagt und gesungen werden müsse, was [mir] im Herzen klang und tönte, andern zur Freude, [mir] selbst zum Heile."(813) The desire to write is ultimately divine and the ability to write a divine gift. If she told herself it was divine, then it ought not to be repressed or controlled like Schopenhauer's will. It ought to be used.

And since, unlike Goethe, society and her family would have prevented her, she considered herself a martyr (like Madame Guyon): "Woraus mir ein Vorwurf gemacht wurde, das war etwas Unentrinnbares und ohne mein

Wissen und Wollen durch eine höchste, göttliche Macht über mich verhängt. Die Leiden, die ich dadurch erduldete, und leiden wollte ich ja! erschienen mir nicht wie gewöhnliche, sondern wie besonders schöne und erhabene, wie die eines Märtytums, und aus diesem Bewußtsein schöpfte ich eine große Widerstandskraft (...)."(814) If that sense of martyrdom gave her the strength to resist total repression of her writing, however, it was not able to prevent her feeling of inferiority vis-à-vis those authors she considered the truly inspired.

Like Meysenbug, whose sense of isolation must have contributed to her pessimism in the 1870s, Ebner-Eschenbach began to consider Schopenhauer more seriously, but in the late 1880s rather than when she first read him in the early 1870s.[35] The resignation which accepts suffering so easily characterizes her later prose works and is anticipated at the end of *Meine Kinderjahre*. After her grandmother's death the thirteen-year-old Marie catalogues the books in her library. In the reading orgies which ensue she is immediately humbled by a biography outlining Lessing's remarkable accomplishments at her own age, and she considers herself insignificant by comparison. Previously the young Marie Dubsky had wanted to write poetry as beautiful as Corneille's. Lessing's biography issues in "eine bittere Zeit der Selbsterkenntnis, voll Sehnsucht und Kümmernis".(877) Comparing herself to other mortals she submits in filial subjugation to the deity, resigning herself to a relatively minor position among mortals and attributing her talent to God, rather than claiming it for herself. In a small sphere and not a large one, she will aim to become important. This passivity and subordination is the same humility and submission she expects of her characters whether it is the dog "Krambambuli" or the orphan "Pavel Holub" in *Das Gemeindekind*. Perhaps it is a step forward if, unlike Lewald, she does not renounce writing altogether on the basis of comparisons of herself with literary greatness, but she clearly lowers her expectations for herself.

The resignation of young Marie which concludes *Meine Kinderjahre* is virtually the same as that expressed by the mature author in the preface. Written in Rome in 1905 this preface describes her visits to the Roman Forum, where she had felt the earth tremble with the marching Roman legions: "Noch ganz erfüllt von den Eindrücken, die ich Tag für Tag empfange, hier in diesem groen Rom, kehre ich in meine Behausung zurück und sollte meine Skizze vornehmen, auf die Druckfehlerjagd ausziehen und entgleisten Sätzen auf die Beine helfen. Das wird mir schwer. Mein Glauben an euer Etwas ist mir entschwunden, ihr armen Blätter. Weil ihr aber eure papiernen Flügel schon entfaltet habt, so fliegt denn, so gut ihr könnt."(749) In the letter to

Rodenberg of 1903 she had acknowledged that her life was poor on external history. Here she succumbs to feeling that as a fault.

Comparing her efforts to grand historical events and personages, Ebner-Eschenbach continually humbles herself, accepting what she feels to be a lower standard. In spite of quoting Sand, "Tout est l'histoire", she must repeatedly convince *herself* of the importance of personal and intimate history while Varnhagen, Arnim, and even Aston had only had to urge it on others. Even Lewald in her assertions of historical continuity had not belittled her own efforts. But Ebner-Eschenbach cannot overcome that more traditional sense of history and her own diminished self-worth for not having participated more fully in it. While it is certainly possible to observe this more traditional "Roman forum" perspective on history, perhaps in this case a more positive appraisal is not out of place. Ebner-Eschenbach does desire strongly to affect history, to influence events beyond the domestic realm. And she does not, ultimately, hide that desire.

The closing episode of the autobiography illumines the connection she made between her sense of pessimistic resignation and her own literary development. Before leaving the library, Ebner-Eschenbach finds a book which provides her with material for a grandly heroic historical play about Richelieu. She reveals she had written on this manuscript for years before burning it. It is not true however that she destroyed all traces of it, at least there are two remaining fragmentary versions of the play.[36] It is as if she wanted to, but ultimately could not forget/burn her dreams of fame and grandeur. Of the drama itself, she wrote: "(Richelieus) Gestalt wuchs und wuchs riesenhaft vor mir empor, bis sie mir – entwuchs und ich begriff, daß ich aus meiner Blindheit über ihre Größe den Mut geschöpft hatte, sie darzustellen. Allmählich waren die Augen mir aufgegangen, ich wußte: Mit all meiner Begeisterung, all meinem Fleiß habe ich nur ein Pfuschwerk zustande gebracht."(883)

After reassessing the drama young Marie feels she must come to terms with her potential. Just as the image of her characters retreated from the glorious heights of history so did her image for herself – or at least she claims it did. But correcting the galleys in Rome she continues to compare herself to History. The pain she had endured as a child, when she was forced to lower her expectations, is still present. In spiral like fashion her life seems destined to repeat itself in the eternal repetitions of Schopenhauer. She closes the autobiography: "Nun stehe ich am Ziel, der Ring des Lebens schließt, Anfang und Ende berühren sich."(747)

Arnim had refused to relinquish her fantasies. Varnhagen persisted in her

dreams no matter how hard the blows history struck and how much she had
to accept in reality. Their dreams had been to reshape history and the meaning of history according to their own needs, so that it might recognize their
needs. Not unlike Meysenbug's earliest claims for herself, Ebner-
Eschenbach's dreams had been of world historical fame. She desires to influence history, but any intimation of needs or vision of a different social
order is gone. In *Meine Kinderjahre* she presents not only the acceptance
of actual defeat, but the justification for lesser hopes and ambitions.

Ebner-Eschenbach had followed Fontane in limiting her story to her first
13 years. A second major structural similarity with his *Meine Kinderjahre*
is the very loosely applied chronology of experience. Events are not arranged
at all by chronology. The portrait of her father, for instance, is structured
according to a list of her father's characteristic traits, for each of which she
provides an anecdote. Although he had not been quite so radical in destroying
chronology, Fontane had also arranged several chapters according to subject matter rather than dates. Like Fontane, Ebner-Eschenbach uses flashbacks and flashforwards to give the reader a rapidly shifting kaleidoscopic
view of the environment in which she had grown up.

However a difference in breadth of vision reveals a fundamental difference in intention as well. At least one of Fontane's intentions had been to
document life in Swinemünde as it existed in the first third of the nineteenth
century.[37] He also hoped to document the life of a Hugenot family in Germany. The source for his material is objective reality. However where
Swinemünde's harbor becomes a focal point for the dreams of the young
Theodor, Ebner-Eschenbach restricts herself to domestic and personal events
and only in one or two cases do her descriptions venture beyond the confines of the family's country estate or city home. Due to her class and sex,
Ebner-Eschenbach's childhood experience with the world could never have
been as broad as Fontane's.

Even so, her experience is narrower than that described by Aston, Lewald,
or the younger Meysenbug. One could argue that her youthful marriage,
the sanctity of which she always upheld, had sheltered her from direct historical experience. However her novels attest to her sensitivity to social issues,
as well as to the effect of historical developments on them (see *Bozena* 1876).
Nevertheless unlike Fontane's her autobiography is absolutely ahistorical.
Her environment is either the Dubsky estate or its park and the persons she
describes are largely members of the immediate family household: governesses, tutors, teachers, a nurse, a family friend, the pastor, a doctor, and
an administrator of the estate. There are no businessmen, no workers, not

even a peasant save the nurse who leaves the family to return to the land. Depiction of objective reality is severely limited; indeed, if Lewald attempted an objective narration, Ebner-Eschenbach attempted an absolutely subjective one.

In her preface Ebner-Eschenbach had written that her ability to remember had increased with advancing years, but the past still did not appear as a powerfully executed painting with a well-lit background. Only isolated images (pictures) emerged sharply from the dusky background: "Phantasie übt ihr unbezwingliches Herrscherrecht und erhellt oder verdüstert, was sie mit ihrem Flügel streift. Sie läßt manches Wort an mein Ohr klingen, das vielleicht nicht so gesprochen wurde, wie ich es jetzt vernehm; läßt mich Menschen und Begebenheiten in einem Lichte sehen, das ihnen eine an sich vielleicht zu große, vielleicht zu geringe Bedeutung verleiht. Ihrer über das Kindergemüt, dessen Entfaltung ich darzustellen suchte, ausgeübten Macht wird dadurch nichts genommen. Das Schwergewicht liegt auf dem Eindruck, den sie hinterlassen haben, und ihn bestimmt die Beschaffenheit des Wesens, das ihn empfing. Dieses Wesen ist treu geschildert, buchstäblich und im Geiste."(747f.) To summarize crassly, the impression left by people or events is determined by the nature of the individual receiving it. "Reality" seems to have no role in this process.

Like Arnim, whose epistolary autobiography is likely not to have accorded with objective historical reality, Ebner-Eschenbach intentionally emphasizes the subjectivity of her narration. The possibility of fictitious elements in autobiography does not concern her, for, according to this statement, we only perceive a fiction and not reality in any case. However the subjectivity of the two autobiographers is quite different. Arnim had sought to infuse objective reality with the ideal, in fact with her own ideality. She assumed the ability to perceive parts of reality adequately. Ebner-Eschenbach asserts that "reality" is imagined by an individual and questions our ability to know anything of it. Unlike Arnim therefore she does not present her development in terms of its ideality, but rather in terms of psychological impressions. Even Ebner-Eschenbach, however, does not fail to emphasize the importance of the *nature* of the individual receiving the information.

At the turn of the nineteenth and twentieth centuries in Vienna such a perspective was not unique and surely not coincidental. In her metaphors for memory, Ebner-Eschenbach had alluded to styles of painting (either with or without well-lit backgrounds), she emphasized impressions, and she subtitled her autobiography "Biographical Sketches". In her case such obvious allusions to Impressionism were almost surely accompanied by an acquaintance with the more recent research on sense perception. Apparently even as a child Ebner-Eschenbach had not been uninterested in science. She had a considerable curiosity about electricity, for instance. In addition, her husband was a scientist and a member of the *Akademie der Wissenschaften*. More specifically Ernst Mach's (1838-1916) studies in sensory perception were popularly known in Vienna after his return in 1895, when he began to give public lectures there.

Insistence on the limitations of sensory experience as a measure of reality is therefore a concern that Ebner-Eschenbach would have shared not only with Arthur Schopenhauer, but with the Neo-Kantians and the man often known as the (first) founder of psychology, Gustav Fechner (1801-1887). Fechner's emerging psychological theories posited an active psyche. In his attempt to refute materialism, he had gone so far as to maintain that the material universe was inwardly alive and conscious. There are parallels between his spiritualism and Schopenhauer's suggestion that non-human life and objects may possess a spirit. Fechner's studies on sensation therefore focused on the interaction of perceptions and their stimuli. In her preface Ebner-Eschenbach had stressed she would report the impressions left on her childhood nature, but that those impressions had been determined *by* that nature. By 1901 Ebner-Eschenbach had not only read Fechner for the second time, she also corresponded about and discussed his work with Joseph Breuer (1842-1925) Freud's former associate and her own doctor and friend.[38]

Well-versed therefore in contemporary scientific developments Marie von Ebner-Eschenbach wrote that the young Marie had puzzled over the concept of synaesthesia. A piano had fascinated her whose keys were painted to correspond to the colors evoked in the senses by a given note (863). Her cousin Moritz had explained the theory behind such an instrument. In *Aus einem zeitlosen Tagebuch*, in a passage written as she began work on *Meine Kinderjahre*, Ebner-Eschenabch experimented with synaesthetic prose.[39] In a letter to Joseph Breuer, dated August 17, 1902 she expressed a desire to write in a less highly structured and more associative manner: "Nur noch aufschreiben, was mir durch den Kopf fährt, es denen mitteilen, die sich dafür interessieren (für diese Durch-den-Kopf-Fahrereien) (. . .)."[40] Though the links between this style of narration and contemporary science appear to be the dominant ones, there are also obvious, though perhaps not direct, links with authors such as Varnhagen and Arnim. Yet as Ebner-Eschenbach carries it out, this style of narration acquires a very different form.

Meine Kinderjahre bears evidence of this desire of hers to write more associatively. It is comprised of impressionistic sketches of her childhood. Characterizations of family and friends are based exclusively on her experience with that person in childhood: her personal impressions. Usually a characterization includes an activity in which Marie participated. Although she occasionally reports what she merely saw or heard, most often she is present at the event. The focus of the autobiography is exclusively on the child, Marie, and the world of adults and others is important only insofar as it affects her childhood. Other events are irrelevant. While she makes allusions to events which occured beyond her thirteenth year, only rarely does she specifically relate something that happened later — her father's death in 1872 or the later life of her beloved governess, Marie Kittl. Otherwise the people she describes have no existence beyond their relationship to the child. Unlike Arnim's highly subjective autobiographical writing therefore she strictly limits herself to what she personally might have known or perceived at the time. The characters are not projections of her own ideality, aspects of her "self", as much as they are imagined impressions on her "self".

Such a consciously subjective view of reality is analgous to a childhood fantasy she had had. Wherever she looked, she felt her eyes conjured up sky, sun, stars, landscapes. Wherever she was not looking was nothing. It was gray, dumb, dead (797f.). In order to unmask the secret — that reality disappeared when she was not looking — she would run very fast and turn around suddenly. Just as the people in her autobiography tend to have little existence, beyond that which the young Marie experienced immediately, so too there was no reality for her beyond what was seen and heard at that moment.

Neither Arnim nor Ebner-Eschenbach wants to project a logic on their autobiographical narrations, but for different reasons. For Arnim that would be an untruthful representation of reality. For Ebner-Eschenbach there is a doubt that objective reality exists. Arnim assumes the authenticity of experience, but knows the difficulty of perceiving and expressing it. Ebner-Eschenbach questions the "reality", the very authenticity of all experience.

All themes in the autobiography are related to her involvement with literature, her attempts to write, the content of her later work, and the rejection of her literary efforts. Writing is the point of departure for her associations. Frequently a work or concept at the end of one sketch will commence the next. Yet the structural lines blur as one sketch evokes and overlaps with another. Seemingly disparate people and events are associated by the subjective vision, not ultimately of the young Marie as she experienced

anything (although Ebner-Eschenbach apparently did rely on childhood
notes), but of the seventy-five-year-old Ebner-Eschenbach as she recalled
them.

The very associative and not causal structure of this work refuses to recognize the existence of objective reality and rules out the possibility of explaining the actions of others or criticizing broader social structures. Attempts
to repress the author's childhood talents are portrayed merely as repetitions
of a fundamental experience, without efforts to draw connections between
one incident and the next or to look behind the pattern for explanation.
She has banished notions of cause and effect, and, in the absence of all references to history, there is of course no suggestion of historical or social
phenomena. The likely infuence of Schopenhauer's demoralizing philosophy contributes to her retreat from history and resignation to what she
perceived as inevitable. Why writing should be shameful had puzzled the
young Marie. At seventy-five however Ebner-Eschenbach still makes no effort to explain such behavior, much less to criticize it.

And yet if she resigned herself to the role of a martyr, it is not without
pride and the conviction that she was right. Ebner-Eschenbach thanks all
who placed hindrances in the path of her endeavors, for: "Je härter und
widerwilliger der Boden war, in dem das Bäumchen meiner Kunst Wurzel
schlagen mußte, desto fester stand es, und je grausamer die Mißerfolge
gewesen sind, desto enger schloß sich das Bändnis zwischen mir und meinem vielbestrittenen Talent."(850f.) Madame Guyon, too, had seen her
earthly trials as God's divine and unalterable plan against which it would
be sinful to rebel. She, too, had been thankful for the lessons she learned
from her tribulations. Ebner-Eschenbach viewed with gratitude attempts
to suppress her drive to write, for they only assured her of her conviction.
Each is thankful for her trials and believes in the divinity of her own instincts. Neither suggests the responsibility of her family or her society in
the development of her inner self. Neither suggests the possibility of af-
fecting changes in the external order. Both resign themselves to pain they
perceive as necessary. It is as though all the engagement with reality, with
the external world since Elisabeth von der Recke first began to make her
family and not God responsible for their oppression of her, as though all
that activity had been eradicated. This very modern text apparently reveals
a very old face.

And yet it is not the same. Camoflaged and in the cracks of this associative narration are the remains of a very different face. With a slight shift
of vision it is discernible. Now it is as though Ebner-Eschenbach wore a mask

to disguise an earlier self. But she has not totally hidden it. As in Frederike Baldinger's autobiography there is another story which somewhat contradicts the one told. But Ebner-Eschenbach's associative structure permits its appearance without breaking any structure. Perhaps she did not totally *want* to hide it. Perhaps she wanted this other self to be discovered as well. As though after years of covering it over, like the song birds, it would not be still or silenced.

The associative structure of the autobiography tends to obscure but not to deny the importance of strong women in her life, either as role models or for support. There is a sociological assumption in this identification that belies the refusal to seek objective connections. A striking preponderance of female figures dominates *Meine Kinderjahre*: her grandmother, her nurse, her step-mothers, governesses, actresses, and even playwrights. Her nurse first fires her imagination with her stories. Her step-mother reads her Swedish feminists like Frederike Bremer (1801-1865) and Emilie Flygare-Carlen (1807-1892). She also gives her Schiller's collected works, "das denkwürdigste Ereignis [ihrer] Kinderjahre".(832)

Of course a young girl in a traditionally structured aristocratic family has contact primarily with women, but Marie seems particularly fascinated with their roles. When her new step-mother arrives, Marie is puzzled to find her crying right after the wedding. When Frau Krähmer's son dies, it is the mother's fate with which she identifies and suffers. Similarly when her brothers' tutor dies, Marie's imagination sympathizes with the mother. The young Marie worships the actress Louise Neuman (1818-1905) and notes two female playwrights for the *Burgtheater* whom she admired, Princess Amalie von Sachsen and Johanna von Weienthurn (1772-1847).

More overwhelming than any of these examples is the scene in which Marie's piano teacher gives a concert. Frau Krähmer, who was to play the clarinet, sat between her two sons on the podium. One of them riveted his glowing dark eyes on the "Meisterin": "fragend, erratend ruhten [seine Augen] auf ihr, und aus ihnen sprach Vergötterung"(790). Thus adored, the artist played and conducted the ensemble. In ecstatic tones the reader learns of the artist's clothing and features: "Mit fanatischer Bewunderung sah ich zu der genialen Künstlerin. . .empor. . .(.)"(790) Although she resolved to kiss the once feared teacher's hand the next time she saw her, she loses her nerve at the crucial moment. But she thought of her often thereafter and even dreamed of her.

The image of the consummate artist surrounded by an adoring audience became a model in literature with Madame de Staël's *Corinne*.[41] This scene may well reveal the influence of de Staël's ideal, for when she dreams of Frau Krähmer, she always sees her in the concert hall, on the podium, between her adoring sons. Unlike "Corinne" however Frau Krähmer is not admired by all. Indeed Marie must defend her to her governess, which she does with vehemence. And there is something pitiable in Frau Krähmer for she is soon to lose her adoring son. This great artist must ultimately be pitied for her suffering, and defended. How the young Marie must have sympathized with and derived strength from this real model!

Of inestimable importance in Marie's childhood was her governess, Marie Kittl. Kittl was the first person to take Marie seriously, to listen to her, to accept the fact that she wrote and wanted to become an author. Marie rewards her with absolute devotion. Even after Kittl left the household, the two women remained in correspondence, and Kittl continued to compliment and encourage the young author. For the older Ebner-Eschenbach however the story of Marie Kittl acquired special poignance. Eventually Kittl gave up her career as governess so that she herself might write. Living on a modest sum which a grateful employer granted her, she attempted to write and publish, but with absolutely no success. Ebner-Eschenbach records Kittl's useless efforts with great empathy: "Ich kenne ihre Sehnsucht und weiß, daß sie ebenso unüberwindlich ist wie die der echten Begabung...aber sie leidet an Unzulänglichkeit."(865) And Ebner-Eschenbach thus avoids more general social criticism of prejudice against women writers.

One more woman must be considered as demonstating the importance of women in Ebner-Eschenabch's childhood. Like "Corinne" this one is also fictional. It is "Queen Anna", the heroine in Marie's play *Richelieu*. With self-irony not quite as severe as Lewald describing her romantic trivialized diaries, Ebner-Eschenbach sketches the characters of the play she never finished. Louis XIII — small of soul, faithless, hard; Richelieu — scheming, relentless, cruel, and powerful; Cinque-Mars — young, noble-minded, blindly trusting his own good fortune; and Queen Anna, the heroine — clever, proud, disdainful of Richelieu's objectionable advances, suffering from his implacable desire for revenge, humiliated by him, but never relinquishing her purity of soul. "Ich liebte Königin Anna von Österreich und wollte schon dafür sorgen, daß jeder, der sie durch mich kennen lernte, sie ebenfalls lieben müßte ...(.)"(880) Not only does the character of Queen Anna represent Marie's ideal of womanhood, a careful look at the list of characters reveals the shadowy outlines of a George Sand novel such as *Indiana*: the cold, uncaring husband; the despicable admirer; the noble-minded young hero; the virtuous, strong heroine. Clearly Schiller had not been the only influence on the shaping of her dramatic ambitions. Only in this very indirect way does Ebner-Eschenbach recall the otherwise unacknowledged impact of George Sand on this budding author.

Ebner-Eschenabch hides nothing of her enchantment with Schiller or with the theater. The same is not true for the early influence of de Staël and Sand. Apparently she felt the same embarrassment about their very influence that she had felt about her earliest work (influenced by Sand)—*Aus Franzensbad*—that it was somehow "illegitimate". Yet just as her own career indicates that the model of a strong, creative woman did not totally give way to resignation and humility, so her autobiography suggests that the memory of these strong women—de Staël, Sand, but also Frau Krähmer, Marie Kittl, and "Queen Anna"—was not entirely erased by her philosophical resignation. She cannot totally ignore an "illegitimate" history that does not accord with her current views.

Having accepted the dominant social values and aesthetic criteria however she could not acknowledge the importance of such women for her development and the suggestion of a more rebellious youth than she wanted to admit. As she had ultimately welcomed the obstacles her family placed in her way as helpful, so she accepted the social injustice she experienced. The subjectivity of this autobiographical form permits Ebner-Eschenbach to conceal, without totally relinquishing, some of her earliest sources of inspiration. The need she obviously felt to hide what had formerly aroused her ambitions and sense of self reveals as much about Viennese culture around 1900 as it does about Marie von Ebner-Eschenbach. Indeed the painful quality of the process of women's socialization and the pressures for resignation are rarely so apparent as in *Meine Kinderjahre*. The costs of Ebner-Eschenbach's success were considerable.

Of course denial of experience had been visible in the contradictions in which Baldinger and Engel had caught themselves. And perhaps the autobiography of Isabella von Wallenrodt comes closest to approximating the radical, unexplicit dichotomy of split consciousness. But even so there is a significant difference. Biographically Ebner-Eschenbach had benefitted from a generation of outspoken women and she herself achieved more than average success with her writing. Her submission had not been financially necessary and had reaped her higher gains. The face that is hidden is not necessarily one that is bitter, though it may be infinitely sad.

More astonishing for the question of women and autobiography is the formal innovation. In the absence of the epistolary tradition of the eighteenth century, Marie von Ebner-Eschenbach has found a formal structure which permits contrary voices to emerge. Working associatively and not in a linear fashion has given her openings into which she can insert information without having to explain the context. Thus, while both she and the later Meysenbug view their lives through the lens of the eternal return posited by Schopenhauer, Ebner-Eschenbach's refusal to apply strictly the category of cause and effect opens her autobiography to at least two voices, including one that had been lost in the final two volumes of Meysenbug's *Memoiren*.

That other voice may not be accorded the attention it was in the epistolary forms, but it can be heard. It may be muffled, but it is not denied as it is in Wallenrodt's autobiography. Nor does it blatantly contradict an explicitly articulated model of development as does Lewald's contradictory experience. Ebner-Eschenbach's other voice half articulates unfulfilled desire and will not be suppressed totally. Ebner-Eschenbach never totally denied her "will", the songbirds she could not silence. Hers is a modest courage, but it is one.

Of the autobiographies of Aston, Meysenbug, Lewald, and Ebner-Eschenbach, the latter most consistently attempts to avoid associations with history or with issues of social injustice, including those particular to women. On the positive side, however, of all the autobiographies discussed in this study — with the possible exception of Baldinger's confused narrative — this is the only one *not* structured around a relationship to a man. For the other authors either marriage or the loss of a lover or husband had represented radical changes in their lives. Those changes influenced the structure of the autobiography, suggesting the financial and/or emotional and social dependence of these women on men. Engel and Wallenrodt experienced marriage as a happy time. Without marriage their financial situation was precarious in the extreme. Had they not lost their husbands we can be reasonably sure we would not have heard from them. Recke, Stägemann, and Arnim all explicitly or implicitly (ex negativo) expose their marriages as putting a stop to the course of personal development prior to their marriage. Recke and Stägemann were well enough off financially to be able to afford a divorce. Arnim not only sought no divorce, her drive to write appears motivated by more than the loss of her husband. She had begun to write — to Goethe to regain her ideal self — during her marriage, but privately. Lewald and Meysenbug structure their autobiographies around unhappy relationships with men. Lewald's rejection by Simon occasioned the depression portrayed in the critical second volume. Meysenbug finds the patterns of her life in rejection by men.

Only Ebner-Eschenbach avoids that structuring on the basis of her relationship to any particular man. This is not merely because she ends her childhood reminiscences at the age of 13; for she projected her entire later life and career into those first thirteen years. It is not that, by implication, her husband especially supported her work after their marriage, encouraging her intellectual and personal growth. Rather his reaction to her writing is perceptively interpreted as the continuation of the more general resistance she had found from her family and society at large. Her struggle to realize her vision of herself did not change when she married. She portrayed herself as having similar struggles, though of different scales, before and after marriage. The determination and conviction she developed as a child she continued to need as an adult. This autobiography suggests a sense of "self" independent of one's relations to family and the opposite sex.

It also suggests a very different general pattern of evolution than that of the autobiographies studied by Bernd Neumann. In those an "identity" evolved until it found an occupation and then it had to accommodate itself to the demands of that role. To the extent that these women autobiographers applied the model of personal development to their life stories, their social role, marriage, has interrupted and diverted that development. Ebner-Eschenbach's perspective of repeated patterns from childhood on poses an entirely different model. There is no essential difference between life patterns early in her childhood and those later, that is why the early ones can stand for the later ones without her having to be explicit. She confronts the same struggles from different sources. Her conviction of her talent is challenged repeatedly. She must have possessed unflagging strength of character.

Lewald and Ebner-Eschenbach both succeeded in the public arena, in a field dominated by men. They were both pioneers and fully conscious of the difficulties they had faced because of their sex. In a general sense their autobiographies represent two very different styles of continuous narration: objective and subjective. And yet, strangely — because both authors were so clearly aware of experiences particular to them as women — neither fully validated that personal experience. Lewald gave priority to the model of Goethe and accepted the logic of a teleological development, even though it did not correspond to her own (narrated) experience. Ebner-Eschenbach failed to establish the connections she saw between her own struggles and those of women in general, even though she was well aware of them and had articulated them in other texts. The associative structure, appropriate for the conception of "reality" as subjective and imagined in any case, did not permit the assertion of any experience as authentic. Neither is an autobiography that would give great comfort to a woman who felt alone in the prejudice she suffered.

Aston, Meysenbug, Lewald, and Ebner-Eschenbach were all born between 1811 and 1830 and belonged essentially to one generation; they shared crucial historical experiences which reverberated profoundly on a personal level. That public experience included youthful fascination with the works of Frenchwomen like Germaine de Staël and George Sand or German women like Rahel Varnhagen or Bettina von Arnim. As different as they were, both French and German authors challenged, in their writing and their lives, traditional role models for younger women. If the term is broadly applied, their efforts, as well as those of their younger admirers could all be described as "liberal". The Revolution of 1848 brought the realization of many of their ideals very close. It must have nourished the sense of promise awakened in the younger authors by their forebears. However those bright outlooks were quickly clouded by their collective experience with one of the harshest periods of political reaction in Germany. As a group all underwent that painful negation of public and private hopes.

Each of these women had entered the realm of public relations. At some point each specifically identified with the capriciously restricted fate of women and, in her own way, each contributed to a new consciousness about the role of her sex in history. Whether they stepped boldly or with caution, however, none crossed that threshold from domestic to public activity unscathed by hostility directed at women who failed to meet social expectations. Of course each reacted differently.

The autobiographies by these four women are spread over a good portion of the late nineteenth century and even into the very early twentieth. They record more than individual reactions to political events. Especially as the individual works reveal the biographical strains of accomodation to disillusionment or to the status quo, they also illustrate the intellectual history of liberalism in general. Read in this way these autobiographies bear witness to a collective tendency to avoid, accomodate, retract, or disguise former associations and ideals unacceptable to the status quo. Dreams which once aroused imaginations and motivated concrete action are treated cynically or relegated to oblivion. The isolation into which the Reaction forced all former adherents of liberal doctrines appears to have made these authors vulnerable to pessimism and resignation.

In the face of that increasing pessimism it is somewhat ironical that as the decades progressed real educational and vocational opportunities for women expanded immensely. Lewald did pioneer the profession of writing for women; others followed, many earning a living from writing for the numerous family-style magazines, like the popular *Gartenlaube*, which flourished in this period. In the 1860s Louise Otto-Peter, whose women's newspaper had been silenced in the years immediately following the 1848, reawakened interest in women's issues by co-founding the *Allgemeiner Deutscher Frauenverein*. With others, she worked to expand educational and vocational opportunities for women – along lines proposed by Fanny Lewald and even the young Malwida von Meysenbug. These efforts to give women the means to economic independence succeeded especially well in the area of teaching, although by the end of the century women were also attending German universities and invading the medical profession.

There would seem to be a kind of paradox here. The women who wrote these autobiographies had believed in these reforms and yet all held their distance from the newly emerging women's movement, never attempting to break out of their new isolation. Despite the real, albeit slow and painful, advance of the material conditions for bourgeois women in general, the autobiographies of these four women exhibit that increasing degree of accomodation, pessimism, and unwillingness to identify with former ideals. Disillusionment did not incapacitate their will to struggle and to find a personal role, but it is painful as readers to witness the degree to which they overlooked and denied their real changes in perspective as well as the changes in expectations for themselves. They evaluated their legitimate accessions to social pressure as the recognition of "truth" – even Ebner-Eschenbach perceived Lessing's talent as greater than hers. Earlier errors are superceded by new insight. It is the same process of evaluation of the past which Foucault had labeled "arrogant" when applied to History. This is the case even for Ebner-Eschenbach who forces herself to recognize the "truth" of her less glamourous talent, when she knows of the prejudice she encountered professionally because of her sex. With the qualified exception of Ebner-Eschenbach, they will not acknowledge or (or cannot remember) the pain of giving up desires or hopes for parts of themselves. The epistolary form allowed a more adequate record of those desires – precisely because it was not narrated from one later, privileged perspective. As a narrative form it had the capacity to be non-teleological – to be "genealogical".

Perhaps the paradox of the simultaneous acceptance of women in certain public occupations and the isolation of these "liberal" women is less of one than it seems. Indeed perhaps it has to do precisely with their failure – whether for social or personal reasons – to envision and give voice to multiple sides of their "selves". Resigned they may well have become, but that had not deterred Rahel Varnhagen and Bettina von Arnim from expressing contrary desires and asserting their alternate vision. In 1819, as that earlier Reaction fell on the also but lately lifted hopes of German liberals in the wake of defeat by Napoleon, Rahel Varnhagen had written Adolph Custine a letter describing her state of mind. Her former friends had begun to shun her and she questioned the power of the new religion (of friendship) as opposed to the old one, meaning Judaism but implying any religion based on authority structures. She was ill, but her doctor — who could not comprehend her entirely — was unable to diagnose the illness. She felt she had been forced to kill parts of herself, to obey new orders. But she wrote about it and still acknowledged unfulfilled dreams. Precisely because she always refused to submit to the established order (contrary to Lewald's portrait of her in *Prinz Louis Ferdinand*) those strands of desire could be read — and had been able to comfort Lewald and give her courage in her isolation. Nor can it be an accident that the letters of Varnhagen and Arnim have held their influence over the imaginations of German women down to the present day. It is *not* caring for the nerves and fibers of the soul that discourages and disables, not nurturing the variety of voices.

For all the influence of Varnhagen and Arnim, the younger German women did not express desire for anything more than integration. Aston, Lewald, Meysenbug, and to a lesser extent Ebner-Eschenbach turned from the multi-vocal narrative structures of their Romantic predecessors and in so doing lost a radical vision of human beings and human life that ultimately not only inspires, but also comforts when it is necessary. Indeed it would seem to provide equilibrium in times of despair. Though it appears more unsettling, the open form which encourages disruptive voices also reassures readers that the author (and reader?) is alive.

Why the women of the younger generation had lost the possibility of expressing those richer visions — even before the failure of the Revolution of 1848 — is a question which exceeds the limits of this discussion. While the answer surely lies in the realm of history and the solidification of power structures, it is also surely one that cannot be answered easily or solely with explanations from that realm. And perhaps we should not forget that as long as we can hear those voices they are not dead. For all her diffidence Marie von Ebner-Eschenbach has shown us that.

THE CASES OF POPP, WEGRAINER, AND VIERSBECK

Until now all of the examples in this study have acquired fictions or "scripts" from middle-class culture and its literary documents, whether novels, philosophical works, or other biographies. But some critics have claimed that working-class culture — and its conceptualization of the individual — was more progressive than bourgeois culture or intrinsically radical. It does not seem unreasonable to expect that the cultural influences on middle-class women differed greatly from those on working-class women. In most cases, we might assume, working-class exposure to the dominant cultural heritage was far more severely limited than that of middle-class women. When nineteenth-century proletarian women write autobiographies, therefore, there are at least two reasons to expect those works to differ significantly from ones by middle-class women. Firstly, and most obviously, their experience will have been very different. But secondly, cultural influences, particular "scripts", manifested in autobiographies of the working class may well have been very different. Three autobiographies written by working-class women will allow us to test these assumptions.

In Germany, the end of the last century saw a definite flowering of working-class autobiography. There had been earlier examples, but the increasing importance of a working-class party, the Social Democracy, occasioned a spate of such publications just at the turn of the century. The mere existence of this party had raised interest in the condition of the working class. Friedrich Engels' *The Condition of the Working Class in England* (1845) alerted well-intentioned middle-class concern, but the very presence of this well-organized opposition occasioned a different kind of political concern as well! Functioning not only passively as a catalyst for general non-party interest in reports of working-class life, the Party also actively encouraged autobiographical writing from workers. As early as the mid-1880s Friedrich Engels had urged Johann Philipp Becker (1809-1886; a revolutionary — vintage 1848 — and co-founder of the First International) to write his memoirs.[2] Engels wished to preserve these valuable recollections of the pre-history of the organized working-class movement. He believed, perhaps naively, that they would form a document no real historian

188

could overlook. Without these memoirs that moment in history would be gone, lost for the movement forever. Historians would either never know of its existence or it would be appropriated by people unsympathetic to their movement. Engels wanted the events of the 1830s told from the Party's perspective for use in the ideological battle with bourgeois historians over the proper view of history.

Curiously, Engels' concern seems directed more at middle-class historiography, than the working-class itself. However this motivation for encouraging autobiographical texts was not necessarily shared by other prominent Party officials. When fragments of Becker's autobiography appeared in the Party journal, *Die neue Welt*, in 1876 Wilhelm Liebknecht had criticized them as not "novelistic" enough.[3] With that Liebknecht appears less interested in historiography than in general readability. Most likely it was a concern that workers enjoy reading such an autobiographical/historical account, and the aim may well have been similar to that of Herder when he urged collections of autobiographical accounts in the eighteenth century: the creation of a sense of common identity. In any case, the Party as a whole clearly lacked a unified perspective on the role of this genre in the proletarian movement.

If these Party fathers disagreed on the ideal function of autobiography within the working-class movement, modern scholars disagree on the actual nature of proletarian autobiography at the turn of the last century. Compared to the quantity of material on bourgeois autobiography, studies on working-class autobiography are rare. This is not really surprising. Nor is it surprising that, unlike the former, studies on working-class autobiography reliably include discussions of autobiographies by women. German socialist thought has a long history of recognizing women as workers. And yet, given the fact that Socialists almost inevitably consider gender differences to represent secondary contradictions, it is also not surprising that they have not isolated issues inherent in women's autobiography.

Petra Frerichs and Ursula Münchow represent two contemporary positions on proletarian autobiography. Münchow, the East German scholar, views these proletarian autobiographies as legitimate heirs to the interrupted humanistic tradition most clearly characterized by Goethe's *Dichtung und Wahrheit*. Claiming this most important German tradition for the working-class, she asserts that only this class has continued the progress toward permitting the harmonious unfolding of personality. Working-class autobiographies outline the socialist process of becoming human ("Menschwerdung") (7) and August Bebel, Adelheid Popp, Wilhelm Moritz Bromme, and Franz

Rehbein thus portray the evolution of socialist personalities. (12) "Der Patriziersohn und Dichterfürst Johann Wolfgang Goethe hatte vor der bürgerlichen Revolution in doppeltem Sinne das Recht, sich als Repräsentant des aufsteigenden Bürgertums zu fühlen und noch unter feudalabsolutistischer Herrschaft eine demokratisch-humanistische Ordnung zu verkünden, in der der Mensch als Mensch und nach seiner Leistung für das Wohl der menschlichen Gesellschaft gewertet wird. Er durfte in diesem Sinne die Forderung stellen, daß der Fleiß und die Tüchtigkeit und die edle Gesinnung der besten Bürger des industriösen Deutschlands in Biographien für die Nachwelt festgehalten werde. Doch die Verwirklichung, die Errichtung der realen humanistischen Ordnung, blieb dem Proletariat vorbehalten." (63-4) It remained for the autobiographies of proletarians to complete the evolution of "humanistic" personalities. Münchow places these autobiographies directly in the tradition of personality evolution established by Goethe and shares, with Dilthey, the assumption about the nature of a "self" as a harmoniously integrated and motivated, apparently discreet individual.

The West German scholar Petra Frerichs, on the other hand, emphasizes the qualitative difference in proletarian and bourgeois autobiography. In the wake of sociologist Jürgen Habermas' assertion of the creation of a bourgeois public sphere beginning around 1800, Oskar Negt and Alexander Kluge attempted to define the evolution of a proletarian public sphere.[4] Wolfgang Emmerich situated his landmark collection of excerpts from working-class autobiography in the context of a "second culture", a proletarian way of life ("Lebensweise") distinct from bourgeois culture.[5] This concept encompasses everything from art to ways of thinking and feeling about the family and social groups. Petra Frerichs has further attempted to apply Lucien Seve's psychological theories about the specificity of proletarian awareness of identity to autobiographical theory.[6]

According to Frerichs, bourgeois autobiography emphasizes the unity of the individual, the evolution of an ego in opposition to the world, the preference for the inner dimension ("Innerlichkeitsdimension"), and the process of writing such a work as a means of self-discovery.(241) Proletarian autobiographies, according to Frerichs, display a sense of collective identity, the evolution of personality in conjunction with a social class, emphasis on objective reality, and the usefulness of autobiography in bringing about collective class consciousness.

So far many, though not all, autobiographers under study here *have* tended to emphasize their inner as opposed to their outer dimension, but, it has been argued, this is has been necessary for *women* who did not identify their "selves" with their bourgeois domestic roles. However, it is difficult to imagine a more radical challenge to the concept of the unity of the individual than that posed by Varnhagen or Arnim. Additionally, it should be emphasized that Aston, Lewald, and Meysenbug also stress that much of their experience is not unique, but shared with women in general. They hope others will benefit from their revelations. Nevertheless, we remain confronted with the opinion that the inwardness manifested in these works is the product of relative luxury. It is a view that cannot be dismissed without investigating autobiographies of proletarian women.

Undoubtedly the most successful and influential of these at the turn of the century was Adelheid Popp's *Jugend einer Arbeiterin* (1909).[7] Although first published anonymously by a bourgeois press, it clearly carried the endorsement of the Social Democracy. None other than August Bebel introduced the author as the "Vorkämpferin ihres Geschlechts"(19) and a "Beispiel der Nachahmung für viele"(20). Bebel, of course, had acheived authoritative status regarding the question of sex roles since his *Die Frau unter dem Sozialismus* (1883) had helped shape both working- and middle-class thought on the emanicipation of women. Even without that stamp of approval, however, Popp's autobiography seemed destined to win the imaginations of proletarian and bourgeois readers alike. It was so popular that a third edition was needed by 1910, but by that time it was no longer necessary to omit the name of the author, for it had remained a poorly kept secret. The fourth edition of 1922 finally appeared, as Popp had long wished, in the Party's press, *Vorwärts*.

The rise of the young Adelheid Dworschak from factory worker to Party activist was a story worth telling, although by now we are properly suspicious of "naturally" shaped stories. Popp begins her autobiography with a description of working-class misery. Unlike other autobiographers, she explains in attempt to set herself apart from bourgeois experience, it is only with pain that she recalls her childhood. Two parents and five children lived in one windowless room. Her father drank heavily and beat his wife. Mercifully perhaps, he died when she was fairly young, and yet in a sense his death made life harder for the family, for now all its members were expected to contribute to its support. Since Adelheid's mother did not believe in the usefulness of education and could not afford textbooks, the ten-year-old Adelheid left school and began working at any job she could find. Just that was not easy, however, and Popp describes desperate periods of searching for work. By the time she is employed in what was considered to be the factory with the best working conditions in Vienna, her experiences have illustrated the double and triple exploitation of young girls in factories. She experiences the poverty, desperation, and humiliation of thousands of working-class women. A friend of her own brother and later a salesman had made undesired sexual advances. The final humiliation came as she confided these events to her mother and brother. Rather than expressing their concern, they chided her for having read too many popular novels and accused her of too lively an imagination.

In fact she did like to read. Not only did that set her apart as a child, it also probably enabled her to escape the dreary conditions of her childhood. Despite her lack of official schooling there can be no doubt that books and religion were the strongest influences on her youthful imagination. And Popp describes them at some length. Very early, she reports, she would devour any reading material that fell into her hands. Friends lent her books or, for two Kreuzer saved from her lunch money, she could borrow books from a lending library. She loved stories about the Wild West and family-style journals with serialized novels. Above all she loved stories about robbers and unhappy queens. Favorite characters were Rinaldo Rinaldini, Katarina Kornaro, Rosa Sandor, Isabella of Spain, Eugenie of France, Maria Stuart. She learned fantasized history from books like *Die weiße Frau im Schloß*, and novels about the Emperor Josef, *Die Heldin von Wörth*. She also liked novels in 100 sequels about poor little girls overcoming terrible obstacles to become a countess, or at least the wife of a factory owner or merchant.

With the consciousness she evolved only later, Popp criticized her youthful literary tastes for removing her from the reality and misery that surrounded her.(37) And yet these novels undoubtedly continued to influence the shape of the narrator's hopes and dreams. As a child she had imagined that a wealthy benefactress, a particular countess, would rescue her from impoverishment.(33) She had hoped that a religious aunt, with a good position, would save her. But she had also imagined herself as heroine, being decorated with the Iron Cross like the Heroine of Wörth(66). These fantasies, which Popp so meticulously recorded, were clearly spawned by the world of bourgeois fiction, of heroes and romance and happy endings.

Nervertheless her tastes evolved. Hospitalized once for an illness contracted because of working conditions, a doctor gave her Friedrich Schiller and Alfons Daudet to read. Popp describes this period as one of the best in her childhood. Not unlike the bourgeois housewife Frederike Baldinger, whose lying-in periods gave her the only opportunity to read, Popp actually enjoyed this enforced bed rest. After her hospitalization she continued reading books like *Raubritter und sein Kind* (50), but she also read the German classics: Lenau, Wieland, Schiller. It would be a while until she learned to appreciate the works of Goethe, but when she did it would be those works he had written about women, in particular: *Die Wahlverwandtschaften, Die natürliche Tochter*, and *Iphigenie*. She does not mention *Dichtung und Wahrheit*, but it is surely not unlikely that she knew it, or of it.[8]

Clearly lack of formal education and time for reading had not totally restricted this working-class woman's familiarity with dominant culture. The literary tradition which Popp claims by naming is decidedly bourgeois, but it is not the liberal/radical one which influenced so many men and women of the 1848 Revolution. It is unlikely she read Rahel Varnhagen or Bettina von Arnim. Apart from her adventurous or Cinderella-like romances, her reading seems to have drawn on what had evolved as the classical canon of German literature, a tradition which included primarily Goethe and Schiller. As autobiographer, Popp may be critical of the popular novels she read as a child, but nowhere does she express a critical opinion of the German classical tradition.

If Popp, the narrator, is openly critical of her childhood taste in literature, she is even more critical of the other great influence on her as a girl. She describes her youthful religious inclinations as absolutely misguided. Fears of falling ill a second time, for instance, led her to undertake a pilgrimmage. That, in turn, led her to criticize the church because it manipulated the needs of believers for its own financial ends. Yet she continued to believe that if she prayed, God would rescue her—like the baroness or well-off aunt? Popp tells of praying for help one day and scraping together enough coins for a small offering. The next day she found a large sum of money on the street (which she gleefully and innocently kept as God's answer to her prayers). The day after she found work. Only when she came to believe in the Social Democracy did she hesitate in her belief in God. She could not understand a deity who allowed its creatures to perpetrate wicked deeds and oppress innocent people.

Like her faith in the classics, however, her faith in religion is not absolutely rejected by the narrator, the Party activist. Rather those influences lend a particular hue to her Socialism as well as her interpretation of her life. Both are tinged with notions of Goethe's entelechie as well as of redemption. Strange as it may seem at first, of all the autobiographies under investigation here, Popp's most nearly approaches the teleological form of Goethe's *Dichtung und Wahrheit*. Her religious beliefs, slightly less important, are for the most part secularized.

In Goethe's entelechial model his talents and desires were met, supported, and encouraged by external realities. That fortuitous circumstance allowed him to evolve his abilities and desires to their fullest and most well rounded. To be sure this did not occur without some opposition, particularly from Goethe's family, but once that was overcome, the intellectual and political climate was propitious. The telos of his being, according to traditional interpretations, was fulfilled. In the highest sense his individuality was allowed to unfold.

Adelheid Dworschak's talents and desires are also convincingly portrayed as fulfilled. In a sense other than she imagined at the time, her youthful fantasies and abilities reach fruition. The narrator Popp distinguishes the youthful Adelheid Dworschak from her colleagues by her passion for reading. Since no other workers are portrayed with a passion for reading, in this regard she appears as unique and individual. When she did not have to work Sundays she could be found reading. Her favorite spot was the cemetery or, when her family could afford a place with a window, by the window. To some extent reading is bound to isolate, yet Popp emphasizes this when she describes herself as withdrawing from her family or from her colleagues during lunch breaks to read by herself. The social side of this endeavor was the fact that she was, from the beginning, a gifted narrator. She entertained family, friends, and colleagues by re-telling the tales she had read. She became very popular for this narrative talent, but it also set her apart.

Without directly saying so, Popp foreshadows her talents and her popular reception as a Party activist. She lays the groundwork for her later evolution, for as she discovers Socialist literature she slowly begins explaining *it*, rather than her novels, to her colleagues at work. She had become a totally new person and those around her who did not share her insights appeared as enemies. "Ich wollte aber bekehren und wollte politisieren'." (76) Her first agitatory success occurs in her own factory when she succeeds in organizing the workers' demand for a holiday on May 1. She feels she had led "eine kleine Revolution".(78) In her own way she had been a heroine.

Dworschak began to attend Party rallies. At first she was only one of two or three women present. In an atmosphere where it was daring for women even to attend such meetings (and apparently unlady-like to applaud the speakers), it was unheard of for one to speak. Yet when she saw only men address the topic of the condition of working-class women, she responded, so she reports, to an irresistible urge to take the podium. It is, not unlike Goethe's *daemon* (or for that matter Ebner-Eschenbach's songbirds), a "natural" force beyond control. Without quite knowing what she was doing, and to the astonishment of all, she addressed her first assembly. She had never even seen a woman speak publicly. In the jubilant reception that greeted her speech she felt "als hätte ich die Welt erobert".(80) Treated afterward as a marvel, a veritable wonder appearing from nowhere, she was encouraged to write her speech for the Party newspaper. Overcoming her mother's opposition, she gradually began touring and speaking for the Social Democrats. Eventually she was invited to take a full-time position with the Party as agitator.

Popp refers to her acceptance of that post as her entrance into "das gelobte Land" (87). For her it represented the highest personal fulfillment. Her life had gained a content (88). Of all the women studied here only Popp convincingly demonstrates that her natural desires and individual talents had coincided with the needs of her immediate society. Far from being thwarted, her interest and ability in reading and speaking were warmly received and nurtured by her colleagues and the Party. She had every reason to be grateful to it. Without it a woman who had left school at age ten would never have been permitted to unfold her talents. This was the work toward which she claims to have been inwardly drawn. Her particular telos appears fully (and convincingly) evolved. Such a successful coincidence of history and personal wishes is seldom achieved.

Petra Frerichs, and Wolfgang Emmerich as well, have relied heavily on the preface to the third (1910) edition to assert Popp's sense of collective rather than individual identity. There Popp had denied that modesty had prevented her from revealing her identity in the first two editions. Rather she had hoped to emphasize the universal class aspects of her experience as opposed to the particularities of her biography. The preface asserted the typical nature of her experience. Such an assertion, however, is undoubtedly characteristic less of proletarian autobiography in particular than of autobiography of any group feeling itself marginal to the social mainstream. Louise Aston, Fanny Lewald, and even so arch an individualist as Malwida von Meysenbug, for instance, all asserted their collective identity with the fate of other women. Moreover, we have seen that while Popp undoubtedly shared experiences and even particular emotions with the working class, she also portrays qualities and talents which were unique to her, at least among her acquaintances.

Indeed the preface to the fourth (1922) edition tended to weight equally her identity as an individual and as a member of a collective. There readers learned that without the encouragement of a comrade, Dr. Adolf Braun, her modesty would, in fact, have prevented her from writing an autobiography. She would never have dared to "enlighten" the public with her memoirs without his encouragement, for she knew that the lives of all working women were the same (23). Thousands could have told the same story so far as the suffering and patience was concerned. But, she noted, her experience could be useful for others because only a few working women had found the way elevate themselves out of an oppressed and enslaved youth. In 1922 (in the edition published by the party) it was precisely her *atypical* reaction to that situation that seemed to justify her telling her story. Although she had waited until 1922 to make such a statement, the 1909 version of the work itself implies just such a sense of self. The unfolding of her particular talents and the evolution of her personality would seem indeed to represent a Goethe-like concept of teleological biography.

The telos evolved remained a personal one: her fulfillment as speaker and writer. To be sure, the class for which she struggled improved its condition, but it did not gain access to "the promised land". If she intended her life as an example to others, that was not possible for the vast majority, whose desires and talents might not be fulfilled by a post with the Party. At some level, Popp confuses her own personal sense of fulfillment and gratitude to the Party with the role of the Party in history. Although she fully credits both herself and the Party for her achievements, and not any supernatural power, both the description of her life and the role of the Party in history carry overtones of a religion she never fully relinquished.

Indeed Popp frequently describes her experience with Socialism in terms commonly reserved for religious experience. The enlightenment she achieves after reading socialist literature for the first time is not unlike that following a divine revelation. The sudden insight and clarity gained by that perspective enthrall and captivate her attention. They permit her to understand and judge her destiny rather than be enslaved by it.(68) When she begins buying the Party weekly, she dresses up as if for church.(70) She enters the office to purchase it as she would enter a "holy place". Not only does she later refer to her work with the Party as "the promised land", she refers to Socialism itself as "welterlösend".

As if recognizing the religious overtones to her description of this ritual, she immediately explains how she gradually worked her way free of her belief in all religious ideas. Yet she is honest enough to admit the inner conflict that resulted. She would argue publicly against the existence of God and heaven, since no God could allow the Czars to send prisoners to labor camps in Siberia. But she would go home and pray to God. In the 1915 continuation of her autobiography, however, she casually mentions that she believes in the "maintenance" (171) of religion (as well as the family), and one suspects that the conflict she had portrayed in the original volume was resolved in favor of God and religion, but against their earthly manifestations.

Indeed the association of Socialism with Christianity becomes much clearer in that 1915 continuation. There she wrote, for instance: "Ich lernte begreifen, daß der Messias, der vor neunzehn Jahrhunderten gekommen sein soll, noch nicht die Erlösung für alle gebracht hat. Aber gleich vielen tausenden Schicksalsgenossen lernte ich auf einen neuen Messias vertrauen und hoffen, auf einen Erlöser, der nicht in Menschengestalt ans Kreuz geschlagen werden kann. Ich lernte auf den Erlöser hoffen, der in den Köpfen und Herzen von Millionen wohnt, der sich aus dem Innersten der Menschen heraus die Welt erobert, um sie so umzugestalten, daß sie dem Glücke aller dient. Dieser Erlöser zaubert nicht. . .aber er gibt den Menschen die Kraft, über die Macht des Goldes zu siegen und die Bahn frei zu machen für die Freuden aller. Ich lernte an den Socialismus glauben, und die Weihnachtsidee, die so lange mein Denken beherrschte und mein Sehnen ausgemacht hatte, trat weit zurück vor dem Verlangen, den Socialismus im Heim der Armen und Unterdrückten als Befreier begrüssen zu können." (120) As much as this passage records her rejection of traditional notions of a mystical savior, it replaces it with a new idea of a Socialist one and redemption on earth. Her own salvation and that of humanity appear in secularized versions of the concepts of redemption and the millenium, and in that sense particularly the story of her life recalls the tradition of religious confession, the highpoint of which is a vision granting clarity and insight, followed by conversion and active engagement on behalf of the redemption of others.

Recalling Popp's childhood fantasies of being saved and of becoming a heroine, it no longer seems out of character for her to have viewed herself as a representative of that general savior, Socialism. In such a case she would fulfill her youthful dreams of heroism and of rescuing others. She exhibits, for instance, some personal satisfaction in having won the workers and her bosses for the idea of a holiday on May 1. She admits her desire to convert, to lead others into the faith. The suggestions of this in the 1909 edition appear visually represented in the fourth edition of *Jugend einer Arbeiterin* (1922), the one which finally saw the fulfillment of her wish for Party publication of her autobiography. That Party edition carried an awkward illustration showing a large number of small figures at the base of a factory, as though they supported it. Two large chimeneys flank the factory and between them looms a large head of a woman (presumably Popp). Arching over her head and joining the two chimeneys is a crown of thorns. In this illustration Popp becomes the heroine she had once dreamed of becoming.

Although she has since renounced militarism and the heroism of battle, it seems likely she still wished to lead her sisters to the same salvation she herself had found in the Social Democracy.

The strength of traditional religious imagery is much stronger in this working-class woman raised in the Austrian Catholic tradition than it has been for any of the middle-class women under study. The religious influence on Wallenrodt and Engel had been rather superficial, and the patheistic mysticism of Arnim exhausted traditional religious patterns. Popp's distinctly millenarian view of the Social Democracy retains far more of those patterns and images. Yet, thanks to the Social Democracy the impact of religious tradition appears decidedly empowering and optimistic. Without that Party the effects of religion on working-class women could be devastating, as we will see in the case of Maria Wegrainer.

Before turning to that work, however, we still want to examine the relative internality of Popp's autobiography, indeed of her conception of herself as an individual. Compared to most of the bourgeois autobiographers, she is relatively restrained with regard to her family life. Her marriage is not portrayed at all in the 1909 edition, she explained later, because she did not want to provide any clues to her identity. Descriptions of her childhood, of course, are another matter. The family portrait, to be sure, illustrates primarily the condition of working-class life and only secondarily her relations with her family. The relationship with her mother is the most precisely described. The young Dworschak was removed from school (which she liked and in which she was doing well) by her mother. She was accused by her of laziness and an overripe imagination when she wanted to avoid a work situation where a man was making advances to her. Her mother never understood her Party work or why she refused to perform all the wifely tasks for her later husband. Although the mother's attitudes are understandable enough, she is described as someone who never understood Popp's less traditional drives or, apparently, the psychological needs, which she does claim to possess. When Bebel and Engels try to convince the mother of the importance of her daughter's work, she merely perceives that two gentlemen old enough to be her father are courting her.

Despite the enormous potential for exploring such resistance to her desires and the psychological struggle between mother and daughter, Popp refrains from pursuing this theme in as much detail as someone like Bettina von Arnim might have. While there is restraint on Popp's part then, it is also possible to assert that she is more candid about (and perhaps more aware of) such a conflict than someone like Wallenrodt or even Ebner-Eschenbach might have been. Indeed she seems not only more willing to admit such familial conflict, she also appears less tortured by confronting it in real life. She merely goes her own way, regardless of what her mother thinks.

But rather than conclude that Popp was less concerned about her inner dimension, we might consider two factors. First, from the age of ten the young Dworschak had been earning income. The emotional independence that almost surely accompanied that relative financial independence had to reduce the psychological tension at home. Popp's mother was not a source of total protection for her; the relationship was more reciprocal from a very early age. While her mother's lack of understanding made Popp uncomfortable, this parent was in no position to restrict her actions. Similarly marriage would not likely change her need to work; it would certainly not remove the knowledge that she could support herself. The lack of inwardness on this score may actually represent less real dependence on family than was typically the case for bourgeois women. She does not need to summon great stores of inner strength to deal with her domestic affairs, because they do not play the same role for her.

Second, the young Dworschak's primary subjective involvement may have focused elsewhere. And indeed Popp actually describes quite extensively — and subjectively — her feelings about her real situation: her precarious financial situation, her terror of falling ill and the religious desires that induced. She details her early reading material to give the reader a sense of her childhood fantasies, which had less to do with domestic affairs or prince charmings than being rescued from poverty by rich women or being the hero herself. Her description of how she became a Socialist is also quite subjective, for she portrays it as answering that internal need. Her timidity at her first rallies and the inner force which drove her to speak for the first time are conveyed as well as the religious awe she felt for the Party. Her work as activist was that toward which her inner being had been striving, and in fact she convincingly demonstrated that she already possessed a sense of "self", gained perhaps from bourgeois literature, which the Party supported and encouraged. Recognizing the difference in perspective, it is difficult to speak of any lack of inner dimension in this autobiography. Indeed the relative importance of that dimension for Popp can again be compared with its importance for Goethe, who portrayed his childhood subjectivity in similar patterns. What is distinctive in Popp's autobiography is that the pattern of inner dimension is less uniquely centered on her family life (including fantasies about men, if the text is taken as accurate), than is the case for most bourgeois women. It is more easily focused on work experiences and financial difficulties, for which there is little sense of guilt or, on the part of the reader, little sense that the author ommited or masked significant portions of her life.

On the other hand, if any emphasis distinguishes Popp's work from Goethe's it is, perhaps surprisingly from Frerichs' perspective, a relative lack of external perspective. To be sure Popp details life in the factories or the very difficulty of looking for work, but her historical perspective is limited. Goethe had drawn on the past fifty years or more of German culture and history, had even compared it with that of neighboring countries. He was aware of domestic politics and foreign revolutions. Although she was an avid reader of history books and newspapers, Popp does not present a picture of history beyond that of the struggle for the right to have May 1 as a holiday. While other (male) socialist autobiographers of the period tend to structure their lives around dates important for the history of the Social Democracy,[9] Popp does not. There is little sense of the place of her efforts in the history or policy of the Party as a whole — or in the history of Austria or the working-class movement as a whole. We know that she was among the first women to become active in the Party, and yet she paints us no picture of Socialist thought about women before or after, no picture of the changing role of women in society at large. Given her strong interest in history it is strange indeed that Popp seems unable to situate herself within it.

And yet, compared with most of the autobiographies we have reviewed, Popp's historical perspective is actually rather large for a woman. Possible exceptions to this would be Regula Engel, Fanny Lewald, and Malwida von Meysenbug. Even in these cases, however, we have seen contradictions and discrepancies, the difficulties confronting women when they attempt to view their lives in relation to commonly accepted notions of "History". The conclusion that can be drawn is that even when a woman like Popp successfully enters history, even when her efforts appear to be warmly received, she is not accustomed to or practiced in seeing herself in relation to larger movements.

Ultimately this probably effected Popp's choice of audience. Not only had Engels wanted Becker to record his memories for the sake of bourgeois historiography, when August Bebel published his autobiography in 1910, it was essentially the history of his role in the evolution of the Social Democracy, that is, more overtly a contribution to historiography. (The very title of that work, *Aus meinem Leben*, moreover, clearly evokes the full title of Goethe's *Aus meinem Leben. Dichtung und Wahreheit* even if the work itself manifests less influence from it than Popp's.) Both of these Socialists seemed to want to address larger bourgeois intellectual audiences. Popp, perhaps more like Liebknecht, seems more concerned with general popularity among the working-class. She engages her passion to stimulate a response from those with backgrounds similar to hers. As she once said of herself, she wants to convert.

There can really be no doubt that this working class woman was heavily influenced in her understanding of her life by bourgeois culture, high and low. It is difficult to view in this autobiography the work of a typical or representative working-class woman. Her passion for reading, for history, for political theory as well as her bald initiative brought her a degree of education which, I think it is fair to say, was uncommon for the majority of the working-class. For these reasons, perhaps, this autobiography does not match Frerichs' outline for a portrait of proletarian autobiography. Her solidarity with her class background and her commitment to better its condition are beyond question. But the solidarity and commitment were no less great for Louise Aston when she wrote *Aus dem Leben einer Frau* to urge middle-class women to take the reigns of fate into their own hands. Like Aston, moreover, her identity is not so bound to her sense of collectivity that she does not conceive of herself as an individual as well. Popp shows the evolution of her individual talents and is grateful for the opportunities the Party has given her to develop them. In order to be able to demonstrate these she has not neglected her inner dimension, she has rendered childhood fantasies. Moreover, as one of Frerichs' characteristics of bourgeois autobiography, the struggle to shape identity cannot be said to occur without pitting herself against society. Although she had the support of the Party (in its role, after all, opposing bourgeois society), she still had to confront not only her bosses, but also the more challenging opposition of her mother. As soon as she had a position to defend, she even perceived colleagues not of her persuasion to be "enemies". Popp's descriptions of her objective situation, the meager Christmasses or the working conditions in factories, may be explicit and concrete, as Frerichs claims they are in proletarian autobiography, but they are no more so than, for instance, Recke's descriptions of her objective situation, being forced to stand for hours by her grandmother's chair or to endure the sexual assaults of her husband. If the former appears more significant to us as readers, we must wonder at the sense of history which respects public, but not private existences.

Popp's autobiography would seem to fulfill more closely Münchow's estimate of working class autobiography as the culmination of the interrupted humanistic tradition that had started with Goethe. Indeed it should be placed within this tradition, a proposal implying that the Party's understanding of the constitution of "individual" was similar to that of the dominant culture.

Of the canon of proletarian autobiography from the turn of the century (and there now *is* one consisting of about 5 or 6 works), Popp's is the only one by a woman. Scholars like Frerichs and Münchow are predisposed toward autobiographies by representatives of the "classic" proletariat, namely factory workers with an affinity for collective action. However, women from a more broadly conceived working-class background, servants or waitresses for instance, also wrote and published autobiographies, and these are seldom, if ever, investigated.[10]

For the modern-day editors of Marie Wegrainer's *Der Lebensroman einer Arbeiterfrau* (1914).[11] this work represents a kind of polar opposite to Popp's. Accepting the interpretation of *Jugend einer Arbeiterin* as a primarily objective autobiography, they consider Wegrainer's primarily subjective(10). While neither statement is quite just, the editors are essentially correct in pointing to a kind of polarity, since Wegrainer's illustrates a working-class perspective that had not benefitted from the insights of the Social Demoncracy. Marie Wegrainer was a pseudonym for Marie Frank (1852-1924), who for a relatively few years worked as a domestic servant. The Social Democracy's lack of interest in organizing domestic help is reflected in this autobiography insofar as the author remains totally oblivious to larger movements or historical connections. She remains a victim of her situation. Frank relates the story of her childhood and her experiences while a domestic servant and then in her marriage. Although her amorous experiences may be highlighted, there are glimpses of the real conditions of her employment and married life.

Not an orphan the infant Marie is, nevertheless, raised in a friendly foster home. Only once does Marie even see her father, after his return from America. Her mother lives in the city and supports her, barely. Like Popp's mother, she sees no use in educating girls and insists that Marie begin earning her living at age 14. By the time the mother remarries and sends for the daughter, Marie has already traveled to Munich in search of employment. Even after joining her mother, there is no family life for her. The mother seems to transfer her hatred for her father to the daughter. Marie's first and truest love is for a wandering painter, Karl Volk. But when her mother discovers they meet secretly her infatuation is merely cause for another row. Oddly enough there is a kind of reconciliation when her step-father makes sexual advances, although both agree she must now leave. Marie returns to Munich to look for work, expecting always that Karl Volk will write. After losing her job when she contracts typhus, she also loses Karl. A letter finally arrives informing her that his family insist he marry advantageously. She is introduced to Leonhard Wegrainer and soon falls in love with this young dandy. She loses her next job when her employer discovers she has a beaux, even though she performs all her duties satisfactorily. Since Leonhard Wegrainer must complete his military service, however, they cannot marry yet, and Marie must look for employment once again.

The Russian countess by whom she is next employed is (apparently) a mistress of King Ludwig II of Bavaria. When the King takes a fancy for the servant and when the countess discovers Marie has been to see him alone she is immediately dismissed. Meanwhile Karl Volk writes that his fiancee will not marry a man who loves another, namely Marie. Although he is full of regret, Marie, in demonstration of her integrity, resolves not to desert Leonhard, for she believes he truly loves her. Without informing her readers about the sequence of events, we next find someone running to fetch the mid-wife. The baby (Leopold's, presumably) soon dies and although utterly forlorn, Marie must endure the insults of the priest. This is the end only of the first, adventuristic and romantic part of the autobiography.

At the beginning of the second it becomes clear that Leonhard's mother does not want him to marry Marie, he also should marry well. Although Leonhard insists, on the day they are married he lets slip, in a drunken stupor, that he has merely rescued his honor by marrying her. The author fairly breezes through her married life, now, mentioning the births of the children and eventually their occupations or marriages. The hardships are many. Trained as a craftsperson, Leonhard has difficulty finding work in an era of manufacturing and his pride will not allow him to enter a factory. He tries to keep up appearances with his friends, but his selfishness only depletes the domestic economy. Marie scrapes their existence together, finally making peace with her husband. The younger son, Gerhard, seems to be her special pride, and it is ultimately for him that she writes her memoirs. She notices that he and his wife are struggling to support his efforts at becoming an artist. She believes the publication of her memoirs would earn enough money to help them and so sits down to record them.

Perhaps the success of autobiographies like Popp's had led others to believe they could earn money in this fashion, but one suspects the idea may have come from a different quarter. Even this brief recapitulation of the content of Frank's work will suggest the flavor of popular romance novels, and the title *Aus dem Lebensroman einer Arbeiterfrau* certainly encourages a suspicion in that direction. If we chose not to question Wegrainer's veracity, and her story is certainly within the bounds of credibility, we must still acknowledge the novelistic treatment of her life. She places distinct emphasis on her amorous difficulties during the few years prior to her marriage and devotes relatively little attention to her many years of marriage and motherhood. After Popp's autobiography we certainly cannot take such a weighting of events for granted. Popp had all but ignored her romantic inclinations in her narration.

Wegrainer's first unhappy love affair, for instance, may be narrated without much artistic flourish, but the elements of a popular romance are there and include an angry mother and lustful step-father. Romance situations abound. They include scenes of jealousy, reconciliation, regret, domestic violence, life threatening accidents, and noble sacrifice. In particular her apparent seduction by the King of Bavaria is narrated in a manner which is anything but naive and which is likely to have been acquired from fiction. Having noted the King's apparent interest in her, Wegrainer merely describes her secret summons to the residence and her journey there alone. The thread of the tale is coyly picked up only as she returns home. A similar coy gap in the narration occurs before she gives birth to her illegitimate child. In general Frank's style may be direct, rather than embellished, but she adds to the novelistic atmosphere of individual scenes by recalling particularities of dress in great detail.

The elements of bourgeois culture, including the focus on amorous affairs with men and the dependence on domestic life illustrated by her changed situation after her marriage, dominate this autobiography. Wegrainer suffers under many, though not all, of the ideological restrictions on middle-class women. Although her inclination may have given her "scripts" from bourgeois fiction, the real condition of poverty soon disillusioned her with regard to ideals of domestic bliss. She does not hide the emotional distance from her husband, although in other respects she would seem not to want to identify herself with it. Novelistic elements, for instance, are underscored by a third-person narration. Names of people and places had been changed. And perhaps it is not insignificant that Frank gives her favorite son's name, Leonhard, to her husband in the *Lebensroman*. (That very son's fame as a writer, moreover, has been the most immediate cause for interest in this autobiography. Leonhard Frank (1882-1961) was a novelist of some reputation in Germany prior to World War II.) It was to help that son that she recorded her life story, a deed she forever kept from her husband.

But the apparent unseemliness of women writing and apparent anxiety over exposing near male relatives kept Frank from using her own name and from telling her own husband, is not unlike that of the authors of those early nineteenth-century autobiographies — Baldinger, Wallenrodt, Recke, Stägemann, and ultimately Varnhagen and Arnim as well. Not unlike Wallenrodt, Recke, and Stägemann she too had taken many motifs from fiction. She also clearly wrote as the nearest means for earning money, as had Engel and Wallenrodt. Frank may have come from a different class background, but how much had really changed for women dependent on families for their existence and emotional support?

Of special importance to this autobiography is its minimal structuring, its division into two parts. The first part concludes with the death of Wegrainer's illegitimate child, the second with the moment of writing, when the author is an old woman. The death of that child represented a spiritual nadir for Wegrainer. Mentally distraught and physically weakened, she must go to her mother's for a rest and remains a year. Frank clearly considered the birth and death of that child to be the fruit of grievous sin. If the first part of her autobiography ends with its death, the words closing the second are: "Durch den schweren Weg, den sie gehen mußte, [ward] alle Schuld gebüßt und ausgelöscht "(185) She views the pain of her married life to be just and divine retribution for her youthful sin. Clearly, religious influence allowed this woman to accept her domestic role as victim. Frank has structured her entire life around that one departure from common morality of which she was not the instigator. Following the most traditional social ethics she blames the victim in this episode, herself, and accepts the punishment for the rest of her life.

The cruelty of a religion that allowed Frank to accept her role as victim contrasts forcefully with the empowering influence of the Social Democracy. But at least as striking is the fact that both Popp and Frank reveal the distinct influences of "scripts" from popular romance novels and of religion. Neither really distances herself from those cultural scripts. Both demonstrate the pervasive influence of bourgeois fictions, whether high or low, on the self-image of working-class women. Popp is more successful in finding both a life and a script that open possibilities for her. She chose from available options. Frank lacks the literary sophistication born of familiarity with the German classics and the historical and personal optimism born of familiarity with the Social Democracy, but both have shown themselves susceptible to the influence of popular literature and religion. Neither seriously questions or undermines the concept of individual as integrated, discreet personality.

Popp's autobiography has acheived the status of a "classic" of proletarian autobiography, and not only among modern scholars. While its popularity in 1909 was greatest in the middle-class,[2] it obviously also inspired other working-class autobiography. For instance, the later autobiography of Ottilie Baader, *Ein steiniger Weg* (1921), took its title from Popp's text.[3] Like Popp, Baader was an activist for the Social Democracy, and many of the themes she develops after World War I resemble those of Popp's. The mere appearance of Popp's work in 1909, however, seems spontaneously to have occasioned autobiographies by other working-class women. One year after the appearance of *Jugend einer Arbeiterin* her publisher, Ernst Reinhart, claimed that only a few of the manuscripts they had since received could be published. He did so in the introduction to the 1910 publication of Doris Viersbeck's *Erlebnisse eines Hamburger Dienstmädchens*, another autobiography by a domestic servant.[4]

Wolfgang Emmerich has grouped this work with others he describes as being written from the perspective of a victim. Whereas autobiographies of class conscious workers portray a dialectical process of development, these works, he claims, remain static and restrict themselves to descriptions of misery.[5] Such a statement, however, is more true of Frank's autobiography, which he fails to mention, than of Viersbeck's. To be sure, Viersbeck envisions no absolute betterment of life, no dream of a life in which there would be no class of domestic servants. However, it is not true that she does not portray some development of character, both an increased mastery over her situation and a heightened sense of what is owed her as a human being. She comes to expect a warm room, the right to her own name, the right not to have her work interrupted, to receive family visits and to take nights off. As she goes from job to job she becomes increasingly sure of her capabilities, she learns to fend for herself on a moment's notice and to demand what she has a right to expect. Her last position of 5½ years she leaves only because she marries. Although she experiences misery, Viersbeck cannot be said merely to describe such a situation. She is not simply the object of history. She clearly takes increasing pride in her work and her person, and she finally occupies what is for her a satisfactory position.

Indeed like Popp Viersbeck not only seems outraged at her shoddy treatment by employers, she also seems concerned to pass on her accumulated wisdom to her peers. She thus details the meanness and stinginess of various employers and summarizes at the end what she has learned in her years of service: "Allen lieben Mitmenschen, die gezwungen sind, ihr Brot an anderer Leute Tisch zu essen, möchte ich zurufen: Tut immer eure Pflicht, voll und ganz; aber dann verteidigt euch auch, wo es nottut."(103) Unrevolutionary advice perhaps, but a defiant recommendation for self-respect. Even without a Party to encourage her Viersbeck recognized the collective fate of domestic servants and hoped to smooth the way for them with the narration of her experiences. When the Party ignored the plight of domestic servants, it not only failed women like Marie Frank, it also lost women like Doris Viersbeck.

If any of these working-class women focuses exclusively on her work experiences, it is Viersbeck. Her family life is hardly mentioned and she ends her autobiography with her marriage, i.e. her exit from the work place, without having described her courtship. Unlike Popp she does not convey any reading or religious experiences. Nor does she narrate any amorous inclinations. What was not the case with Popp's autobiography is the case here. The subjective element is missing. But so, too, is any horizon beyond her several experiences in domestic service. She demonstrates no interest in history. Viersbeck describes, for what inevitably will be a bourgeois and not a working-class audience, only what life is like as a domestic servant.

None of the influences observed in other works appears here. Despite its sense of collectivity this is not a working-class autobiography of pre-socialist affinities. Nor does Viersbeck merely describe her victimization. Moreover, although the author demonstrates of her increasing sense of self and abilities, this work cannot comfortably be placed in any tradition of bourgeois humanism, which imagines the natural unfolding of a harmoniously constituted human being. There is no obvious evidence of any other element of bourgeois culture, or religion. There is no obvious influence from any quarter. While we cannot assume she did not read popular or even classical works of literature, they do not appear to have influenced the recollection of her life.

This work appears naive, but more than that if anything distinguishes it from others it is Viersbeck's uncomplicated pride in her capabilities and her straightforward insistence on respect for her person. Financial independence, no doubt, had much to do with the expression of this self-respect, but one wonders whether familial expectations that she would work as an adult also did not prepare her for accepting that self-confidence. Viersbeck, however, with her lack of inner dimension, relates little of that family experience.

This is not a very exciting autobiography formally, stylistically, or even with regard to its content, but in the simple, uncomplicated expression of self-respect it appears in some ways quite hopeful. That is a sad commentary on the fate of German women in the nineteenth century. How hard had bourgois women like Baldinger, Engel, Wallenrodt, Recke, Stägemann, Varn-hagen, Arnim, Lewald, Meysenbug, and Ebner-Eschenbach had to strug-gle for self-respect! Some never achieved it. Of those who did, none really expressed straightforward pride in her capabilities. Expression of pride in one's abilities has always been mixed with shows of modesty, comparisons to really great talents, excuses of altruistic motives, over-exertion in its very demonstration. It has never been simple and direct. Even Popp only informs readers of her good work habits in connection with her organizing, although she had to be a model worker in order not to be fired. Moreover apart from the May 1 holiday, she never expresses simple pride in her ability as an or-ganizer.

As unique and as hopeful as Viersbeck's self-respect is, one must finally ask whether her pride was not possible only because the role of domestic servant posed no challenge to traditional images of women? In that case, and one suspects it to be so, the very absence of an obvious and particular influence here constitutes the more general acceptance of dominant cul-ture. Viersbeck had no desire to assume the life patterns of men. She en-countered no fundamental opposition in her efforts to fulfill her talents in the area of domestic service. Nor had she sinned grievously as a woman, as had Frank. Her life, as she described it, was unproblematic for the tradi-tional thread of social fabric.

Essentially the story of an apprenticeship to an acceptable trade, Viers-beck's autobiography is reminiscent in its objectivity and restriction to work experience to sixteenth-century chronicles "die von Hunger und Armut berichten, aber auch von menschlicher Freude und von Stolz über bezwun-gene Nöte erfüllt sind."[15] It narrates the author's acquisition of a profes-sion. As such it falls into one of Niggl's categories for antecedents of late eighteenth-century autobiography, the autobiography of profession. Af-ter four centuries a woman can relate with dignity how she learned a trade. This was not the first time; even in the late seventeenth century Glückel of Hameln recorded her business adventures![7] But the relative rarity of such a document gives pause, as does the fact that domestic service is not a trade with great public status. It is, however, a trade most commonly associated with women, and with their roles as wives and mothers, so that the very nar-ration of such a story is in fact a landmark.

If anything distinguishes these autobiographies from those of bourgeois women it has less to do with a challenge to bourgeois concepts of the in-dividual than the absence of domestic restrictions on these women's lives. The difference lies in the naturalness with which these authors explore the work they did and, with the possible exception of Wegrainer, the lack of problems posed by the ideology of the bourgeois domesticity. These autobiographers did not feel the need to struggle with traditional forms of autobiographical narration in order to write and publish their life stories. Given the timely interest in working-class autobiography their "confessions" of working-class life were welcomed. Nor were they in a position of having to explain why they led lives which did not conform to bourgeois ideology. In different forms perhaps these had been the very issues also confronting the writing and publishing of women's autobiographies around 1800. These differences did not mean working-class women did not adopt "identities" for themselves derived from bourgeois culture. Indeed in a fundamental way not even Adelhaid Popp challenged the middle-class definition of "individuality", the foundation of middle-class culture. But these women were not forced into the self-contortions of their better-off sisters, who were faced with upholding domestic relations or breaking them irrevocably. Neither did they undermine the assumptions of identity of that culture. They aspired, rather, to acquire it.

CONCLUSION

Those women in nineteenth century Germany who attempted to write a "History" of their lives with a telelogocial perspective have revealed the inadequacy of that formula for their experience: in particular Fanny Lewald and Adelhaid Popp. According to the concept, a rich and harmonious unfolding of an integrated "self" required a fertile soil and adequate nourishment. These were not present for Lewald, who found her way out of her personal dilemma with a great deal of good luck. Certain aspects of experiences particular to her sex could not be fully validated within this context: the constraints of family, her personal identification with women. Moreover she was ultimately *not* able to establish the intimate connection to history implied by such a perspective; rather that relationship to public history, as she described it, was quite distanced. In places she painted a panoramic background, but without clear connections to her own life. It is as if she rode through history as she once rode through that economically deprived village, peering into the lighted windows as she passed, encased and protected by her carriage.

Adelhaid Popp appears to have found a fertile and receptive ground for the unfolding of her character; but it is within the framework of a Party in opposition to the entire social order. The nurturing ground of the Party does not necessarily reflect a more general public receptivity. And even so she does not establish her personal connection with the concept of public history—either in terms of the history of the Party or in terms of German history. It may be implicit in her millenarian view of the Party, but her own connection with that is not articulated. Given the historical position of women it is unlikely that any one of them would be able to succeed in modeling her life on this pattern. Nor is it necessarily desirable that this type of closure become possible.

The epistolary forms, in their variety, seem best able to provide the possibility of avoiding teleological approaches. They also seem best able to dis/close the particularity of experience which does *not* accord with dominant history, and that includes experience particular to women. They allow a "genealogical" approach to personal history. They do not necessarily assume a unified "self", which would almost necessarily be one that con formed to a conception of dominant history. Rather they permit the surfacing of non-consistent aspects of personality. For women they permit the articulation of contrary emotions, the articulation of a "self" in opposition to the established order. It was only when women like Recke and Stägemann availed themselves of this form that they permitted themselves to express such sentiments.

It would seem therefore that it was only from the vantage point of a nonharmonious concept of "self" that women were able to articulate a "self" at all. For Baldinger, Engel and Wallenrodt subordinated their "selves" to the dominant order, i.e. tradition. In a religious tradition the inner voice calling one away from other conventional responsibilities could be attributed to God, viz. Madame Guyon. And while in a secular framework men could be "called" to particular professions, women could not. For them it took the form of a still, small voice within which had to assert some fundamental integrity of "self". That voice needed encouragement and required friendship.

The perspectives of Rahel Varnhagen and Bettina von Arnim appear the most viable. Couched firmly within a philosophy acknowledging the dependence of inner growth on that of one's friends and the rest of society, they continually urged the necessity of interrogating personal desires and asserting their rights as well as the authority of one's deepest and most generous convictions — gently (though not necessarily quietly or modestly) but persistently. This meant opening one's "self" to others, exposing one's "self" painfully and repeatedly to disappointment and risking ridicule; so friends were necessary for sustenance. Involvement in and for the "self" meant involvement in and for others as well. Strangely, repeated well-placed risks seem the best security against pessimism and resignation, against forms of internal "suicide", suggested by the continuation of Meysenbug's autobiography, to some degree by Ebner-Eschenbach's, and by the actual biography of Louise Aston. Under certain circumstances nothing may adequately guard against such forms of internal masochism. From the vantage point of today it is impossible to judge what was possible under the oppressive isolation enforced by the political Reaction after 1850 in Germany. To outward appearances it would seem that some form of desperate internal "suicide" of desires *was* necessary. It remains a curious fact, and one worthy of pursuit elsewhere perhaps, that those voices, like Aston's, who militated for change had acquired perspectives that countered their own efforts.

Under the circumstances any notion of slow, but steady historical progress for women throughout the nineteenth century is difficult to support.

It is an indisputable fact that the variety of public positions available to women at the end of the century was greater than at the beginning. Women like Fanny Lewald and Marie von Ebner-Eschenbach were the stars. But the costs of such recognition, the forms of internal "suicide" — even to women so generally esteemed — make it seem a pyrrhic victory. Not even Ebner-Eschenbach felt unrestrained enough to describe some of her most meaningful literary experiences — those with rebellious women authors. She could allude, in only the most circuitous manner, to disappointment at the lack of receptive understanding from her husband. Even she felt constrained to suppress powerful desires. The autobiography is filled with an unspoken, but infinite sadness at unfulfilled dreams, with resignation.

It is as though by entering the world of History contrary voices and desires are silenced. Those autobiographies by women which posed most radically an alternate vision also challenged most radically the bourgeois notion of harmonious, autonomous individualism. They were written in the early nineteenth century. They were the ones most conscious in their form of the dividedness as well as collectivity of the individual. They were the ones most aware of the subtleties and internalization of cultural oppression. As women only marginally engaged in public affairs naturally their works were restricted largely to the private sphere. Indeed they were not even published during the lifetimes of their authors, but remained hidden. Their lives may have been restricted by social convention, but their visions were not. Stägemann, Varnhagen, and Arnim all dreamed of a different social order in which those talents reserved for women, talents for friendship and nurturing, would be valued for and by all. These women nurtured the recalcitrant parts of their own souls, and refused to relinquish any dreams.

As women were admitted into the public domain one might think their appetite and contrariness would be appeased and progress recognized. But, instead of becoming truly reconciled women like Meysenbug and Ebner-Eschenbach became bitter and/or pessimistic. Their success, and peace of mind, depended upon repressing formerly held beliefs. In a sense Meysenbug's later life returned to the early nineteenth-century salon forms. She became known for her friendships with famous men like Friedrich Nietzsche, Alexander Herzen, Richard Wagner, and Romain Rolland. She asserted the importance of freely chosen families and became a model for them. But her later writings have lost the glimmer of utopian vision. She came to regard her own efforts in Hamburg on behalf of workers, prostitutes, and women in general as falsely conceived and repudiated that part of her past. Dreams can evolve, of course, and need not remain the same forever. And

Meysenbug would have her readers believe this was the case for her. But her autobiography reveals every bit as much of a forced repression of her hopes as was the case for Ebner-Eschenbach. When hopes, no matter how unrealistic, are so brutally repressed, "killed", it is difficult to speak of progress.

As women assumed public roles one would also expect them to portray a sense of interaction with public events. Despite the increased inclusion of such events into some of these autobiographies, however, there continues to be strong evidence of women's lack of ease with them. This was as apparent in Engel's removed observations of great historical events as in Lewald's awkward relation to the process of history and Popp's virtual omission of larger historical moments. In some ways Lewald's autobiography is the most interesting in this regard, for her intentions are so clearly to place her own experience within that public historical framework. However, there is no continuity of history which she perceives as immediately relevant to her personal development, there are only disconnected moments. Under these circumstances, again, it is difficult to claim progress.

For reasons that are now obvious, female autobiography reveals what is at best a strained relation to the tradition of male autobiography. Indeed it is highly irregular in the degree to which it even attempts to follow that tradition. And when it does, the results are very different in tone and quality. This awareness alone suggests that the history, if not the very definition, of the genre requires profound revision. It is simply inaccurate to assert that male forms alone constitute the parameters of this genre.

On the other hand, neither can it be asserted that there is a particularly female tradition of autobiography. To be sure, as other scholars have observed, the pattern of women's lives has been to restrict their experiences to the family. Family and interpersonal ties have been far more important for their personal development and for their perception of the world in general, than for that of men. These differences inevitably play themselves out in autobiographies by women. But while the "plot" or line of character development may change as a result of this, the full formal implications of such differences have seldom, if ever, been realized. An autobiographical form consistent with an active awareness of this difference would modify the very nature of the narrator/autobiographer. Her identity as autobiographer would be shared with family or friends. Only the authors of epistolary autobiography have moved successfully in this direction, in particular Varnhagen and Arnim. Neither in their own time, nor today, however, has this form been recognized as a radical and alternative form of autobiography. Although drawing on female talent and experience and exploiting a form specifically associated with women, these works began no tradition. Rather than adopt this more noticeable and noteworthy form, nineteenth-century women like Lewald and Meysenbug returned to more traditional narrative forms. Rarely have women fully and consistently recognized the necessity for alternative forms. Although there may be particular and specific developmental patterns to women's lives, therefore, it is not really possible to speak of a tradition of women's autobiography.

Especially in view of these epistolary works, however, it is also not possible to claim that up until today all women's writing has merely imitated and aped the voice and views of male authors. Around 1800 Wallenrodt, Recke, Stägemann, Varnhagen, and Arnim evolved a form that appears to be particularly female. However, while this particularity should be emphasized it probably should not be overemphasized. German romantics, sometimes labelled androgynous, were notoriously open to the qualities of women. And despite Varnhagen's statement to the effect that men and women were two different nations, she and others relied in great measure on the philosophical writings of men. If women were more consistent and concrete in applying theoretical notions of multiplicity, an absolute difference there is not.

Even those women, moreover, who were less radical in their formal experimentation can hardly be said to simply ape the voice of men. Most frequently their lives did not fit the molds, but Aston knew it and Meysenbug and Ebner-Eschenbach knew it as well. If Popp's autobiographical form is reminiscent of Goethe's that is not only a sign of bourgeois influence. In her youth Popp's life was probably less significantly different from that of a working-class boy's than were the lives of bourgeois girls from bourgeois boys. When she begins attending rallies she may wish she were a man in order to participate, but not only does she soon discover she knows more about politics than most working-class men, she soon begins to act politically herself—and is rewarded. Sometimes there may be reasons for the approximation of form and voice.

With a more differentiated understanding of this autobiographical heritage comes a more differentiated respect for these women and their struggles. None may provide a model for absolute imitation: from Wallenrodt's hypocritical servility in her defiant struggle for survival to the simple and yet limited pride of Viersbeck, from Lewald's formal accomodation without relinquishing the reality of her experience to the radical yet essentially private insights of Varnhagen and Arnim — who nevertheless avoided revealing information regarding their important relationships to men. But from all something may be learned.

TRANSLATIONS

INTRODUCTION

(footnote 3) "Autobiography in the narrower sense concerns itself above all with the inner development of its hero. It is not only a retrospective of what has been lived, but also and primarily introspective."

(footnote 4) "the education of a soul and the development of its character"

(footnote 6) "the sheer limitless multiplicity of autobiographical writings in the universal-historical connection of the human spirit to European culture"

(I,11) "The history of autobiography is, in a certain sense, the history of human consciousness."

(IV/2, 926) "of understanding the historical as rational, the accidental as organic"

(I, 15) "the human being in the art of great individuals"

(IV/2, 917) "To approach Goethe's autobiography as a historically conditioned work and link in an ever-evolving genre is difficult. . . (we) sense. . . the artist's spirit, the organizing will, the comprehension of world and humanity which is at work in this narration, and history. . . reveals itself as a grand work of art centered in itself, in which for the first time the full reality of an individual being is truly conceived as self-end."

(I,6) "Autobiography is not a literary genre like any other. . . no form is foreign to it."

(I,6) "autobiography has moved in all these forms, and when it is itself and a person of individuality presents him/herself in it, then it destroys all these genres or creates through its very being an incomparable form"

(footnote 20) "Everything that issues from human social interaction shall pass me, excite me and move me so that it might in turn be moved by me. And in the way in which I take it up and treat it I will find my freedom and by externalizing build my originality."

Chapter 1: THE CASES OF BALDINGER, ENGEL, AND WALLENRODT

Kästner (rough translation)

On the Inaugural Dissertation of Frau Doctorinn***
That cures are often benignly hasty
Is proven, Madame Doctor, by yet another example:
That your sex often certain ailments cures
Pleasantly and quickly, but not at all surely.

Baldinger

(17) "I am supposed to record the history of my intellect? As if I had so much that

215

it would be worth the trouble to explore its course."

(38) "I don't know if I should take credit when friends honor me because of my intellect. If you follow me step by step to the peak where even Kästner and Lichtenberg became my friends, I think even the most stupid person would benefit from both intellectually. Does it merit admiration that I have become adequate through such good company?"

(15) "a far too insignificant creature. . .that (she) should demand one read about the education of (her) intellect."

(16) "Few women owe their husbands as much as I owe you. This will reassure the reader, who interprets obedience to you as vanity on my part."

(36) "My love for the sciences grew the more I knew about them."

(26) "always to be free and independent of the whole world"

(18) "(She) was the most upright woman I have ever known, but in her intellect, a *woman*, further distinguished by nothing."

(20) "she had never read anything intelligent and the days of her youth were not the most advantageous for women's education"

(27) "I had imagined men must all be more clever than women since they assume all authority over us. But I found precious few who, on the basis of superiority of intellect, had that right. This made me an enemy of a whole sex."

(27) "irrational"

(38) "As a woman I have become adequate, how small I would have been as a man!"

(32) "had all the disposition of a saint, (she) was pious, a Vestal Virgin, was carried away in raptures."

(35) "Since the higher powers of my soul always outweighed the lower ones, I don't know if (my husband) has always found his desires satisfied by me, as a woman . . .I tried to correct my faults by expanding my mind, I preferred friendship to animalistic love."

Engel

(34) "But I am not writing a war history and may only relate as many of these incidents as touched my life. . ."

(59) "I beg forgiveness if I have begun to politicize a little, I promise only to relate what I have heard. . .(.)"

(110) "since I now commence the tale of my trip to the continent of North America, I must remind the reader in advance, that I traveled neither as naturalist, statesperson, nor merchant. . .What I observed of the customs and manner of living I in my naivete will report as I saw it"

(87) "Our fourth son Florian. . .was probably already dead when I saw my beloved husband fall. . .My youngest son Joseph, only ten years old, fought at my side, his head torn to pieces by a bullet, I saw an eye and his brain spattered in front of me."

(89) "The loss of my beloved spouse was enough cause for quiet reflection about myself, my continuing fate and my future existence. . ."

(9) "may the dear reader excuse the little outburst of my feelings at this point. . ."

(191) "The general trust which I encountered from all true scholars of history, from

all favorably disposed readers and friends of truth after the publication of the first part of my memoirs, the desire to know about these events and even personal solicitation has led me to the second fragment or rather continuation of my life story."
(238) "famous and important people in hospitality"
(238) "distinguished (I venture to say it and whoever reads my life story will not doubt it) among women, not only in Zürich, but in all parts of Switzerland and even beyond its borders; bearing the stamp of battles fought and surrounded by my 21 children, since they have carved our name in the indestructible stone of France...(.)"
(237) "I have now arrived on board my life's path of longing, encircled by the walls of my dear native Zürich, the city of my birth and education. Cut off from it for more than two years by the stormy waves of an uncertain sea, now to one side, now to the other, now forwards, now backwards, like a ship without a navigator tossed by the wild rage of the waves I pined for it. Misfortune broke over me like a gush of water, even if the dear sun sometimes still shone."
(195) "O! the pain! like a harbinger of my previous fates which displayed all the colors of my misfortune..."
(193) "O how melancholy thoughts gnawed in my bosom...(.)"
(218) "O! What sorrow pierced my soul at this hour. I could not cry any longer, my spirit was saddened by the deadening stream of thoughts."
(195) "the words fail me, dearest reader!"
(233) "O I cannot paint my situation with words, I cannot make it symbolic...(.)"

Wallenrodt

(I,8) "where and how I myself attracted so much misfortune and unfavorable opinion."
(iv) "a practical accounting"
(I, 546) "The world, or at least a portion of it, shall read these letters. How fortunate if here and there they teach an artless, happy creature, too lively to reflect on every action, to turn inward and take care!"
(II,35) "Providence lets none of its creatures out of its sight and weaves all our fates to our best end."
(II, 599) "How much I hope that the candid confessions of these disadvantages, caused by myself and which have given me sleepless nights for more than 18 years and caused the most gnawing concern, so much—truly— unearned bad opinion, how much I hope these confessions will be a warning to young and lively people."
(I,140) "A child who freely gives all away should be taught to keep his little possessions for himself, since he would otherwise experience a shortage. If he wants to be generous everywhere, one should show him that this is a virtue only under certain conditions...(.)"
(I, 595) "uncommonly sweet"
(I, 595) "that I felt it was a burden I bore, and who doesn't tire of that finally?"
(I, 597) "I cherished the man whose chains I wore...but I felt the weight too."
(I,6) "Other people I had perhaps irritated with a little satire or with proof that

218

I saw, heard and discerned. They were disposed therefore to degrade me as much as possible, in every way they could think of."

(I, 596) "as soon as I wanted, my will won out, but in order to reap this advantage I had to adjust myself to him without appearing to force myself."

(II, 612) "When I was married I was supposed to learn Italian, English and even Latin; but nothing got beyond the introductory stage. Many confinements, household tasks and social diversions interrupted everything."

(II, 615f.) "if I had more attention and time to devote to elegance and could have read more, if my head, filled with hundreds of unpleasantries, had always been capable of the precision I loved so well. But precision only shows itself in the works of a well-practiced author, who had nothing but his material in his head and doesn't need to bend the essential train of thought around thousands of fatal secondary ideas."

(II, 648) "hastiness and failure to refine"

(I, 161) "Now prepare yourselves for the last and most entertaining adventure of my married life"

(footnote 16) "The entire education of daughters must be oriented around the male sex. To please men and be useful to them, to keep their love and respect, to care for them, advise them, comfort them, make their lives comfortable and sweet, this one must teach them from childhood on."

(footnote 17) "(Women) use their books like watches. They carry them so that they can be seen, and yet they are usually not working or not set according to the sun."

CHAPTER 2: THE CASES OF RECKE AND STAEGEMANN

Elise von der Recke

(105) "the science to which I was educated consisted in entertaining company with modesty and excelling in society."

(127) "absolutely nothing gentle or agreeable in his character"

(88) "the tender union of hearts between good, like-minded souls had early been my heart's need and the joy of my life"

(278) "I hid from everyone just how unhappy my marriage was; only to the preacher on my parents' estate, that honorable and also worldly wise man, did I bare my entire situation and the melancholy mood of my soul which began to feel this earthly life as a burden."

(viii) "whether in their full range and precise expression or in shortened and revised form cannot be determined. The former rather than the latter is to be assumed."

(I, 159) "Later entry in another hand, not corresponding to the content of the volume"

(II, 313) "And now, since I no longer have Sophie and so that I might always judge clearly the state of my heart, I tested myself this morning in my diary and I will continue to develop, in these pages, just as candidly my most secret feelings and thoughts, like I used to do in the blessed hours of the most intimate outpourings of my soul with my Sophie."

(II, 313) "refuge in (her) diary".

(230) "Oh! Sternheim was much better, more worthy of love and more unhappy than I."

(281) "the powers of the soul are exercized through suffering"

(224) "the thought that blessed spirits surround me, that they live in my heart, gives me strength to remain cheerful when I see myself misunderstood and despised by the person whose life I would so gladly make happy"

(213) "as if we had no soul and only a piece of flesh"

(8l) "And how different was that which I showed outwardly from that which took place inside."

(72) "Do not look at things from the point of view of nature. If you do, the people will appear more blameworthy than they were. Everything must be seen in God who permits such things in order to further my salvation and so that I do not fall into perdition."

Stägemann

(7) "I attempted, to the best of my ability, to merge poetry and truth in conversation with her and found a strange satisfaction in being able to express my feelings without speaking of myself."

(8) "(I) let the friend, which my fantasy created, often represent the voice of reason, while I gave myself over totally to the outpourings of my heart."

(10) "the true expression of my soul"

(II, 95) "an isolated self"

(II, 32) "And marriage. . .despite all the disagreeabilities to which we must submit, is still the most practical arrangement of bourgeois society to protect our rest and safety, and even the peace of our heart."

(8) "in a vain battle with (her) abilities and inclinations and yearned as much for truth as for the completion of any portion of (her) being. The force of circumstance ultimately decided, for due to (her) deep love for (her) family daily life gradually became so interwoven with (her) interests that all choice disappeared."

(9) "I had to live the second part of my life for others, as I had lived for myself until then. . .as though nothing of what I once loved, what I had once practiced with such unspeakable diligence could carry over into the second half of my life.— Like the separated link of a chain, my past lay behind me. . .(.)"

(9) "It is not primarily the daily practice of art which makes us happy, so much as the power through which it clarifies, uplifts, and beautifies everything, through which it blesses us if we bring it no other sacrifice than that flamed by love and devotion, kindled in purity in our innermost soul."

(II,40) "Oh Meta! Can I help it if the sense for natural freedom, which should be holy to everyone, is kindled by my misfortune, when a hundred others would suffocate?— Has this feeling not been awakened by educating my mind— and must we become stupid and dull before we can be happy and make others happy?"

(II,41) "who would be my provider and my friend in the strictest sense of the word"

(II, 103f.) "I dreamed of independence and learn that a woman only finds her true independence, that is, the most beautiful and free exercise of her abilities, in an orderly life, even one with the most difficult responsibilities. What appears, under other circumstances, to be weakness is sanctified here. Denial and devotion no longer battle against the pride of a female heart. Subordination to the will of another which once cast my glance to the ground, which once my pride wanted to tear forcibly from me, has become, under the rule of order, my triumph. . . My peacefulness has erected a thick bower around those for whom I care. No burning ray of too lively gaiety penetrates it, nor destructive storm of suffering."

(II,105) "a holy place, entered only seldom and only by a few. Here between high flowering foliage stands her piano, here hang her favorite paintings and drawings, among them a Madonna I once painted for the Count."

(I,187) "foretaste of heaven"

(I, 51) "quiet efficacy"

(I, 205) "peace and quiet in my family circle"

(II, 84) "a more beautiful, spiritual pleasure"

(I, 170) "propriety without pretense, generosity full of self-confidence"

(II, 82) "To be sure I once had an ideal (of myself) and I can still only relinquish my belief in it with the better part of my existence."

(I, 94) "our pastoral idylls of (Salomon) Gessner"

(footnote 16) "The inner form of autobiography is. . .circular: from the visible time of narration which also (temporarily) marks the end of life, the beginnings of one's own life are taken up and then narrated sequentially to the end determined by existence and narrative technique. In the narration, which represents a gradual reduction in the distance of narrated time, the identity of the narrating and narrated "I" is continually established by drawing it out of the content of the life."

(footnote 17) "even with a consistent first person narrative every consciously excerpted depiction can only occasionally mediate between the narrating and the narrated "I" and tends to the epic emancipation of the depicted events."

(footnote 18) "to a very pleasant and very edifying vehicle for passing time. . .not something for idle women, but also for the thinking mind."

(4f.) "What a bold thought, my friend, to hand over to cold and alien judgement a correspondence thrown on paper without a real goal or plan and without careful construction!"

Chapter 3: THE CASES OF VARNHAGEN AND ARNIM

Varnhagen

(II, 576) "the inner economy"

(I, 265) "What a friend you have chosen, discovered! and uncovered!. . .I can loan my soul as though doubly organized and have the remarkable power to double myself without confusing myself."

(II, 305) "the heavy, dark, patient earth would yield its fullness for all peoples; they would not need to war, to lie, and proclamations for legitimation!"

(I, 266) "I am as unique as the greatest phenomenon on earth. The greatest artist, philosopher, or poet is not above me. We are of the same cloth, in the same rank, and belong together. . .but life was assigned to me."

(II, 414f.) "And I will write you letters where the soul can take a stroll, and not a goal-directed, purposeful trip on well-trodden, dusty highways. We want to walk on fresh, small, abstract paths that even we do not know: and follow the play of the clouds as we go, and enjoy the magic of the light and even follow, if we choose, the darkness!"

(III, 55f.) "I want a letter to be the portrait of the moment in which it was written: and it shall be primarily a likeness, as high as any demands of art on ideal enoblement. . . Happy are the lovely images of a laughing moment of nature which, far from all human invention, could serve the most artistic as a model!"

(II, 516) "form, color, and content"

(I,92) "How can one describe the indescribable: at best! at best narrate it? At best? No, absolutely not, positively not."

(footnote 10) "Language is not at my command, not German, not my own; our language is our lived life; I have invented mine myself. I could make less use than many others of the tired phrases, that's why mine are often clumsy and full of all kinds of errors, but always genuine. . ."

(I, 574) "I write letters in which blossoms and fruit lie, together with the roots, and the earth on them from being pulled out of the ground. And little worms."

(II, 548) "The letters of Mich Angelo, and Annibal Carucci (sic). . .sweeten my days. Their troubles are pushed into the distance: their striving, their activity, their desires, their heart and spirit stand there more clearly; for me especially, since I learn so much about people from their letters. History and all of time become clearer to me in such correspondence than through famous historians."

(II, 570) "Do not be frightened off by diverse precautious digressions in the book, poor Lavater had to bend with the spirit of the times; it was the — perhaps presumptuous — Enlightenment. He does it with grace, and impatience; in it we learn about that time and its difficulties and to judge our own more energetically as a former one, and watch him tread flat steps with great audacity."

(II, 570) "That's how narrow minds inhibit the rare and beautiful flights of our most illustrious!"

(I, 266) "So that *one* image would capture the existence. Even pain, as I know it, is a life; and I think I am one of those models which humanity should construct and then no longer needs, and no longer can."

(I, 466f.) "I know what joy, what comfort a little spark of truth in a piece of writing has held for me! Only that gives the past life, and the present shape; and an artistic perspective from which to be seen; only sentiments, observations enlivened by a story create leisure, divine time and freedom; where otherwise only shoving and pushing and squeezing and a dizzy seeing and doing is possible; in the real life of a conditioned, limited day as it presents itself to us! Not because it is my life, but because it is a true one; because I often said things, with tiny, unintentional flair, that would represent truth for a researcher, such as I also am, and even things which will supplement history. And finally, because I am a marvel of nature, a

corner-person in nature's concept of humanity, because nature threw me, and did not lay me, in grizzly battle with whatever fate found to hound me. Each one of nature's fighters, of greater history's fighters, is thrown into a historical moment in which he must fight, as in battle with an animal in an arena; fortunate veterans continue to affect the consciousness of nature and humans; unfortunate ones are dashed. When I was already dashed, thoughts and innocence elevated me to a position between heaven and earth. In short, I cannot say how it stands with me; I want nothing more. No plan, no image; the earth staggers and vanishes under the goods of life; the gift of life is everything! To see, to love, to understand, not to want anything, to submit in innocence. To exalt being, not to want to hammer, to discover, to improve: and to be cheerful and always gooder! May my brothers see me just as I was and will be ! But I myself want to examine my letters and discard; and not in forty, fifty years, as you wrote, but much sooner. I want to live when it is read." (I, 154f.) "And friendship is a preparatory egoism for that education. . ."
(I, 89) "only by igniting itself to real life does this seed of self-activating properties rouse itself, that electric spark which builds and constructs world history through great persons. . ."
(footnote 16) "A letter is always like a novel for me. . . Paper is so faithless a messenger that it forgets the glance and the tone, and often even carries the wrong meaning."

Arnim

(footnote 21) "a portrait transfigured by poetry and born of her spirit"
(footnote 22) "She continually rewrote what did not appeal to her until it acquired the ease of style of something that had been hastily thrown on paper. Her style in her quickly written letters is much heavier than in her books."
(I, 96) "I am so proud in you, because you often speak to me as though it were the voice of wisdom which I have long listened for in the distance and is now so near to me in you that I cannot distinguish it from myself."
(footnote 24) "Günderode was my mirror; I let every tone echo in her and characterized her with my feelings and impressions. Revelations came to me by practicing to express myself for her."
(footnote 25) "I love my own spirit, you are the gate through which I enter it."
(I, 188) "I am the product of my love for you."
(II, 513) "You said, you love yourself in me."
(footnote 26) "Read my book more than once. . . Open it here and there in every mood. You will surely find a resonance there. . ."
(II, 452) "Writing is not close enough, it reflects on itself too much."
(II, 434) "but shouldn't there also be an immediate revelation of Poesie', one which penetrates the marrow deeper and more terribly, without the firm boundaries of form?—Which reaches into the spirit more quickly and more naturally, even less consciously, but creating, cultivating another spirit?"
(I, 317) "Oh slave epoch in which I was born!"
(footnote 29) "(Clemens Brentano's) correspondence with his sister, Bettina, is a

remarkable monument to the polarities at work in him. He plays the precocious tutor to his younger sister. . . Apparent everywhere is his secret fear of himself, of his own demon, which he recognizes like a terrifying mirror image of himself in his equally gifted sister and whom he therefore fights with all his strength. . . ."

(I, 85) "arbitrary, autocratic will"

(I, 100) "This great planet, de Gachet, unsettles me too much when it comes too close to me. — She spoke of the heavenly bodies, their subtle emanations, and the mutual attraction of planets in their orbits, and of inner meaning in the ocean of feelings, and I was totally stupefied. What do I seem to her that she says such things to me! — She held me firmly in her arms, I might have joined the devil; I was ashamed that I had to listen to her, captured in her arms, and understood nothing. . . (.)"

(II, 216) "A person shall always perform the greatest deed and no other. "

(II, 217) "Thinking is praying"

(II,224) "to do what is great and not to regard prejudice"

(II, 243) "True education arises from exercizing the powers which reside within us"

(II, 243) "Each person shall be curious about herself and work to bring her whole self to the surface like a piece of metal ore."

(II, 302) "No, my dear grandmama, it seems to me that I am called to do that."

(II, 458) "deceitful, petty characters"

(II, 550) "People do not understand what freedom is. They want to conquer it, that is already to kill it. One cannot conquer freedom, it must appear in us as a divine power, it is the law from which the spirit constructs itself. Inner restraint and outer freedom are doubly heavy chains, because an intoxication accompanies them which binds and confuses the senses."

(II, 406) "the past belongs to each day of life"

(II, 317) "but it is not appropriate for a book, for it is finished straight off, and what should happen next?"

(II, 313) "If you stop at every Hawkweed and Forget-me-not, we will not get very far."

(II, 217f.) "I feel that you are right and know that I am too timid, and cannot outwardly defend what I inwardly hold to be right against their reasons drawn from lies. I grow silent and am ashamed precisely when others ought to be ashamed, and it goes so far that I ask forgiveness of people who have been unjust to me out of fear that they might notice it."

(III, 98f.) "Ah, since her death she has probably left me the better part of her spiritual abilities."

(Goethe) "So let me seem until I become, take not my white dress from me"

(III, 515) "innate to every human being and is the origin of all longing for a divine life. . ."

(III, 137) "that I will enter the ordinariness of daily, common life and that this world in which my senses are alive will recede, that which I should cover protectively I will betray. . .where uninhibited childlike wisdom will give me a sign I will offer spite and know better. . ."

(III, 137f.) "You are my protective altar, I will flee to you. This love, so powerful, which commands us and the understanding that comes to me through it and the revelations, they will by my protective walls, they will free me from those who would straighten me out."

(III, 275) "all of nature mirrors to me what I should say to you...everything is arranged by God, so that love conducts the correspondence between us..."

(III, 125) "a heartspring that could flow nowhere else..."

(III, 226) "You look at me in the spirit and your glance draws thoughts out of me. Often I must say what I don't understand, what I only see."

(IV, 13) "You are in the midst of my inner being, it is no longer one, it has become two in me."

(III, 244) "the task of love between friends is to solve the riddle of nature, so that each learns of his more profound nature through and in the friend."

(III, 246) "if I tell you the truth, then your soul must overflow into mine — I believe that."

(II, 238) "Your spirit lives in me and enflames me."

(III, 519f.) "Shouldn't one make fun when a passion which had only commenced outlasts everything real and asserts itself in a heart whose amorous aspirations have long been ridiculed as foolishness?"

(IV, 63) "by becoming aware of sensuous beauty we cultivate in us a spiritual reflection of it, a heavenly transfiguration of that which we sensuously love..."

(IV, 86) "Oh learn through my prattle beautiful dreams which lend you wings and float through the cool ether with you. How gloriously you tread on these dream carpets! How you churn your way through the thousand-fold veil of fantasy and become more and more clear, more and more distinct, you, yourself..."

(II, 46f.) "There are three things out of which a person arises. Not merely a portion of him or one aspect of him, but the person himself, together with all aspects of him, and his seed and kernel reside in these three things, which are the elements out of which all of created nature once again creates itself in the person."

(II, 46f.) "But faith is firming and without it everything hovers and acquires no form and dissipates in a thousand ways."

(II, 48) "thought perishes in itself because it is the attire of temporality and not a visible aspect of the eternal spirit."

(II,48) "Evil therefore is suicide, for the will to destroy is temporal."

(II, 48) "Goodness is when the eternally divine transforms the mundane itself and makes everything in it God."

(II, 48) "Reason is a pillar firmly implanted in human beings, however, it is also eternal and a support of heaven...in its roots lie time, but as the spirit evolves out of matter, so eternity evolves out of this time and climbs in reason to eternity, and through reason the human being leaves the mortal and becomes immortal."

(footnote 34) "One forgets how to write here where the whole day, the whole year, the whole dear, long life nothing happens which would make one want to lift an arm or a leg. I know of no activity which injures the head more than doing nothing and experiencing nothing...Ah, how my aspirations for life have sunk and the less I demand, the more it bargains me down, and it will allow me only to turn my-

self into a rascal or a scoundrel."
(footnote 38) "the most pure, the most simply beautiful and charming of anything she had written"

Chapter 4: THE CASES OF ASTON AND MEYSENBUG

Aston

(footnote 1) "Life is fragmentary, art is supposed to create a whole!"
(154) "That was the first chapter in her marriage. . ."
(27) "Money was my destiny — it shall remain my destiny which I willingly follow and against which I no longer battle."
(150f.) "You would sell me, treat me like an object, like your property!. . .You have no right to determine my love and my honor. I will preserve the holiest rights of my heart and my life — this is the point, that must separate us forever."
(1f.) "who believe that to live the comfort of a quiet, peaceful life is to exhaust the highest goal and the entire value of existence."
(2) "utopias of petty bourgeois imaginations"
(154f.) "She saved her better self from the brutal force which conspired against her in a hundred forms! *She saved the sanctity of marriage by destroying it!* But still she had not conquered one force which was more powerful than position or money or freedom and which, if driven underground, soon emerged, a constellation to govern her life from now on; a power which in its innate, hereditary holiness broke all forms sanctified by laws and conventions — *love.*"

Meysenbug

(footnote 7) "second baptism. . .at the hand of the Revolution".
(I,78) "Every diligent striving turns finally from the inner outward to the world."
(I,155) "battle without end, a path which leads through lonely, desolate deserts."
(I,155) "Will you accept the task and not fear the sacrifices which it will demand of you? Will you be ready to see your heart, with its eternally burning thirst for beauty, continually crucified?"
(I,183f.) "A veil fell from my eyes. I perceived that I was no longer the gentle, pliable creature, who in order not to affront anyone submitted to everyone and pursued the path which all pursued out of obedience and desire to please. I sensed that I was becoming an individual with convictions and with the energy to admit them. Now I grasped that this was my crime."
(I,364) "which (she) had endured because (she) had wanted to shape (her) life according to (her) convictions"
(I, 234) "The great right of the individual to everything that is necessary for it to become everything it can become presented itself to me with bitter clarity. That it was permissable to break every authority in order to attain this right was no longer a matter of any doubt for me."
(I, 268f.) "threefold tyranny of dogma, convention, and the family"
(footnote 8) "the spoils of a heart which had suffered thoroughly"

(v.f.) "the same right to the evolution of all their abilities"

(v.f.) "a modest portrait of one of those lives of unkown trail blazers who seek the way while still in the shadow of night when a new idea wants to break a path in history and who, when they are not treated as fools or criminals, are taken for idealists demanding the impossible."

(I, 11) "independent creature"

(I, 168, 181) "the highest flowering of life" and "the most beautiful and noble flowering of my being"

(I, 199) "Love and freedom had become. . .one in me"

(I, 184) "an individuality (sic) with convictions and with the energy to defend them"

(I, 313) "an individuality . . .who exercizes a certain power"

(I, 367) "In Theodor's grave, in that of the school, I also buried my youth, my hope, the joyful courage, which still believed in fulfillment in the future."

(footnote 12) "that had one important fundamental thought. . .which arose independently in my soul even before I knew Schopenhauer"

(I,245) "to want to die in order not to suffer any longer is weakness. Live for the Ideal, to complete the good in and around you!"

(I, 245) "the badge of one's personal dignity which emerges untinged out of every battle and conquers all disappointments"

(footnote 14) "(those persons) who give their lives for an idea, who kill the will to live for the sake of what is objective and recognized".

(I, 246)"how could a man ever perform his public duty in its full dimensions if there were no great woman's heart standing by him at the home's hearth, prepared to take part in his great interests and to sacrifice for them, when it had to be, even her personal happiness?"

(I, 158) "After a while the fleeting phenomena of the world, the phantasmagoria of the imagination, the stormy desires sank, as in a dream . . . For a long, long time I gazed out and had lost the feeling of my individuality."

(I, 276f.) "and by opening myself to the universe it sometimes seemed as though the ephemeral suffering of this world was not worth the many tears shed for it."

(II, viiif.) "memorial wreathes"

(II, 246) "family of free choice"

(III,223) "Faithfulness was fundamental to my character and yet that strange perversity, in which fate sometimes likes to appear, always drove me out anew, from the firm ground which I had won for myself to the inconstancy and uncertainty of new relationships. Painfully, it tore my heart loose from whatever it had lovingly embraced and refused my spirit to exercise steady concentration on one task and to experience the joy of success."

(III, 223f.) "the blessed unity at the root of things in which all restlessness of phenomena has ceased as well as the completion which we sought in the dark impulse"

(III,274) "gave my life its finishing touch"

(III, 75) "These thoughts led me to *one* conclusion, namely, that we who thought we had demolished all idols and false gods had voluntarily erected a new graven

image: namely the people."
(II, 276) "essential component of female nature"
(III,270) "holy task of the mother in the highest ethical sense"
(III,264) "(M)otherliness welled up in me"
(III, 271) "the motherly profession"
(III, 271) "That woman could fight just as true a battle for the sake of her holiest
convictions and, for their sake, break the restrictions of social conditions, just as
well as man — this view of mine had not remained theoretical, I had realized it. Fur-
thermore, that woman could rely on herself and earn herself an honorable posi-
tion through work and a life which commanded respect — in this, too, I had remained
true to my principles."
(III, 164) "in the land of deception, in the realm of madness"
(III, 164) "(t)he heart on which we repose grows cold and the lips which whispered
words of love or announced lofty wisdom grow silent; the human race which we
wanted to aid shrugs its shoulders and crucifies or ridicules us."
(III, 296) "It dawned on me that as once in Italy after the failure of the union of
Lombard cities and with it the failure of a dream for complete political freedom,
longing fled to the realm of art and there created a transfigued humanity, an ideal
fatherland, so too every, even the greatest accomplishment in the political arena
would remain defective, like everything which devolves to the limitations of the
mundane."
(III, 284) "The bound God in us must liberate itself from the limits of individuation in which the stormy urge to live has banished it. The long, painful struggle
with existence has no other meaning than the resurrection after the crucifixion of
which the ego, that which is personal, dies in order to live eternally as the universal."
(III, 297) "our personal history ends then"

Chapter 5: THE CASES OF LEWALD AND EBNER-ESCHENBACH

Lewald

(footnote 6) "In (autobiographies) only those things are important which make the
life of the narrator that specific life, and people and events have no significance
for us except as they influence this *one* life.—Goethe felt this..."
(2/1, 116) "We all welcomed every last one of those works with surprise and with
great consensus..."
(2/2, 67) "For me the encounter with female actresses had quite a specific significance, because it brought before me the model of independence and personal
significance, for which my whole soul longed."
(2/2, 20f.) "There came to me then, in christian terms, a solace and a source of hope
quite as though from heaven for it was communicated to me through someone already dead, through Rahel Varnhagen von Ense ...(.) (It was) a revelation and a
salvation ...consummated for me by the posthumous letters of this woman. What
most profoundly depresses a person is the idea of suffering a special fate ...(.)

Whatever I had encountered, whatever uncomfortable, embarrassing, and painful thing I had had to endure and to suffer, Rahel Levin had known it all, had been through it all, had conquered all with her innate power, and been able to settle herself in a position in which she found that for which she longed: the possibility of enjoying and accomplishing according to the innate needs of her nature."

(3/2, 46) "From my first small novel to these confessions about myself I have considered it my highest task to serve, by creating my works, the goals and interests which have been my ideal and my religion since I learned to think."

(3/2, 230) "that to win freedom and recognition for yourself is also to win it for others. For that is what is beautiful and encouraging in freedom, that it cannot be acquired for oneself alone."

(1/1, 5) "The sight of others' laborious struggles strengthened me in my work and endurance. Favored and happy lives gave me hope of success and striving after similar satisfaction. And when I saw people, whom I had to rank above me, struggle with misfortune or even succumb to the circumstances around them, then that guarded me against foolish demands for so-called absolute and effortless happiness. It directed me toward active patience and taught me to enjoy with double awareness every second and to acknowledge with double gratitude both the advantages that my background had given me and that which I had achieved by my own power."

(1/1, 4) "And what once appeared, in the heat of the moment, to be mysterious, separate and without connection, coincidental, inconsequential or even brutal and unjust, that acquires shape in the glance that surveys the entirety. Then one's own and others' deeds, errors and pains, our thinking and striving, our failures and successes come to us as just so many causes and effects. Every life carries its own logical connection in itself."

(1/2, 226) "I earned considerable appreciation and found lively admiration for my verses. From that day on my girl friends considered it absolutely settled that I was a poet."

(3/2, 147) "my task is mainly to explain the connection between my life and my writing."

(3/2, 302) "I had become master of my freedom, my situation, myself, and thus finally able to use them and enjoy them."

(3/2, 78) "I do not know if all people and especially other women experience the need for independence and personal freedom as urgently as I did..."

(1/2, 119) "...the drive for a separate independence never again ceased..."

(2/2, 254) "When I read these words the blood rushed quickly and warmly from my heart to my head. I looked at my father, he must have read the joy in my eyes. It was like a vision in the desert of the promised land, it was the prospect of emancipation, it was the realization of my thought, the fulfillment of a wish which I had not dared to admit to myself."

(3/2, 29f.) "In my youth my life's prospects had been limited. Now they broadened from day to day and I had difficulty accustoming myself to it. Everything was totally different from what I had wished. As far as a person could foresee in my sixteenth year, I was destined to become the wife of a christian pastor and to live in a quiet village in the Harz mountains. I had thought of that as the greatest happiness, had painted it for myself in rosy colors...Of everything for which I had once yearned and striven there was nothing now for which I longed. Now none of it could have given me the happiness it once might have."

(3/2, 225f.) "For as long as I can remember I have known with a fair amount of certainty what I wanted and I have not lost the goal from sight for long."

(3/1, 18) "This pleasure in (my) characters was soon accompanied by the bliss of being able to say through them everything that had lain in my heart for years and of being able to say it without having anyone chastize me, or contradict me, without having to moderate myself and be discreet and without having to say it in self-defense."

(3/1, 60f.) "I cannot repeat often enough what a joy working was for me, what a pleasure creating gave me. The moment in which I could sit down at my desk and pick up my notebooks passed like a stroke of magic...I was happy, free, powerful, and undaunted. I continuously had a sense of my power and a certain feeling of success as well."

(3/2, 34) "We have it so much within our power to grind the glasses through which we see the world and to choose the color in which we want to see our fate. Whoever leans toward viewing the world and its duties in a somber light normally lacks insight and self-knowledge and above all the proper love."

(3/2, 305) "the highest love, the fulfillment of all my wishes"

(256) "this inner necessity of the world order, to which one must submit"

(III, 105) "that the ground must be healthy in which happiness shall grow"

(footnote 11) "the disconnected quality of her sudden ideas and her manner of expression had acquired something uncanny, unbeautiful, and unsettling for me"

Ebner-Eschenbach

(footnote 16) "The poisonous atmosphere of the revolution is portrayed too faithfully in it."

(footnote 24) "As they are detailed here for us in truly female fashion and taken up anew from one act to the next, don't these petty domestic squabbles give the petty impression of family gossip exposed to the public eye?"

(footnote 26) "illegitimate child".

(footnote 33) "The whole future, my entire life, so poor in external events, is already anticipated there. It was inevitable that I would become the wife of my dear cousin and an author."

(footnote 34) "In later years I saw this tiny event experienced countless times by me and by others on a different scale and in a different form."

(808f.) "Everything repeats itself in life. The fundamental tone to which the fate of the greatest and the smallest is tuned appears again and again. The mute rejection with which the most faithful and best loved greeted my first poetic stammerings would be accorded my little writings by others, also loyal and dearly loved, well into my most mature years."

(813) "Grandmama interrupted the explanation with a severity I had not yet ex-

perienced from her and one which remains inexplicable to me to this day."
(813) "unjust and sinful"
(814) "the painfully humiliating feeling of possessing a secret, innate flaw"
(811) "I might just as well have carried a brood of songbirds around with me and gotten them to be silent."
(811) "poor, childish stammering of verse"
(813) "that everything that chimed and resonated in my heart had to be said and sung to give others joy and me salvation"
(814) "They reprimanded me for something unavoidable, something destined for me without my knowledge or desire by the highest divine power. The pain I suffered because of that, and I wanted to suffer, did not seem to be the usual, but rather especially beautiful and noble, like that of martyrdom, and in this awareness I mustered a great resistance. . ."
(877) "a bitter period of self-recognition full of longing and grief"
(749) "Still filled with the impressions I receive day by day in this grand Rome, I return home and am supposed to pick up my sketch and venture out in hunt of typographical errors and help fallen sentences to their feet. I find that difficult. My faith in your something has disappeared, you poor pages. Since you have already unfolded you paper wings, fly then, as well as you can."
(883) "(Richelieu's) character grew and grew like a giant in front of me, until — it outgrew me and I comprehended that only in my blindness for its grandeur had I mustered the courage to portray it. Gradually my eyes opened, I knew, with all my enthusiasm, all my diligence I had only created a hodge-podge."
(747) "Now I stand at the goal, the ring of life closes, beginning and end touch."
(747f.) "Imagination exercizes her invicible right to rule and brightens or dims what she strifes with her wing, lets many a word sound in my ear which was perhaps not spoken as I now perceive it, lets me see people and events in a light which lends them perhaps too great, perhaps too small a significance. The power it exercizes over a child's spirit, whose development I have tried to portray is not thereby diminished. The emphasis lies on the impression it left behind and which is determined by the nature of the being that received it. This being is faithfully rendered literally and in spirit."
(footnote 40) "To write down only what passes through my head, to share it with those who are interested in it (this passing-through-the-head). . ."
(850f.) "(the) harder and more resistant the ground in which the little tree of my art was forced to take root, the firmer it stood. And the more horrible the failures, the tighter grew the bond between me and my much contested talent."
(832) "the most noteworthy event of (her) childhood."
(790) "questioning, guessing (his eyes) rested on her and they spoke adoration"
(790) "With fanatic admiration I looked up to the brilliant artist. . ."
(865) "I recognize her longing and know that it is just as invicible as genuine talent. . .but she suffers from inadequacy."
(880) "I loved Queen Anna of Austria and wanted to make sure that everyone who met her through me would also love her."

Chapter 6: THE CASES OF POPP, WEGRAINER, AND VIERSBECK

(63-4) "Before the bourgeois revolution the patrician's son and poet-king, Johann Wolfgang Goethe, had doubly the right to consider himself the representative of the rising bourgeoisie and still to proclaim, under the very rule of absolute feudalism, a democratic-humanistic order in which a person would be valued as a person and according to his efforts on behalf of humanity. Thus he could demand that the hard work, diligence, and noble sentiments of the best citizens in an industrious Germany would be preserved for posterity in biographies. But the realization, the establishment of a real humanist order remained for the proletariat to complete."

Popp

(19) "vanguard of her sex"
(20) "model for many to imitate"
(78) "I wanted to convert, however, and to politic'."
(78) "a little revolution"
(80) "as though I had conquered the world"
(87) "the promised land"
(120) "I learned to understand that the Messiah who was to have come 1900 years ago had not yet brought redemption for all. But like many thousands who shared my fate I learned to trust and hope in a new Messiah, a redeemer who could not be nailed to a cross in human form. I learned to hope for a redeemer who lived in the heads and hearts of millions, who conquered the world from the innermost depths of humanity in order to reorder it so that it served the happiness of all. This redeemer performed no magic. . . but he gives humans the strength to conquer the power of gold and to clear the path for the joy of all. I learned to believe in Socialism, and the idea of Christmas, which had ruled my thoughts for so long and comprised my longing, receded in the face of the desire to be able to greet Socialism in the home of the poor and oppressed as a liberator."

Wegrainer

(185) "By the difficult path I had had to travel, all guilt was repented and absolved."

Viersbeck

(103) "I would like to proclaim to all dear fellow human beings who are forced to eat their bread at other people's table: Always perform your duty, fully and completely; but then defend yourself where it is necessary."
(footnote 16) "which report hunger and poverty, but are also filled with human joy and pride at conquering need"

NOTES

INTRODUCTION

¹ One British researcher of autobiography even rejected those works in which a "fictional" element played a large role, for example Goethe's *Dichtung und Wahrheit*. See Anna Burr, *The Autobiography. A Critical and Comparative Study* (Boston: Houghton, Mifflin, 1909), pp. 68f, 207.

² Friedrich von Bezold, *Über die Anfänge der Selbstbiographie und ihre Entwicklung im Mittelalter* (Erlangen, 1893), p. 3.

³ *Ibid.*

⁴ Hans Glagau, *Die moderne Selbstbiographie als historische Quelle* (Marburg, 1903), p. 53.

⁵ For examples of recent scholarship in this vein, see Roy Pascal, *Design and Truth in Autobiography* (London, 1960); Wayne Schumaker *English Autobiography: its emergence, materials and form* (Berkeley, 1954); Bernd Neumann *Identität und Rollenzwang. Zur Theorie der Autobiographie* (Frankfurt/M., 1970); Georges May *L'autobiographie* (Paris, 1979).

⁶ Georg Misch, *Geschichte der Autobiographie* I (Frankfurt/M., 1969), p. 6. All further quotations from Misch will be cited in the text by page only.

⁷ See Neumann, *op. cit.*; Klaus-Detlef Müller, *Autobiographie und Roman. Studien zur literarischen Autobiographie der Goethezeit* (Tübingen, 1976); Günter Niggl, *Geschichte der deutschen Autobiographie im 18. Jahrhundert. Theoretische und literarische Entfaltung* (Stuttgart, 1977).

⁸ Jost Hermand and Evelyn Beck, *Interpretive Synthesis. The Task of Literary Scholarship* (New York, 1975), p. 26.

⁹ *Ibid, p. 27.*

¹⁰ cited in Michael Ermarth, *Wilhelm Dilthey: The Critique of Historical Reason* (Chicago, 1978), p. 88. Original given as *Manuscripts from the Berlin Nachlass. Literatur-Archiv der deutschen Akademie der Wissenschaften, Berlin* 49/218-20.

¹¹ Ermarth, p. 90.

¹² See especially Werner Mahrholz, *Deutsche Selbstbekenntnisse. Ein Beitrag zur Geschichte der Selbstbiographie von der Mystik bis zum Pietismus.* (Berlin, 1919); Neuman, *op. cit.*; Müller, *op.cit.*

¹³ Ursula Münchow, *Frühe deutsche Arbeiterautobiographien* (Berlin, 1973) and Wolfgang Emmerich *Proletarische Lebensläufe. Autobiographische Dokumente zur Entstehung der Zweiten Kultur in Deutschland* (Reinbek bei Hamburg, 1974).

¹⁴ Roland Barthes, "The Death of the Author" in Stephen Heath ed., *Image-Music-Text* (New York, 1977), pp. 142, 144. Further citations from this essay will be noted in the text by page only.

¹⁵ Michel Foucault, "What is an Author?" in Donald F. Bouchard ed., *Language,*

Counter-Memory, Practice. Selected Essays and Interviews (Ithaca, 1977), p. 116. Further citations from this essay will be noted in the text by page only.

[16] Michel Foucault, "Nietzsche, Geneology, History" in *Language, Counter-Memory, Practice*, pp. 139-164. All citations from this essay will be noted in the text by page only.

[17] See Silvie le Bon, "Un Positivisme désespéré", in *Esprit* 5 (1967), 1317-1319. (cited in Foucault, p. 114)

[18] cited in Ermarth, p. 73. (original given as Wilhelm Dilthey, *Gesammelte Schriften* (Stuttgart, 1914-77) 4, p. 539.)

[19] Ermarth, p. 45f.

[20] Friedrich Schleiermacher, *Monologen: Nebst den Vorarbeiten*, Die philosophische Bibliothek, Vol. 84, ed. Friedrich Michael Schiele (Leipzig, 1914), p. 70.

Chapter 1: THE CASES OF BALDINGER, ENGEL, AND WALLENRODT

[1] Bernd Neumann, *Identität und Rollenzwang. Zur Theorie der Autobiographie* (Frankfurt/M.: Athenäum Verlag, 1970).

[2] Klaus-Detlef Müller, *Autobiographie und Roman. Studien zur literarischen Atuobiographie der Goethezeit* (Tübingen: Niemeyer, 1976).

[3] Günter Niggl, *Geschichte der deutschen Autobiographie im 18. Jahrhundert. Theoretische Grundlegung und literarische Entfaltung* (Stuttgart: Metzler, 1977).

[4] Müller, pp. 74-126; Niggl, pp. 26-38.

[5] Renate Feyl, *Der lautlose Aufbruch. Frauen in der Wissenschaft* (Darmstadt: Luchterhand, 1983), p. 9.

[6] Abraham Gotthelf Kästner, *Gesammelte Poetische und Prosaische Schönwissenschaftliche Werke* I (1841: rpt. Frankfurt/M.: Athenäum, 1971), p. 13.

[7] Feyl, p. 65.

[8] Feyl, p. 68.

[9] Jeannine Blackwell, "An Island of Her Own: Heroines of the German Robinsonades from 1720 to 1800" in *The German Quarterly* 58/1, p. 6.

[10] Frederike Baldinger, *Lebensbeschreibung* (Offenbach: Ulrich Weiss und Carl Ludwig Brede, 1791). All citations will be given in the text by page only.

[11] Regula Engel, *Frau Oberst Engel* (Zürich: Artemis, 1977). All citations will be given in the text by page only.

[12] Isabella von Wallenrodt, *Das Leben der Frau von Wallenrodt in Briefen an einen Freund. Ein Beitrag zur Seelenkunde und Weltkenntniss* (Leipzig: Stiller, 1797). All citations will be given in the text by page only.

[13] Christine Touaillon, *Der deutsche Frauenroman des 18. Jahrhunderts* (Vienna: Braumüller, 1919), p. 323.

[14] Niggl, pp. 65-72.

[15] Kay Goodman, "Autobiographie und deutsche Nation. Goethe und Herder" in Wolfgang Wittkowski ed. *Goethe im Kontext* (Tübingen: Niemeyer, 1984), pp.

260-282.
[16] in Feyl, p. 76.
[17] in Feyl, p. 41.
[18] in Feyl, p. 76.

Chapter 2: THE CASES OF RECKE AND STAEGEMANN

[1] Neumann, *op. cit.*

[2] Eckermann, *Gespräche mit Goethe* (Weimar: Kiepenheuer, 1918), p. 253, compare also p. 216. (October 22, 1828 and July 5, 1827)

[3] Ritta Jo Horsley, "A Critical Appraisal of Goethe's *Iphigenie*" in *Beyond the Eternal Feminine. Critical Essays on Women and German Literature*, ed. Susan L. Cocalis and Kay Goodman (Stuttgart: Akademischer Verlag Hans-Dieter Hein, 1982), pp. 47-74.

[4] Elisa von der Recke, *Aufzeichnungen und Briefe aus ihren Jugendtagen*, ed. Paul Rachel (Leipzig: Dietrich, 1900). All quotes will be from this edition and cited within the text by page only.

[5] Elise von der Recke, *Mein Journal. Elises neu aufgefundene Tagebücher aus den Jahren 1791 und 1793/5*, ed. Johannes Werner (Leipzig: Koehler & Amelang, 1927). All quotes are from this edition and cited within the text by page only.

[6] Niggl, p. 70.

[7] Ruth Perry, *Women, Letters, and the Novel* (New York: AMS Pres, 1980).

[8] Rachel concurs in this judgement. See Rachel in Recke, *Aufzeichnungen*, p. 232.

[9] For a lengthier discussion of the emancipatory aspects of la Roche's novel see Ruth-Ellen Boetcher Joeres, "Das Mädchen macht eine ganz neue Gattung von Charakter aus!" Ja, aber ist sie deshalb eine Feministin? Beobachtungen zu Sophie von La Roches *Geschichte des Fräuleins von Sternheim*" in Ruth-Ellen B. Joeres and Annette Kuhn ed. *Frauen in der Geschichte* (Düsseldorf: Schwann, 1985), pp. 92-116.

[10] Theodor Diestel, "Rachel, Paul, Elisa von der Recke *Aufzeichnungen aus ihren Jugendtagen*," in *Euphorion*, 8 (1901), 387-397.

[11] Jean Marie Bouvier de la Motte Guyon, *Das Leben der Frau J. M. B. von la Mothe Guion von ihr selbst beschrieben* (Berlin: Sander, 1826). All quotes are from this edition and cited in the text by page only.

[12] Elisabeth Stägemann, *Erinnerungen für edle Frauen. Nebst Lebensnachrichten über die Verfasserin und einem Anhange von Briefen* (Leipzig: Hinrichs, 1846), p. 7. All quotes are from this edition and cited in the text by page only.

[13] Gustav Kühne, "Einleitung" to Elisabeth Stägemann, *Erinnerungen für edle Frauen* (Leipzig: Hinrichs, 1858), p. 3.

[14] Müller, pp. 107-121.

[15] *Ibid.*, pp. 64ff. and 290-330.

[16] *Ibid.*, p. 56.

[17] *Ibid.*

[18] Friedrich von Blanckenburg, *Versuch über den Roman* (1774; rpt., Stuttgart: Metzler, 1965), p. vii.

[19] Müller, p. 118.

[20] Johann Gottfried Herder, *Sämmtliche Werke*, ed. Bernhard Suphan, XXIII (Berlin, 1881), pp. 228ff. and 321. See also Kay Goodman, "Autobiographie und Deutsche Nation. Goethe und Herder", *op.cit.*

Chapter 3: THE CASES OF VARNHAGEN AND ARNIM

[1] For more detailed information on the Berlin salons see: Ingeborg Drewitz, *Berliner Salons* (Berlin: Huade and Spener, 1965); Deborah Hertz, "Salonieres and Literary Women in Late Eighteenth-Century Berlin," *New German Critique, 14* (1978); Deborah Hertz, *The Literary Salon in Berlin, 1780-1806: The Social History of an Intellectual Institution*, Diss. University of Minnesota, 1979; and Edith Waldstein, *Bettina von Arnim and the Literary Salon: Women's Participation in the Cultural Life of Early Nineteenth-Century Germany*, Diss. Washington University, 1982.

[2] Wolfdietrich Rasch, *Freundschaftskult und Freundschaftsdichtung im deutschen Schriftum des 18. Jahrhunderts* (Halle: Niemeyer, 1936), pp. 36-62.

[3] *Ibid.*, pp. 130-133.

[4] *Ibid.*, pp. 247-259.

[5] Agnes Heller, "Enlightenment Against Fundamentalism," *New German Critique*, 23 (1981), 13-26.

[6] Georg Steinhausen, *Geschichte des deutschen Briefes. Zur Kulturgeschichte des deutschen Volkes* (1889; rpt., Dublin: Weidmann, 1968), II, pp. 320-325. For further information on the history of letters in Germany, see Reinhard Nickisch, *Die Stilprinzipien in den deutschen Briefstellern des 17. und 18. Jahrhunderts* (Göttingen: Vandenhoeck Ruprecht, 1969).

[7] Waldstein, pp. 230-244.

[8] Shub Pinson Koppel, *Modern Germany, its history and civilization* (New York: Macmillon, 1954), pp. 23-49.

[9] Hannah Arendt, *Rahel Varnhagen. Lebensgeschichte einer deutschen Jüdin aus der Romantik* (Frankfurt a. M.: Ullstein, 1959).

[10] Rahel Varnhagen, *Rahel. Ein Buch des Andenkens für ihre Freunde*, ed. Karl August Varnhagen von Ense (1834; rpt., Bern: Herbert Lange, 1972), II, 33. All quotes, unless otherwise noted, will be taken from this edition of her letters and cited within the text by page only.

[11] Kay Goodman, "The Impact of Rahel Varnhagen on Women in the Nineteenth Century", in Marianne Burkhard, ed., *Gestaltet und Gestaltend. Frauen in der deutschen Literatur* (Amsterdam: Rodopi, 1980), pp. 125-153.

[12] Doris Starr Guilloton, "Rahel Varnhagen und die Frauenfrage in der deutschen Romantik: Eine Untersuchung ihrer Briefe und Tagebuchnotizen," in *Monatshefte*, 69 (1977), pp. 391-403.

[13] Elke Frederiksen, "Die Frau als Autorin zur Zeit der Romantik: Anfänge einer weiblichen literarischen Tradition," in *Gestaltet*, pp. 83-108.

[14] Waldstein's dissertation is one of the few studies to treat these works as novels.

[15] In Ingeborg Drewitz, *Bettine von Arnim. Romantik-Revolution-Utopie* (Mün-

chen: Heyne, 1969), p. 150.

[16] In Gisela Dischner, *Caroline und der Jenaer Kreis. Ein Leben zwischen bürgerlicher Vereinzelung und romantischer Geselligkeit* (Berlin: Wagenbach, 1979), p. 87.

[17] Bettina von Arnim, *Sämtliche Werke*, ed. Waldemar Oehlke (Berlin: Propyläen, 1920), I, pp. 205f. All quotes, unless otherwise noted, will be taken from this edition and cited within the text by page only.

[18] Karl August Varnhagen von Ense, ed., *Briefe von Stägemann, Metternich, Heine und Bettina von Arnim* (Leipzig: Brockhaus, 1865), p. 264.

[19] *Die Andacht zum Menschenbild. Unbekannte Briefe von Bettine Brentano* (1942; rpt., Bern: Herbert Lang, 1970), p. 237.

[20] Waldemar Oehlke, *Bettina von Arnims Briefromane* (Berlin: Mayer & Müller, 1905).

[21] Bettina von Arnim, *Werke und Briefe*, ed. Gustav Konrad (Frechen: Bartmann, 1959), I, p. 557.

[22] Bettina von Arnim, *Goethes Briefwechsel mit einem Kinde* (Berlin: Hertz, 1890), p. xx.

[23] See Oehlke, *Sämtliche Werke*, I, xlv.

[24] *Ibid.*, lv.

[25] *Ibid.*, liv.

[26] In Oehlke, *Briefromane*, p. 5.

[27] *Ibid.*

[28] In Körner, I, p. 548.

[29] Christa Wolf, "Einleitung", in Karoline von Günderode, *Der Schatten eines Traumes* (Berlin: Der Morgen, 1979).

[30] Oehlke, *Werke*, II, 8.

[31] Waldstein, p. 50.

[32] Reinhold Stieg, ed. *Bettinas Briefwechsel mit Goethe* (Leipzig: Insel, 1922), p. 409.

[33] Drewitz, p. 98.

[34] Cited in Christa Wolf, "Nun ja! Das nächste Leben geht aber heute an. Ein Brief über die Bettine" in Bettine von Arnim, *Die Günderode* (1975; rpt., Frankfurt/M.: Insel, 1982), p. 468.

[35] Drewitz, p. 151.

[36] Oehlke, *Sämtliche Werke, III*, p. 9.

[37] Drewitz, p. 151.

[38] Cited in Körner, I, p. 546.

[39] *Ibid.*

[40] For more information on women novelists in this period, see Renate Möhrmann, *Die andere Frau. Emanzipationsansätze deutscher Schiftstellerinnen im Vorfeld der Achtundvierziger-Revolution* (Stuttgart: Metzler, 1977, pp. 60-117.

Chapter 4: THE CASES OF ASTON AND MEYSENBUG

[1] Louise Aston, *Aus dem Leben einer Frau* (Hamburg, 1847), preface. All quotes

238

are cited within the text by page only.

² Upon being asked to leave Berlin, Aston defended herself publicly. She denied most of the charges, but not that of having formed a club for emancipated women. See Louise Aston, *Meine Emancipation, Verweisung und Rechtfertigung* (Brussels, 1846).

³ *Ibid.*, p. 16.

⁴ Germaine Goetzinger, *Für die Selbstverwirklichung der Frau: Louise Aston* (Frankfurt a.M., 1983), p. 16.

⁵ Cited in Goetzinger, *ibid*, p. 46.

⁶ Goetzinger, p. 58. (Although she aknowledges the textual and real life parallels, Goetzinger finds the elaborations too extreme and refers to *Aus dem Leben einer Frau* as a novel. p. 59)

⁷ Malwida von Meysenbug, *Memoiren einer Idealistin* (Berlin, 1900) I, p. 35. All quotes are from this edition and will be cited within the text by page only.

⁸ Karl August Varnhagen von Ense, ed., *Rahel. Ein Buch des Andenkens für ihre Freunde* (Berlin, 1833), p. 145.

⁹ See Friedrich Nietzsche, *Werke in drei Bänden*, ed. Karl Schlechta (München, 1956) III, pp. 1118, 1125, 1137, 1140.

¹⁰ Dora Wegele, *Th. Althaus und M.v. Meysenbug. Zwei Gestalten des Vormärz* (Marburg, 1927), p. 30.

¹¹ For biographies of these women see Ruth-Ellen Boetcher Joeres, *Die Anfänge der deutschen Frauenbewegung: Louise Otto-Peters* (Frankfurt a.M.: 1983) and Maria Wagner, *Mathilde Franziska Anneke in Selbstzeugnissen und Dokumenten* (Frankfurt a.M.: 1980)

¹² Berta Schleicher, ed., *Briefe von und an Malwida von Meysenbug* (Berlin, 1920), p. 19.

¹³ Berta Schleicher, ed., *Im Anfang war die Liebe. Briefe an ihre Pflegetochter von Malwida von Meysenbug* (München, 1931), p. 322.

¹⁴ Schleicher, *Briefe*, p. 17.

Chapter 5: THE CASES OF LEWALD AND EBNER-ESCHENBACH

¹ See Anna Blos, *Frauen der deutschen Revolution* (Dresden, 1928).

² Ironically, but perhaps not accidently, that same Hahn-Hahn had been the woman with whom Heinrich Simon had fallen in love, forsaking Lewald.

³ Marieluise Steinhauer, *Fanny Lewald, die deutsche George Sand. Ein Kapitel aus der Geschichte des Frauenromans im 19. Jahrhundert* (Berlin, 1937), p.90.

⁴ Fanny Lewald, *Gefühltes und Gedachtes* (1838-1888), ed. Ludwig Geiger (Dresden and Leipzig, 1900), p. 37.

⁵ Fanny Lewald, *Meine Lebensgeschichte* (Berlin, 1861/2),l/l, p.l. All quotes are from this edition and cited within the text by page only.

⁶ *Gefühltes und Gedachtes*, p. 34.

⁷ Johann Wolfgang von Goethe *Schriften,8* (Stuttgart, 1950), pp. 13f.

[8] Kay Goodman, "Autobiographie und deutsche Nation. Goethe und Herder" in Wolfgang Wittkowski ed. *Goethe im Kontext* (Tübingen, 1984), pp. 260-283.

[9] The novelist Friedrich Spielhagen, for instance wrote: "Es ist schön zu sehen, da einem Menschen, der mit festem Willen und reiner Überzeugung seinen eigenen Weg geht, eben fast Alles möglich ist" and compared her work to Goethe's. Friedrich Spielhagen, "Fanny Lewald," in *Gartenlaube*, 42 (1862), 661.

[10] Fanny Lewald, *Prinz Louis Ferdinand* (Breslau: Josef Max, 1849) I, 20.

[11] H.H. Houben, ed. *Gespräche mit Heine* (Frankfurt/M.: Rütten & Loening, 1926), 735.

[12] Käthe Offergeld, *Marie von Ebner-Eschenbach. Untersuchungen über ihre Erzählungstechnik* (Munster, 1917), pp. 34f.

[13] Mechtild Alkemade, *Die Lebens- und Weltanschauung der Freifrau Marie von Ebner-Eschenbach* (Graz und Würzburg, 1935), p. 110; and Anton Bettelheim, *Marie von Ebner-Eschenbach. Wirken und Vermächtnis* (Leipzig, 1920), pp. 96f.

[14] Karl Gladt, Preface to Marie von Ebner-Eschenbach, *Das Waldfräulein*, (Vienna, 1969), p. 17.

[15] Bettelheim, p. 106.

[16] *Ibid.* p.112.

[17] Some of these productions were: 1863 *Die Heimkehr* (Berlin); 1864 *Die Veilchen* (Vienna); 1867 *Das Geständnis* (Prague); 1868 *Marie Roland* (Weimar); 1869 *Dr. Ritter* (Vienna); 1873 *Das Waldfräulein* (Vienna); 1874 *Männertreue* (Koburg);1874 *Untröstlich* (Vienna). The well-known actress Julie Rettich incorporated *Die Schauspielerin* into her repertoire. See Gladt.

[18] Bettelheim, pp. 120f.

[19] Hans Albert Koller, *Studien zu Marie von Ebner-Eschenbach* (Hamburg, 1920), p. 8; and John Preston Hoskins, "The Life of Marie von Ebner-Eschenbach," in *The German Classics* (New York, 1914), XIII, pp. 336f.

[20] See Gladt, p. 24; and Else Riemann, *Zur Psychologie und Ethik der Marie von Ebner-Eschenbach* (Hamburg, 1913), p. 13.

[21] Bettelheim, p. 130.

[22] *Ibid.* p. 131.

[23] Moritz Necker, *Marie von Ebner-Eschenbach. Nach ihren Werken geschildert* (Leipzig und Berlin, 1900), pp. 29f.

[24] Cited in Anton Bettelheim, *Marie von Ebner-Eschenbach* (Berlin, 1900),p. 89.

[25] Gladt, Necker, and Bettelheim (both 1900 and 1920) all describe these plays.

[26] Marie von Ebner-Eschenbach, *Aus einem zeitlosen Tagebuch* in *Erzählungen. Autobiographische Schriften* (München, 1958), p. 719.

[27] Alkemade, p. 78.

[28] *Ibid.* p. 77.

[29] *Ibid.*

[30] 1901 Isolde Kurz; 1902 Emile Mataja; 1903 Hermine Villinger; 1904 Enrica Handel-Mazzetti; 1905 Helene Böhlau; 1906 Marie Eugenie delle Grazie; 1907 Ricarda Huch; 1908 Gisele Freiin von Berger; 1909 Hermine Cloeter; 1910 Erika Rheinsch-Spann. In Bettelheim (1920), p. 289.

240

³¹ Lisa Barck-Herzog, "Hermine Villinger — Marie von Ebner-Eschenbach. Eine Dichterfreundschaft. Nach Briefen von Hermine Villinger dargestellt," *Deutsche Rundschau*, 9 (1961), 845-49.

³² See Hans-Heinrich Reuter, "Theodor Fontane," in Benno von Wiese, ed., *Deutsche Dichter des 19. Jahrhunderts. Ihr Leben und Werk* (Berlin, 1969), pp. 557-98. Also Theodor Fontane, *Meine Kinderjahre*, in *Werke in Fünf Bänden* (Berlin, 1969), I, p. 237.

³³ Bettelheim (1920), p. 40.

³⁴ Marie von Ebner-Eschenbach, *Meine Kinderjahre*, in *Erzählungen. Autobiographische Schriften*, pp. 843f. All quotes are from this edition and are cited in the text by page only.

³⁵ See Bettelheim (1920) pp. 157 and 221; also Alkemade, p. 238.

³⁶ Bettelheim (1920), pp. 31f.; and Gladt, pp. 15-17.

³⁷ Fontane, p. 73.

³⁸ Robert Kann, ed., *Marie von Ebner-Eschenbach — Dr. Breuer. Ein Briefwechsel 1889-1916* (Vienna, 1969), pp. 41-48.

³⁹ Ebner-Eschenbach, *Aus einem zeitlosen Tagebuch*, p. 706.

⁴⁰ Kann claims that the posthumously published *Aus einem zeitlosen Tagebuch* itself represents such an attempt. Kann, p. 49, and pp. 179f.

⁴¹ For an introduction the history of the Corinne' tradition in English and American literature, see Ellen Moers, *Literary Women* (Garden City, 1976).

Chapter 6: THE CASES OF POPP, WEGRAINER, AND VIERSBECK

¹ See for instance Wolfgang Emmerich, ed., *Proletarische Lebensläufe. Autobiographische Dokumente zur Entstehung der Zweiten Kultur in Deutschland* (Reinbek:Rowohlt, 1974)I, p.27f.

² Petra Frerichs, *Bürgerliche Autobiographie und proletarische Selbstdarstellung. Eine vergleichende Darstellung unter besonderer Berücksichtigung persönlichkeitstheoretischer und literaturwissenschaftlich-didaktischer Fragestellungen* (Frankfurt a.M.:Haag & Herchen, n.d.) p.262..

³ cited in Ursula Münchow, *Frühe deutsche Arbeiterautobiographien* (Berlin: Akademie, 1973), p. 9.

⁴ Oskar Negt, Alexander Kluge, *Öffentlichkeit und Erfahrung. Zur Organisationsanalyse von bürgerlicher und proletarischer Öffentlichkeit* (Frankfurt a. M.: 1972).

⁵ Emmerich, p. 32. Emmerich also relied on the work of Raymond Williams, *Gesellschaftstheorie als Begriffsgeschichte. Studien zur historischen Semantik von 'Kultur'* (München:1972) and Wolfgang Jacobeit and Ute Mohrmann, *Kultur und Lebensweise des Proletariats. Kulturhistorische-volkskundliche Studien und Materialien* (Berlin/DDR: 1973).

⁶ Frerichs, p. 266. Lucien Seve, *Marxismus und Theorie der Persönlichkeit* (Frankfurt a.M.: 1972).

[7] Adelheid Popp, *Jugend einer Areiterin* (Berlin: Dietz, 1977). All quotes are from this edition.

[8] Emmerich asserts that Popp never read *Dichtung und Wahrheit*. However, given the fact that she mentions having read so much Goethe, it seems imprudent to claim that she had never read his autobiography. Emmerich, p. 22.

[9] Münchow, p. 63.

[10] A recent exception to this is Mary Jo Maynes' overview of the distinctions in themes and issues addressed in a wide range of proletarian autobiography from this period. See Mary Jo Maynes, "Feministische Ansätze in den Autobiographien von Arbeiterinnen" in Ruth-Ellen B. Joeres and Annette Kuhn ed. *Frauen in der Geschichte VI* (Düsseldorf: Schwann, 1985), pp. 164-182. (Soon to appear in *German Women in the Eighteenth and Nineteenth Centuries. A Social and Literary History* (Indiana University Press).)

[11] Marie Wegrainer, *Der Lebensroman einer Arbeiterfrau* (Frankfurt a.M.: Campus, 1979).

[12] Emmerich, p. 26f.

[13] Ottilie Baader, *Ein steiniger Wed* (Berlin: Dietz, 1979).

[14] Doris Viersbeck, *Erlebnisse eines Hamburger Dienstmädchens* (München:Ernst Reinhardt, 1910).

[15] Emmerich, pp. 24,29.

[16] Münchow, p. 55.

[17] *The Memoirs of Glückel of Hameln* (New York: Schocken, 1977).

"E D•

NEW YORK UNIVERSITY OTTENDORFER SERIES. NEUE FOLGE

Bd. 1   Rosenbauer, Brecht und der Behaviorismus. 102 Seiten, 1970.

Bd. 2   Zipes, The Great Refusal, Studies of the Romantic Hero in German and American Literature. 158 Seiten, 1970.

Bd. 3   Hughes, Mythos und Geschichtsoptimismus in Thomas Manns Joseph Romanen. 116 Seiten, 1975.

Bd. 4   Salloch, Peter Weiss' «Die Ermittlung». Zur Struktur des Dokumentartheaters. 170 Seiten, 1972.

Bd. 5   Peter/Grathoff/Hayes/Loose, Ideologiekritische Studien zur Literatur, Essays I. 260 Seiten, 1972.

Bd. 6   Seitz, Johann Fischarts Geschichtsklitterung zur Prosastruktur und zum grobianischen Motivkomplex. 252 Seiten, 1974.

Bd. 7   Vaget/Barnouw, Thomas Mann-Studien zu Fragen der Rezeption. 158 Seiten, 1975.

Bd. 8   Baron/Mühsam/Heidesieck/Grimm/Theisz, Ideologiekritische Studien zur Literatur. Essays II. 158 Seiten, 1975.

Bd. 9   Silbermann, Literature of the Working World. A Study of the Industrial Novel in East Germany. 118 Seiten, 1976.

Bd. 10   Rosellini, Thomas Müntzer im deutschen Drama. Verteufelung. Apotheose und Kritik. 176 Seiten, 1978.

Bd. 11   Antosik, The Question of Elites. An Essay on the Cultural Elitism of Nietzsche, George and Hesse. 204 Seiten, 1978.

Bd. 12   Becker, A War of Fools. The Letters of Obscure Men: A Study of the Satire and the Satirized. 190 Seiten, 1981.

Bd. 13   Van Cleve, Herlequin Besieged. The Reception of Comedy in Germany during the Early Enlightenment. 203 Seiten, 1980.

Bd. 14   McKnight, The Novels of Johann Karl Wezel. Satire. Realism and Social Criticism in Late 18th Century Literature. 311 Seiten, 1981.

Bd. 15   Stern, Gegenbild, Reihenfolge, Sprung. An Essay on Related Figures of Argument in Walter Benjamin. 121 Seiten, 1982.

Bd. 16   Poore, German-American Socialist Literature, 1865–1900. 225 Seiten, 1982.

Bd. 17   Berman, Between Fontane and Tucholsky: Literary Criticism and the Public Sphere in Imperial Germany. 175 Seiten, 1983.

Bd. 18   Blevins, Franz Xaver Kroetz: The Emergence of a Political Playwright. 295 Seiten, 1983.

Bd. 19   Grimm, Texturen – Essays und anderes zu Hans Magnus Enzensberger. 236 Seiten, 1984.

Bd. 20   Reutershan, Clara Zetkin und Brot und Rosen... Literaturpolitische Konflikte zwischen Partei und Frauenbewegung in der deutschen Vorkriegssozialdemokratie. 264 Seiten, 1985.

Bd. 21   Teraoka, The Silence of Entropy or Universal Discourse. The Postmodernist Poetics of Heiner Müller. 240 Seiten, 1985.

Bd. 22   Kirchberger, Franz Kafka's Use of Law in Fiction. A New Interpretation of «In der Strafkolonie», «Der Prozess», and «Das Schloss». 212 Seiten, 1986.

Bd. 23   Kaiser, Social Integration and Narrative Structure. Patterns of Realism in Auerbach, Freytag, Fontane, and Raabe. 230 Seiten, 1986.

Die Bände 1, 2, 4, 5 und 6 sind direkt beim Athenäum-Verlag in Frankfurt/M. zu beziehen. Alle übrigen, sowie die später erscheinenden Bände werden durch den Verlag Peter Lang AG, Bern hergestellt und ausgeliefert.